Robotics and Generative AI in Healthcare

A New Era of Innovation

Editors:

Deepika Kumar
Department of Computer Science and Engineering
Bharati Vidyapeeth's college of Engineering,
New Delhi, India

Gargi Mishra
Department of Computer Science and Engineering
Bharati Vidyapeeth's college of Engineering,
New Delhi, India

Jude D Hemanth
Department of Electronics & Communication Engineering
Karunya Institute of Technology and Sciences,
Coimbatore, India

CRC Press
Taylor & Francis Group
Boca Raton London New York

CRC Press is an imprint of the
Taylor & Francis Group, an **informa** business
A SCIENCE PUBLISHERS BOOK

First edition published 2026
by CRC Press
2385 NW Executive Center Drive, Suite 320, Boca Raton FL 33431

and by CRC Press
4 Park Square, Milton Park, Abingdon, Oxon, OX14 4RN

CRC Press is an imprint of Taylor & Francis Group, LLC

Library of Congress Cataloging-in-Publication Data (applied for)

ISBN: 978-1-041-08468-6 (hbk)
ISBN: 978-1-041-13596-8 (pbk)
ISBN: 978-1-003-67058-2 (ebk)

DOI: 10.1201/9781003670582

Typeset in Times New Roman
by Prime Publishing Services

Preface

The convergence of robotics and generative artificial intelligence (GenAI) represents a transformative juncture in the history of healthcare. Over the past few decades, the landscape of modern medicine has been shaped by revolutionary technologies, yet none have captured the imagination of scientists, clinicians, engineers, and policymakers as profoundly as the integration of intelligent machines and generative learning systems. This book delves into this convergence with a focused lens on the emerging tools, frameworks, applications, and challenges that define this new paradigm.

The aim of this book is twofold. Firstly, it seeks to bridge the technical intricacies of GenAI and robotics with their tangible, real-world applications in the medical domain. Secondly, it aims to stimulate thoughtful discourse around the ethical, social, and operational implications that emerge when these technologies permeate sensitive ecosystems like healthcare. Drawing from a wide range of interdisciplinary research, clinical case studies, engineering advances, and data science innovations, this book addresses both foundational knowledge and applied research. It is crafted for a diverse audience-researchers, healthcare professionals, policy makers, and students-who are navigating the convergence of AI and robotics in healthcare delivery.

The Context of Transformation

Healthcare systems globally are under increasing pressure to deliver high-quality, cost-effective, and personalized care. Rising life expectancies, chronic disease burdens, workforce shortages, and escalating costs are challenging traditional healthcare delivery models. Simultaneously, the explosion of biomedical data, advancements in machine intelligence, and progress in robotics have created fertile ground for innovation.

Generative AI, powered by models like GANs, VAEs, Diffusion Models, and Large Language Models, offers the ability to synthesize realistic content, whether it be medical images, patient narratives, or biochemical structures. Meanwhile, robotics has evolved beyond mechanical automation to intelligent agents capable of perception, decision-making, and autonomous operation in clinical environments. These advancements are not isolated; they are deeply interwoven. Generative AI enables robots to better understand human intent, simulate procedures, and adapt to unpredictable situations. In turn, robotics gives physical form to the decision-making and learning capabilities of AI, making them actionable at the point of care.

This book is structured into thirteen chapters, each offering a comprehensive and curated exploration of key themes. Let us now introduce the reader to the trajectory of the content.

Chapter Summaries and Thematic Overview

Chapter 1, Introduction to Robotics and Generative AI in Healthcare, lays the foundational framework for the entire volume. It introduces the reader to the transformative role of robotics and GenAI in the healthcare ecosystem. By exploring applications such as surgical automation, assistive rehabilitation, and synthetic data generation, this chapter sets the tone for understanding the dual engines of change. The synergy between robotics' precision and AI's adaptability is highlighted, along with early use cases in diagnostic decision-making, personalized therapies, and procedural automation. The chapter concludes with a visionary outlook on how technology is redefining care pathways.

Chapter 2, Engineering Healthcare: Key Technologies and Systems in Healthcare, shifts focus to the infrastructural and technological backbone supporting these innovations. The discussion spans a wide spectrum—from robotic-assisted surgeries and biosensors to electronic health records and telemedicine. Engineering disciplines are at the heart of this transformation, creating tools that extend human capacity, improve diagnostic accuracy, and streamline operations. However, the chapter also provides a critical reflection on interoperability, digital equity, and the governance challenges that need to be addressed to ensure inclusive adoption.

Chapter 3, Generative AI: A Comparative Analysis of Architectures, Evaluation Metrics, and Emerging Challenges, delves deeper into the technical architectures of GenAI. It offers a comparative study of GANs, VAEs, Diffusion Models, and LLMs, examining their respective strengths and limitations across domains. Attention is given to the metrics used to evaluate generative quality, stability, scalability, and computational efficiency. Beyond the technical layers, this chapter discusses critical challenges such as bias propagation, misuse in deepfakes, and questions surrounding data provenance and intellectual property. It calls for the development of standard evaluation protocols and ethical governance frameworks to guide the responsible deployment of GenAI in sensitive domains like healthcare.

Chapter 4, Foundation of Generative AI: Concepts, Models, and Applications, complements the previous chapter by offering a conceptual deep dive into how GenAI models function. The content is accessible yet technically rich, helping readers build a nuanced understanding of key model types and their capabilities. Real-world applications are examined in domains including text generation, image synthesis, video creation, and structured knowledge extraction. The versatility of

GenAI is underscored through its potential in domains as diverse as education, art, and medicine. This chapter provides the cognitive scaffolding required to appreciate the more domain-specific discussions in the subsequent chapters.

Chapter 5, Generative AI in Healthcare: A New Frontier for Diagnostics, presents a data-driven investigation into how generative models can improve diagnostic accuracy through data augmentation and anomaly detection. Using the ChestX-ray14 dataset, the chapter demonstrates how GANs and VAEs can be leveraged to enhance image-based classification systems. It shows a measurable improvement in diagnostic metrics—such as AUC, precision, and recall—when synthetic data is used to augment training datasets. This case study not only validates the clinical utility of GenAI but also introduces ethical considerations around data synthesis, such as transparency, fairness, and privacy.

Chapter 6, Revolutionizing Clinical Practice with Generative AI, expands the horizon by showcasing the systemic transformation enabled by GenAI. It explores use cases including AI-assisted radiology reports, automated clinical documentation, and synthetic EHR generation for training AI models while maintaining patient privacy. The chapter emphasizes the value of multimodal integration—combining imaging, lab data, and clinical notes—to create holistic decision-support systems. Additionally, it highlights mitigation strategies against AI "hallucination" through prompt engineering and retrieval-augmented generation (RAG). It advocates for validation, transparency, and stakeholder collaboration to ensure clinical reliability and trustworthiness.

Chapter 7, Empirical Evaluation using Generative AI Models for the Multiclass Classification of Retinal Diseases Images, presents a high-impact use case for SRGANs in classifying complex retinal disorders. By generating synthetic training images for eye diseases like DME and CNV, the chapter shows how data scarcity can be overcome to create more robust classifiers. A custom CNN, trained on both real and synthetic data, achieves near-perfect classification accuracy, setting a benchmark for future medical image analysis models. The empirical rigor and technical depth of this chapter offer an invaluable resource for practitioncrs working in diagnostic AI.

Chapter 8, Implementing Robotics and Generative AI in Healthcare: Challenges and Opportunities, offers a pragmatic perspective on the systemic implementation of these technologies in real-world settings. While the promise of AI-augmented robotics in surgery, rehabilitation, and administration is undeniable, this chapter confronts the ground realities of integration. Topics include clinician training, interoperability standards, ethical guidelines, and infrastructural readiness. The chapter emphasizes the need for multidisciplinary collaboration between clinicians, engineers, ethicists, and policy makers to co-design future-ready healthcare ecosystems.

Chapter 9, Generative AI in Healthcare: Transforming Delivery and Redefining Patient–Provider Dynamics, transitions the discussion to the macro-level implications of GenAI on care delivery models. Personalized medicine, accelerated drug discovery, and intelligent clinical assistants are discussed as transformative applications. However, the chapter also raises red flags around algorithmic bias, transparency, and patient trust. It highlights the importance of regulatory alignment with HIPAA and GDPR frameworks to ensure data privacy and fairness. The evolving dynamics between providers and patients—mediated by intelligent agents—are explored through a socio-technical lens.

Chapter 10, Revolutionizing Healthcare: The Synergy of Blockchain and Robotics for Secure, Transparent, and Efficient Operations, introduces a new dimension to the discourse by integrating Blockchain Technology (BT) with robotics and GenAI. Blockchain's decentralized, immutable architecture offers promising avenues for ensuring data integrity, traceability, and secure automation in robotic workflows. Use cases include secure surgical logs, automated drug delivery systems, and clinical trial validation. The chapter also discusses the limitations—such as regulatory hurdles and implementation costs—and proposes collaborative strategies for scalable deployment.

Chapter 11, Future Directions and Emerging Trends in Robotics and AI, paints a compelling picture of what lies ahead. From quantum-enhanced AI to neuromorphic computing and explainable robotics, this chapter surveys the frontiers of innovation. It discusses critical themes such as human–robot collaboration, ethical AI, autonomous agents, and cybersecurity. The chapter anticipates the challenges posed by job displacement and AI bias, advocating for socially responsible innovation. Coupling generative AI with edge computing and sustainable design is projected as the next evolutionary step toward more human-aligned and eco-conscious healthcare systems.

Chapter 12, Generative Artificial Intelligence Development, Models, Healthcare Applications, and Future Directions: A Review, synthesizes the developmental trajectory of GenAI with its implications for healthcare. It charts the evolution of foundational models, explores applications in diagnostics and therapy, and outlines systemic bottlenecks such as data governance, ethical regulation, and clinical adoption. The chapter ends with a forward-looking review of emerging GenAI models and their potential to further revolutionize healthcare delivery. It serves as both a retrospective and prospective account of GenAI's ongoing journey in medicine.

Chapter 13, Leveraging Data Science and Generative AI to Explore Human Behavior and Health Issues, underscores the confluence of behavioral science, data analytics, and GenAI. Understanding patient behavior, mental health trends, and population-level dynamics are increasingly essential to modern medicine. This chapter introduces methodologies that combine structured and unstructured data—including sensor outputs, clinical narratives, and social determinants of health—to uncover patterns that inform preventive care and policy making. By contextualizing generative outputs with behavioral insights, this chapter advocates for a more holistic, patient-centric approach to healthcare innovation.

A Call to Action

This book arrives at a moment of inflection. The convergence of robotics and generative AI offers an unprecedented opportunity to redefine not just how care is delivered, but how health itself is understood, protected, and promoted. However, this opportunity comes with a responsibility to ensure that innovation is inclusive, ethical, transparent, and aligned with human values.

We must ensure that our models do not encode historical inequities. We must train our systems not just to be intelligent, but to be wise. We must teach our robots not just to act, but to empathize. And we must remember that behind every data point, every scan, and every algorithm, there is a human being—vulnerable, hopeful, and deserving of dignified care.

As you embark on this intellectual journey through the pages ahead, may this book inspire inquiry, collaboration, and above all, compassion. The era of intelligent healthcare is not a distant future—it is already unfolding. Let us shape it thoughtfully, courageously, and inclusively.

Contents

Preface *iii*

List of Contributors *xi*

1. Introduction to Robotics and Generative AI in Healthcare 1

2. Engineering Healthcare: Key Technologies and Systems in Healthcare 15

3. Generative AI: A Comparative Analysis of Architectures, Evaluation Metrics, and Emerging Challenges 31

4. Foundation of Generative AI: Concepts, Model and Applications 58

5. Generative AI in Healthcare: A New Frontier for Diagnostics 72

6. Revolutionizing Clinical Practice with Generative AI 94

7. Empirical Evaluation using Generative AI models for the Multiclass Classification of Retinal Diseases Images 113

8. Implementing Robotics and Generative AI in Healthcare: Challenges and Opportunities 131

9. Generative AI in Healthcare: Transforming Delivery and Redefining Patient–Provider Dynamics 147

10. Revolutionizing Healthcare: The Synergy of Blockchain and Robotics for Secure, Transparent, and Efficient Operations 159

11. Future Directions and Emerging Trends in Robotics and AI 171

12. Generative Artificial Intelligence Development, Models, Healthcare Applications, and Future Directions: A Review 194

13. Leveraging Data Science and Generative AI to Explore Human Behaviour and Health Issue 213

Index 229

About the Editors 231

List of Contributors

Aakanksha Mahajan
CSmE, PIET, Samalkha, India.

Ajay Sharma
Amity University, Noida, India.

Amritanshu Raj
Department of Computer Science and Engineering, JIMS Engineering Management Technical Campus, Greater Noida, Uttar Pradesh, India.

Anupam Tiwari
Department of Computer Science and Engineering, The Institution of Electronics and Telecommunication Engineers, New Delhi, India.

Arpit Singh
Information systems and Analytics, Jindal Global Business School, Sonipat, India.

Ayush Kaushik
Department of Computer Science and Engineering, JIMS Engineering Management Technical Campus, Greater Noida, Uttar Pradesh, India.

Bhawna Suri
Department of Computer Science and Engineering, Bhagwan Parshuram Institute of Technology, GGSIPU, Delhi, India.

Disha Tuteja
ECE, Guru Tegh Bahadur Institute of Technology, New Delhi, India.

Hemang Vats
ECE, Guru Tegh Bahadur Institute of Technology, New Delhi, India.

Jolly Parikh
Department of Computer Science and Engineering, Bharati Vidyapeeth's College of Engineering, New Delhi, India.

Kashvi Aggarwal
Computer Engineering, TIET, Patiala, India.

Kushagra Kalra
Information Technology, BPIT, GGSIPU, New Delhi, India.

Mukesh K Sahu
Department of Electronics, Hansraj College, University of Delhi, India.

Neha Sharma
Department of Computer Science and Engineering, Chitkara University Institute of Engineering & Technology, Chitkara University, Rajpura, India.

Nupur Chugh
Department of Computer Science and Engineering, Bharati Vidyapeeth's College of Engineering, New Delhi, India.

Palak Girdhar
Department of Computer Science and Engineering, Bhagwan Parshuram Institute of Technology, GGSIPU, Delhi, India.

Parinay Goel
Information Technology, BPIT, GGSIPU, New Delhi, India.

Pavneet Singh
Department of Computer Science and Engineering, Bhagwan Parshuram Institute of Technology, GGSIPU, Delhi, India.

Pooja Gupta
Computer Science and Technology, MAIT, Delhi, India.

Prateek Mishra
CSE, Asia Pacific Institute of Information Technology, Panipat, India.

Prateek Thapar
Department of Computer Science and Engineering, New Delhi, India.

Rakhi Joon
Department of Computer Science and Engineering, Bharati Vidyapeeth's College of Engineering, New Delhi, India.

Raman Dhand
ECE, Guru Tegh Bahadur Institute of Technology, New Delhi, India.

Renuka Sharma
Department of Computer Science and Engineering, JIMS Engineering Management Technical Campus, Greater Noida, Uttar Pradesh, India.

Ronit Mathur
Department of Computer Science and Engineering, JIMS Engineering Management Technical Campus, Greater Noida, Uttar Pradesh, India.

Ruchi Goel
Computer Science and Engineering, MAIT, Delhi, India.

Sagar Panchal
CSE, Asia Pacific Institute of Information Technology, Panipat, India.

Samyak Jain
Actuarial department, EXL, Delhi, India.

Sandeep Banerjee
Department of Computer Science and Engineering, Bharati Vidyapeeth's College of Engineering, New Delhi, India.

Shailendra Singh Gaur
Information Technology, BPIT, GGSIPU, New Delhi, India.

Shilpa Gupta
Department of Computer Science and Engineering, JIMS Engineering Management Technical Campus, Greater Noida, Uttar Pradesh, India.

Shranya Suri
Government Doon Medical College, Dehradun, India.

Shubhra Dixit
Amity University, Noida, India.

Shweta Taneja
Department of Computer Science and Engineering, Bhagwan Parshuram Institute of Technology, GGSIPU, Delhi, India.

Smit Kumar
Deutsche Bank, Germany

Stephin George
ECE, Guru Tegh Bahadur Institute of Technology, New Delhi, India.

Suman
CSE, BPIT, Delhi, India.

Surbhi Gupta
Amity University, Noida, India.

Urvi Maniar
School of Engineering, Republic Polytechnic, Singapore.

Vedika Puri
Department of Physics, Hansraj College, University of Delhi, India.

Vijay Bharti
CSE, Asia Pacific Institute of Information Technology, Panipat, India.

Vivek Chaurasiya
Snap Inc, Santa Monica, U.S.A.

Yagyadatta Goswami
Department of Electronics, Hansraj College, University of Delhi, India.

Yugnanda Malhotra
Department of Electronics and Communication Engineering, Bharati Vidyapeeth's College of Engineering, New Delhi, India.

1 Introduction to Robotics and Generative AI in Healthcare

Nupur Chugh[1], Sandeep Banerjee[2], Rakhi Joon[3*] and Vivek Chaurasiya[4]

This chapter explores the growing impact of advanced technologies on modern medicine. It examines the key characteristics, advantages, and applications of both robotics and generative artificial intelligence (AI) in healthcare. The discussion highlights how robotic systems enhance surgical precision, improve patient care, and facilitate rehabilitation through greater accuracy, convenience, and safety. Additionally, it outlines how generative AI can accelerate drug discovery, tailor treatment plans, and generate synthetic medical data for research and model training. The authors further describe how the integration of these technologies is transforming clinical decision-making, patient diagnosis, and workflow management—ultimately enabling more personalized care and faster recovery for patients.

1.1 Overview

The fusion of robotics and artificial intelligence (AI) is reshaping healthcare, driving a transformative shift in patient treatment, diagnosis, and innovation. Generative AI, in particular, is gaining recognition for its role in data synthesis, clinical reasoning, and autonomous systems. This synergy isn't merely automation—it redefines how clinicians interpret data, make decisions, and interact with patients. Together, robotics and AI hold the promise of enhancing clinical outcomes, streamlining workflows, and improving overall healthcare efficiency.

Despite its complexity and intolerance for error, healthcare is gradually embracing robotics in highly specialized roles. Robotic systems now support precise, minimally invasive surgeries, enable real-time feedback in rehabilitation, and facilitate remote consultations through telepresence. In hospitals, automated transport and logistics are improving operational efficiency and resource distribution.

[1-3] Department of Computer Science and Engineering, Bharati Vidyapeeth's College of Engineering, New Delhi, India.
[4] Snap Inc, Santa Monica, U.S.A.
E-mail: nupur.chugh@bharatividyapeeth.edu[1]; sandeepbanerjee25@gmail.com[2]; vivekchaurasiya@gmail.com[4]
* Corresponding author: rakhi.cse@bharatividyapeeth.edu

DOI: 10.1201/9781003670582-1

Generative AI is reshaping healthcare's data foundations, enabling the creation of synthetic patient records, diagnostic-quality images, and structured clinical narratives for training and research—especially where data privacy or rare case limitations exist. Additionally, AI-powered decision support tools help clinicians explore diagnoses, evaluate treatments, and improve patient outcomes with greater speed and confidence. As robotics and generative AI converge, healthcare is shifting from automation to intelligent, personalized collaboration. Future systems will unify human expertise with machine intelligence—enhancing safety, accessibility, and efficiency in medical care. Recent advances in multimodal LLMs, GANs, diffusion models, and reinforcement learning have accelerated the development of intelligent, integrated care systems. These models can process diverse inputs—text, images, signals, and sensor data—enabling nuanced reasoning and human-like interaction. Their integration enhances situational awareness, adaptability, and responsiveness in clinical settings. This convergence fuels cross-disciplinary innovation across computer vision, NLP, bioinformatics, robotics, and medical sciences, driving breakthroughs in surgical assistance, real-time diagnostics, patient monitoring, and autonomous healthcare technologies.

1.2 Historical Context and Technological Evolution

Medical robotics gained prominence in the 1980s with the PUMA 560 robot arm performing stereotactic neurosurgery—marking a pivotal integration of robotics into medicine (Satava, 2002). This innovation laid the groundwork for future advances, notably the da Vinci Surgical System, which redefined robotic-assisted surgery through 3D visualization and minimally invasive procedures executed with superior precision and dexterity. Its master-slave teleoperation model reduced recovery time and surgical risks (Lanfranco et al., 2004). Medical robotics has expanded far beyond surgery, with applications in rehabilitation, infection control, and elder care. Wearable exoskeletons aid neuroplastic recovery by helping immobile patients regain movement. Prosthetics embedded with sensors provide intuitive control and feedback, improving the quality of life for amputees. Autonomous disinfection robots enhance hospital hygiene—especially during pandemics—by reducing infection risks. Social robots now assist the elderly by monitoring health, managing medication routines, and offering emotional support, advancing integration across the continuum of care.

Generative AI has rapidly advanced with the emergence of deep models—evolving from GANs and VAEs to transformer-based architectures like GPT-4, DALL·E, and Stable Diffusion. These models, trained on vast datasets using self-attention mechanisms, now exhibit exceptional fluency, contextual understanding, and creative output. In healthcare, this shift is particularly impactful: generative AI enables high-fidelity synthesis of medical images (MRI, CT, X-ray), supports training diagnostic models without breaching patient privacy, and generates structured clinical narratives from unstructured data. It also simulates disease progression using multimodal patient inputs, facilitating predictive analytics and personalized care. Crucially, synthetic data helps address privacy and scarcity challenges, making generative AI pivotal for developing intelligent, privacy-preserving healthcare systems (Biswal et al., 2023).

Integrating generative AI into robotics offers transformative potential for healthcare, pushing boundaries of autonomy, perception, and decision-making. By enriching reinforcement learning with large language models (LLMs), robots gain semantic understanding and high-level reasoning, adapting dynamically to real-world clinical environments. The fusion of multimodal data—images, sensor inputs, and textual knowledge—enhances diagnostic and navigational accuracy, even under noisy or incomplete conditions. In surgical robotics, generative models simulate intraoperative scenarios and enable real-time adjustments to anatomical changes or complications. This evolution signals the rise of contextual, intelligent robotic agents capable of collaborative decision-making and adaptive care. As generative AI matures, it will redefine human–machine interaction in clinical practice—reducing errors, personalizing treatment, and propelling the development of smart, responsive healthcare systems.

1.3 Scope and Purpose of this Chapter

This chapter provides a foundational overview for researchers exploring the intersection of robotics and generative AI in healthcare. It aims to:

- Explain key technologies and recent advancements in medical robotics and generative AI
- Outline historical milestones and emerging research trajectories
- Present integration strategies, enabling tools, and systemic implementation challenges
- Examine real-world applications and ethical considerations in clinical adoption

By contextualizing current developments, it promotes new research questions, interdisciplinary collaboration, and thoughtful evaluation of AI-driven healthcare's societal impact.

1.4 Robotics in Healthcare

Robotics has significantly transformed healthcare delivery by enhancing precision, operational efficiency, and patient outcomes. Its applications span surgery, diagnostics, rehabilitation, logistics, and medical training. Surgical robotics, notably the da Vinci Surgical System, exemplifies this impact—enabling minimally invasive procedures with superior control and reduced surgeon fatigue. These systems contribute to faster recovery, reduced pain, and fewer post-operative complications. Rehabilitation robots and wearable exoskeletons play a critical role in recovery for patients with stroke, spinal cord injuries, or neuromuscular impairments. By enabling repetitive, high-intensity motion training, they support physical therapy and allow for continuous progress monitoring—leading to better outcomes and reduced long-term dependency. Service robots are increasingly used in hospitals to automate routine logistics—transporting medications, linens, and supplies, and performing room disinfection using UV light or chemical sprays (Ranschaert et al., 2019). By relieving healthcare staff from repetitive tasks, these systems improve productivity and free up time for direct patient care. Telepresence robots are increasingly used in rural and underserved areas to bridge healthcare gaps. These mobile platforms facilitate remote consultations via video and audio, enabling specialists to engage directly with patients regardless of location—enhancing access and continuity of care. Robotic technology is increasingly applied across diagnostics, prosthesis design, pharmacy automation, and medical training. These systems enhance diagnostic accuracy, support personalized care, and improve clinical education. As technologies advance, robotics is poised to play a critical role in predictive medicine, elderly care, and tailored treatment—reshaping the future of healthcare delivery.

1.5 Surgical Robotics

Surgical robotics represents the most advanced and transformative application of robotics in healthcare. Robotic-assisted surgeries (RAS) enhance surgical precision through 3D imaging, improved ergonomics, tremor reduction, and fine instrument control. These systems enable minimally invasive procedures with smaller incisions, reduced blood loss, shorter hospital stays, and faster patient recovery.

The da Vinci Surgical System, developed by Intuitive Surgical, is a leading example of robotic surgery technology. It comprises a surgeon console, a patient-side cart with articulating robotic arms, and a vision cart for real-time imaging and processing. This integrated setup allows surgeons to perform complex procedures with exceptional precision and dexterity, surpassing conventional methods (Lanfranco et al., 2004).

Robotic surgery has been applied across diverse medical specialties, including urology, gynecology, cardiothoracic, gastrointestinal, and general surgery. India's first da Vinci system was installed at AIIMS, New Delhi in 2006—a landmark in national surgical history. Since then, robotic-assisted procedures have grown rapidly, with over 12,800 surgeries (e.g., prostatectomy, hysterectomy, myomectomy, nephrectomy, colorectal) performed across 66 centers by 2019. Ongoing advancements and expanded training are expected to further broaden its reach and impact.

Robotic-assisted surgery offers substantial benefits over traditional open procedures, including enhanced precision, reduced blood loss (typically 100–200 ml vs. 250 ml), smaller incisions, shorter hospital stays (1–3 days), and faster recovery (2–3 weeks). Advanced visualization and seamless robotic motion enable complex yet minimally invasive operations, improving patient satisfaction and outcomes. However, widespread adoption faces challenges such as high system costs, lengthy surgeon training, and limited access in underserved regions. Addressing these issues is essential for equitable integration into surgical care.

Table 1.1 Comparison of Open, Laparoscopic, and Robotic Surgery Outcomes

Surgery Type	*Avg. Recovery Time*	*Avg. Blood Loss*	*Hospital Stay*	*Cost*
Open Surgery	6–8 weeks	400–600 ml	7–10 days	Moderate
Laparoscopic	3–4 weeks	200–300 ml	3–5 days	Lower
Robotic-Assisted	2–3 weeks	100–200 ml	1–3 days	High

1.6 Rehabilitation and Assistive Robotics

Robotic rehabilitation systems are revolutionizing recovery for patients with stroke, spinal cord injuries, and other neurological impairments. By enabling repetitive, high-intensity, task-specific training, they effectively promote neuroplasticity and functional restoration. Unlike traditional therapy, robotics offer consistent, measurable support across extended sessions and varied settings—overcoming human limitations in stamina and variability.

Rehabilitation robots support upper and lower limb recovery post-neurological injury. The ArmeoSpring exoskeleton aids voluntary movement and joint control in stroke patients through natural arm trajectories and progressive resistance. For lower limbs, gait trainers like Lokomat and EksoGT help patients relearn walking patterns safely—especially beneficial during early recovery when independent mobility is impaired. Recent innovations in soft robotics —like flexible gloves and exosuits—use lightweight pneumatic or cable-driven actuation to aid hand movement and object grasping, crucial for fine motor rehabilitation. Integrated biosensors, motion capture, and AI feedback systems provide real-time performance metrics, enabling therapists to personalize treatment plans, track patient progress, and adjust training intensity to optimize recovery.

1.7 Service and Social Robots

Service and socially assistive robots (SARs) are gaining prominence in non-clinical and semi-clinical settings by improving hospital logistics and expanding patient care. Beyond operational efficiency, these robots provide emotional, cognitive, and social support to vulnerable populations—including the elderly, children, and chronically ill patients.

In hospitals, service robots like Aethon's TUG autonomously handle routine logistics—delivering medications, supplies, meals, and lab samples—helping reduce staff workload and freeing time for patient care. Socially interactive robots, such as Zenbo and Pepper, use voice, facial recognition, and display interfaces to enhance communication and engagement, particularly benefiting elderly and cognitively impaired patients.

Decontamination robots, such as Xenex LightStrike, have gained traction for infection control, especially during the COVID-19 pandemic. Using high-intensity pulsed UV light, they sterilize hospital rooms and high-touch surfaces, reducing pathogen exposure and enhancing hygiene without human involvement (Yang et al., 2020).

Socially assistive robots (SARs) are increasingly used in rehabilitation centers, eldercare facilities, and home-care settings. They offer emotional support, medication reminders, and gamified cognitive therapy—boosting mental health and engagement. As automation advances, SARs play a vital role in building resilient, patient-centric healthcare ecosystems. Socially Assistive Robots (SARs) are designed to promote emotional well-being and provide companionship, particularly for older adults and individuals with cognitive or developmental challenges. Unlike robots built for physical tasks, SARs focus solely on enhancing psychological health through interactive engagement. Notable examples include *Paro*, a robotic seal used in dementia care that calms users through gentle tactile responses, helping reduce anxiety and stimulate memory recall. Another widely recognized SAR is *Pepper*, a humanoid robot from SoftBank Robotics that communicates using voice, gestures, and facial recognition to foster empathetic interactions, identify emotions, and alleviate feelings of isolation.

Social and Service Robots are increasingly deployed in nursing homes, recovery centers, and mental health facilities where staffing and companionship gaps exist. They help reduce stress, loneliness, and behavioral challenges in patients while alleviating emotional strain on caregivers. As shown in Table 1.2, their key roles include enhancing patient morale, enabling personalized interaction, and improving long-term care quality. This reflects a promising shift toward person-centered robotics in healthcare.

Table 1.2 Roles and Benefits of Service and Social Robots in Healthcare

Robot Type	*Primary Function*	*Setting*	*Key Benefits*
Service Robot	Logistics, disinfection	Hospitals	Efficiency, safety
SAR (Paro, Pepper)	Emotional and cognitive aid	Elderly, mental care	Engagement, emotional support

1.8 Generative AI

Generative Artificial Intelligence (Generative AI) refers to machine learning methods capable of producing new data that mimics the statistical patterns of training data. Unlike discriminative models that focus on prediction, generative models learn the underlying distribution to synthesize high-fidelity outputs. Prominent architectures include Generative Adversarial Networks (GANs), which employ a generator-discriminator framework, Variational Autoencoders (VAEs) for probabilistic encoding, and Transformer-based models like Generative Pre-trained Transformer (GPT), which have significantly advanced natural language generation and application.

Generative AI is reshaping healthcare across diagnostics, drug discovery, personalized medicine, and imaging. In drug development, it enables the design of novel molecules with targeted properties, accelerating the preclinical phase by simulating biological interactions before costly lab testing. This significantly shortens development timelines and reduces expenses (Zhavoronkov et al., 2019; Mak & Pichika, 2019).

Generative AI is driving major advances in medical imaging by enhancing low-quality scans and generating synthetic datasets to address data scarcity, especially for rare conditions. It can simulate uncommon pathologies for training purposes and improve image clarity. Techniques like GANs expand and enrich diagnostic training sets, strengthening the accuracy and resilience of AI-based image analysis.

Transformer-based generative models are increasingly applied in clinical documentation and EHR management, automating transcription, summarizing patient history, and offering predictive insights to support clinical decisions. They also enable highly personalized treatment planning by modeling individual responses to therapies based on medical history, genetic profile, and lifestyle data—advancing precision medicine.

The rise of high-performance computing and abundant anonymized health data has accelerated the adoption of generative AI for faster, more accurate, and cost-effective healthcare solutions. However, responsible implementation demands careful attention to ethical concerns—particularly data privacy, model transparency, and rigorous clinical validation.

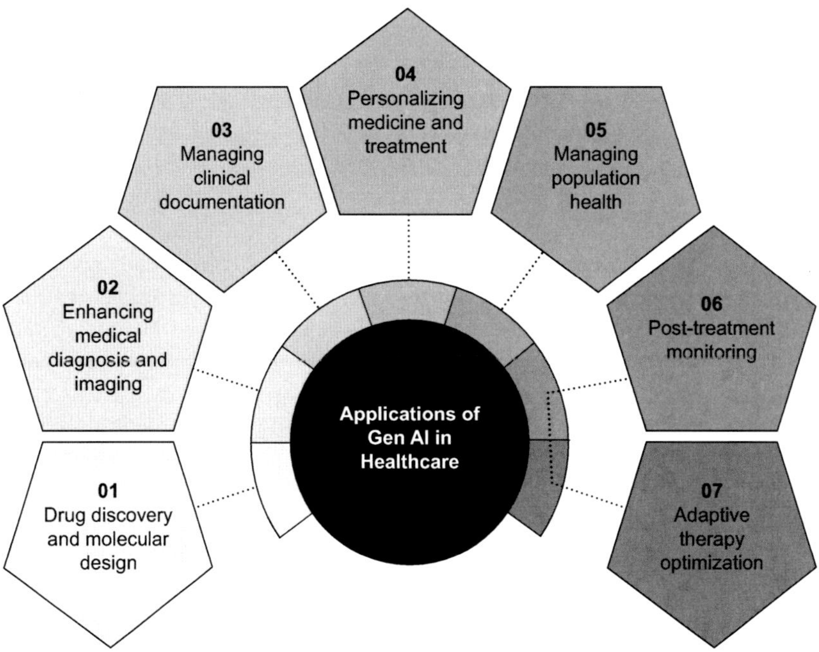

Fig. 1.1 Conceptual Diagram of Generative AI Applications in Healthcare

1.9 Applications

1.9.1 Drug Discovery and Molecular Design

Generative AI is revolutionizing drug discovery by dramatically reducing development time and cost. Traditional drug pipelines often span over a decade and cost billions, but generative models can design novel molecules with desired therapeutic properties and predict bioactivity and toxicity before synthesis (Zhavoronkov et al., 2019). Firms like Latent Labs and Insilico Medicine leverage deep generative models with reinforcement learning to identify candidates for diseases like fibrosis and cancer. Notably, Insilico Medicine achieved preclinical validation for a fibrosis drug in just 18 months (Mak & Pichika, 2019). Enhancing Medical Diagnosis and imaging

Generative AI is significantly advancing medical imaging by improving diagnostic precision and image quality. Generative Adversarial Networks (GANs), in particular, enhance low-resolution or noisy scans, enabling the restoration of high-fidelity images rich in diagnostic detail. These models are applied in critical fields like radiology, pathology, and dermatology to support accurate and robust analysis (Yi et al., 2019).

Generative models are increasingly applied in radiology to produce synthetic MRI and CT scans, serving two key roles: expanding limited datasets and enhancing image resolution. This is particularly valuable for training AI diagnostic tools, where annotated medical images may be scarce due to privacy constraints. Synthetic data improves model generalizability and robustness, enabling stronger real-world performance.

Modern generative models, such as image-to-image translation techniques, can reconstruct one imaging modality from another—for example, generating a CT scan from an MRI. This enables multi-modal diagnostics without requiring repeated tests, reducing patient exposure to cost, time, and radiation.

Generative AI is poised to transform medical imaging beyond diagnostics by supporting preoperative planning and automating annotation and segmentation of anatomical structures—easing radiologists' workload. As computational methods advance, these models offer promising diagnostic enhancements, particularly in low-resource settings lacking high-quality imaging tools. The resulting improvements in image fidelity, reduced reliance on manual annotation, and broader accessibility position generative AI as a cornerstone of future imaging innovation (see Table 1.3).

Table 1.3 Impact of Generative AI in Medical Imaging

Use Case	*Benefit*	*Model Type*
Image Enhancement	Improved resolution & clarity	GAN
Modality Translation	Generate missing imaging types	CycleGAN
Data Augmentation	Increase rare pathology datasets	VAE, GAN
Anomaly Detection	Identify deviations from normal scans	Diffusion Models

1.9.2 *Managing Clinical Documentation*

Generative AI is streamlining clinical documentation by using language models trained on large-scale EHRs to auto-generate notes, reports, and summaries with minimal human input—freeing up time for patient care. Integrated AI assistants can transcribe real-time doctor–patient interactions into structured records. Models like GPT-4 and Med-PaLM have shown strong contextual understanding, with pilot studies reporting up to a 70% reduction in clinician documentation time (Liu et al., 2023).

AI assistants integrated into hospital workflows can transcribe real-time doctor–patient interactions into structured clinical notes. Generative models like GPT-4 and Med-PaLM have shown strong contextual accuracy in summarizing and recommending patient care based on input data. Early studies report up to a 70% reduction in clinician documentation time with these AI-powered tools (Kumar et al., 2022).

1.9.3 *Personalizing Medicine and Treatment Plans*

Generative AI is transforming personalized healthcare by analyzing and simulating complex biomedical data. By integrating patient-specific inputs—such as genetic profiles, medical history, lifestyle, and prior treatment outcomes—these models can predict individual responses to therapies. This predictive capability empowers clinicians to craft highly tailored, efficient treatment plans aligned with each patient's unique profile.

Generative AI holds immense promise in oncology, where treatment decisions are complex and highly individualized due to tumor heterogeneity and variable patient responses. These models can simulate outcomes by analyzing genomic data, tumor markers, and historical clinical profiles—helping oncologists assess how different drug combinations might interact with a patient's cancer subtype and genetic makeup. This enables more informed, personalized treatment plans with higher efficacy and reduced adverse effects.

Generative AI enables dynamic, personalized treatment by continuously adjusting recommendations based on longitudinal patient data. This adaptability supports better outcomes and quality of life in cancer care and is increasingly relevant in cardiology, neurology, and chronic disease management. As these models advance, simulating and optimizing therapy will become central to precision medicine and the evolution of healthcare delivery. Managing Population Health

Generative AI holds transformative potential for public health by leveraging vast, real-time data sources—such as EHRs, epidemiological records, and wearable device outputs—to detect unseen patterns, forecast emerging health trends, and predict epidemics with exceptional accuracy. Early identification of anomalies can trigger timely interventions, optimal resource allocation, and containment strategies. Additionally, these models can simulate the impact of policies or health campaigns to refine approaches for vaccination, education, and care delivery, fostering a dynamic, evidence-based strategy for improving population health outcomes.

1.9.4 Post-treatment Monitoring

Remote Patient Monitoring Systems (RPMS) are rapidly integrating with generative AI to enhance predictive and preventive healthcare. By analyzing continuous physiological data from sensor-equipped wearables like smartwatches and fitness trackers, generative models can detect subtle anomalies before deterioration occurs—enabling timely, personalized interventions.

Predictive models using generative AI go beyond simple detection by anticipating health risks based on current and historical patient data. For example, they can forecast post-surgical complications—such as infections, thrombosis, or delayed healing—using real-time biometrics and medical history. This enables clinicians to proactively adjust treatment plans, schedule follow-ups, and implement preventive care to reduce risk and enhance recovery.

Generative AI enhances patient engagement by delivering automated, context-aware feedback to both clinicians and patients. Through timely alerts, personalized insights, and predictive notifications, it promotes adherence to treatment and empowers early interventions—reducing hospital readmissions and improving overall quality of life.

Integrating remote monitoring with generative AI marks a shift toward proactive, data-driven healthcare. This synergy enables personalized, adaptive care—especially for patients with chronic conditions or post-surgical needs—by leveraging real-time insights for timely intervention.

1.9.5 Adaptive Therapy Optimization

Adaptive therapy optimization is a forward-looking application of generative AI in precision oncology and chronic disease care. Unlike standard fixed-dose regimens, adaptive therapy uses patient-specific clinical, molecular, and physiological data to adjust treatment over time. The goal is to maintain long-term disease control, delay resistance, and minimize treatment-related toxicity.

Generative AI significantly enhances adaptive therapy by enabling sophisticated predictive modeling using multimodal data—such as patient-specific genomics, tumor imaging, medical records, and treatment history. These models simulate disease progression, drug interactions, and resistance dynamics, helping clinicians personalize treatment strategies with optimal timing, dosage, and duration to maximize therapeutic benefit (Schork, 2015; Gatenby et al., 2009).

In oncology, generative AI can model tumor evolution under drug pressure, guiding timely adjustments to therapy and dosage to prevent resistance while maintaining disease control. Robotic systems enhance this approach by delivering precise, reproducible treatment aligned with adaptive protocols, minimizing error and ensuring consistent drug delivery (Topol, 2019).

Adaptive Gen AI- and robotics-driven therapy mark a major shift in personalized, evidence-based clinical care. By enhancing outcomes and quality of life, this integration also helps cut healthcare costs—reducing overtreatment and minimizing long-term consequences of drug resistance.

1.10 Challenges of Robotics and Generative AI in Healthcare

While robotics and generative AI offer immense promise in healthcare, their widespread adoption raises complex challenges. Key concerns include technical limitations, data privacy, ethical risks, regulatory compliance, and integration into existing clinical workflows. Addressing these requires careful, multidisciplinary strategies to ensure responsible and effective implementation.

1.10.1 Data Privacy and Security Risks

Generative AI in healthcare relies on extensive patient data, often containing highly sensitive personal information. This raises serious concerns around privacy, security, and ethical handling. Ensuring compliance with regulations like HIPAA and GDPR is essential but challenging. Misuse or breaches can result in legal consequences, public mistrust, and harm to affected individuals. As generative AI becomes embedded in clinical workflows, robust and transparent data governance is critical (Mesko, 2023).

1.10.2 Bias and Fairness

Generative AI models are inherently vulnerable to biases embedded in training datasets, often due to historical inequities, underrepresentation of certain ethnic groups, and skewed sampling. These biases can lead to inaccurate diagnostics, inappropriate treatment recommendations, and flawed risk assessments—especially for minorities, women, elderly patients, or those with rare conditions. Such disparities may worsen existing health inequalities unintentionally. For instance, Obermeyer et al. (2019) revealed that biased algorithms resulted in systematically poorer care for disadvantaged populations. Addressing this requires diverse data sourcing, fairness audits, and bias mitigation throughout the AI development pipeline.

1.10.3 Lack of Explainability

Many deep learning-based generative AI models function as opaque "black boxes," producing complex outputs without clear reasoning. This lack of explainability undermines trust, especially in healthcare, where clinicians must justify treatment decisions and communicate effectively with patients. In high-stakes contexts like oncology or emergency care, unexplained AI outcomes could lead to serious consequences. To address this, there's growing focus on Explainable AI (XAI) and hybrid models that merge generative capabilities with transparent, human-interpretable logic (Amann et al., 2020).

1.10.4 High Costs and Infrastructure Demands

AI-driven healthcare systems offer precision and innovation but come with high costs—from purchasing advanced robotic platforms to maintaining AI diagnostics and training staff. These financial demands limit adoption in smaller or rural facilities, widening the healthcare divide and restricting access to cutting-edge treatments. Bridging this digital gap will require scalable technology, new funding models, and strong public-private partnerships to ensure equitable access across regions (Mesko, 2023).

1.10.5 Regulatory and Legal Uncertainty

The regulatory landscape for AI and robotics in healthcare is fragmented and underdeveloped across many regions, posing major hurdles to innovation and clinical adoption. Despite their potential to improve diagnostics and surgical precision, the lack of clear legal and ethical frameworks creates ambiguity—especially around accountability. For instance, if an AI system delivers a harmful diagnosis or treatment, it remains unclear who bears responsibility: the developer, clinician, or healthcare institution.

Regulatory ambiguity around AI and robotics in healthcare creates legal risks for institutions, often deterring clinical adoption despite clear benefits. Existing approval systems are ill-equipped to evaluate dynamic, continuously learning technologies that evolve post-deployment.

The European Commission (2022) and other regulators are introducing frameworks like the EU AI Act to classify and manage AI applications by risk level. However, these efforts are still in early stages and lack broad adoption. Without clear, enforceable regulation, the transformative potential of AI and robotics in healthcare may remain unrealized.

The growing use of automation and generative AI in healthcare raises concerns about job displacement, particularly for roles involving routine administrative tasks like transcription, billing, scheduling, and diagnostics. While these tools enhance efficiency and reduce errors, they can also lead to anxiety and resistance among staff worried about redundancy or diminished responsibilities.

Integrating AI into clinical workflows creates a growing need for professionals with interdisciplinary skills—blending medical expertise with knowledge of AI, data analytics, and machine learning. Addressing this shift requires new training programs, certifications, and curricula to prepare the next generation of AI-ready healthcare leaders. Yet, technological progress outpaces workforce reskilling, widening the skills gap. Bridging it demands collaboration between academia, health systems, and tech providers to position automation as a tool that complements, rather than replaces, human-centered care.

Conclusion

Robotics and generative AI are reshaping healthcare by enhancing precision, efficiency, and personalization in patient care. Their applications span surgical robotics, rehabilitation, drug discovery, synthetic data generation, and clinical documentation—driving better diagnostics, faster research, and improved patient outcomes.

To fully realize the benefits of robotics and generative AI in healthcare, critical challenges must be addressed. Key concerns include data privacy, algorithmic bias, and opaque decision-making processes, which hinder trust and ethical use. High costs, unclear regulations, and workforce skill gaps further limit widespread adoption. Successful integration demands coordinated, cross-disciplinary collaboration among clinicians, technologists, ethicists, and regulators.

As healthcare enters the digital age, robotics and generative AI must be implemented in a human-centric way—supporting, not replacing, medical professionals. These technologies should enhance decision-making, reduce administrative burden, and improve access and consistency of care. Looking ahead, sustained innovation, ethical safeguards, and inclusive policy development will be vital to shaping a healthcare ecosystem where AI and human expertise work in harmony for better outcomes and long-term sustainability.

References

[1] Amann, J., Blasimme, A., Vayena, E., Frey, D. and Madai, V. et al. (2020). Explainability for artificial intelligence in healthcare: A multidisciplinary perspective. *BMC Medical Informatics and Decision Making*, 20(1), 310. https://doi.org/10.1186/s12911-020-01332-6.

[2] Biswal, S., Ray, A. and Paul, S. (2023). Generative AI in Healthcare: Opportunities, Challenges, and Ethical Considerations. *Journal of Medical Artificial Intelligence*, 6(1), 101–117. https://doi.org/10.21037/jmai-23-20.

[3] Choi, W. (2022). Effects of robot-assisted gait training with body weight support on gait and balance in stroke patients. *International journal of environmental research and public health*, *19*(10), 5814.

[4] European Commission. (2022). *Regulation on AI and medical devices*. https://ec.europa.eu/health.

[5] Gatenby, R.A., Silva, A.S., Gillies, R.J. and Frieden, B.R. (2009). Adaptive therapy. *Cancer Research*, 69(11), 4894–4903. https://doi.org/10.1158/0008-5472.CAN-08-3658.

[6] Kumar, S., Dey, D. and Sinha, R. (2022). Transforming EHRs: The rise of generative AI in clinical documentation. *Health Informatics Journal*, 28(3), 231–244.

[7] Lanfranco, A.R., Castellanos, A.E., Desai, J.P. and Meyers, W.C. (2004). Robotic surgery: A current perspective. *Annals of Surgery*, 239(1), 14–21. https://doi.org/10.1097/01.sla.0000103020.19595.7d.

[8] Lanfranco, A.R., Castellanos, A.E., Desai, J.P. and Meyers, W.C. (2004). Robotic surgery: A current perspective. *Annals of Surgery*, 239(1), 14–21. https://doi.org/10.1097/01.sla.0000103020.19595.7d.

[9] Liu, Y., Ott, M., Ghosh, S., Zhang, Y. and Chang, S. et al. (2023). Generative AI for clinical documentation: Opportunities and challenges. *Journal of Biomedical Informatics*, 139, 104333.

[10] Mak, K.K. and Pichika, M.R. (2019). Artificial intelligence in drug development: present status and future prospects. *Drug Discovery Today*, 24(3), 773–780.

[11] Mesko, B. (2023). Challenges of AI implementation in healthcare. *The Medical Futurist*. https://medicalfuturist.com

[12] Obermeyer, Z., Powers, B., Vogeli, C. and Mullainathan, S. (2019). Dissecting racial bias in an algorithm used to manage the health of populations. *Science*, 366(6464), 447–453. https://doi.org/10.1126/science.aax2342.

[13] Ranschaert, E.R., Morozov, S. and Algra, P.R. (2019). *Artificial Intelligence in Medical Imaging: Opportunities, Applications and Risks*. Springer.

[14] Satava, R.M. (2002). Emerging technologies for surgery in the 21st century. *Archives of Surgery*, 137(2), 189–193. https://doi.org/10.1001/archsurg.137.2.189.

[15] Schork, N.J. (2015). Personalized medicine: Time for one-person trials. *Nature*, 520(7549), 609–611. https://doi.org/10.1038/520609a.

[16] Topol, E. (2019). *Deep Medicine: How Artificial Intelligence Can Make Healthcare Human Again*. Basic Books.

[17] Yang, G.Z., Nelson, B.J., Murphy, R.R., Choset, H., Christensen, H. et al. (2020). Combating COVID-19—The role of robotics in managing public health and infectious diseases. *Science Robotics*, 5(40), eabb5589. https://doi.org/10.1126/scirobotics.abb5589.

[18] Yi, X., Walia, E., and Babyn, P. (2019). Generative adversarial network in medical imaging: A review. *Medical Image Analysis*, 58, 101552.

[19] Zhavoronkov, A., Ivanenkov, Y.A., Aliper, A., Veselov, M.S., Aladinskiy, V.A. et al. (2019). Deep learning enables rapid identification of potent DDR1 kinase inhibitors. *Nature Biotechnology*, 37(9), 1038–1040.

2 Engineering Healthcare: Key Technologies and Systems in Healthcare

Pooja Gupta[1], Ruchi Goel[2] and Kashvi Aggarwal[3*]

Smart technologies have reshaped daily life, and their rapid advancement has positioned engineering as a transformative force in healthcare. This chapter highlights key domains—robotic-assisted surgery, EHRs, real-time diagnostics, telemedicine, biosensors, biomechanics, and genetic engineering—showing how these innovations improve diagnostic precision, enable personalized treatments, enhance safety, and lower costs. However, challenges remain around data privacy, regulatory compliance, and equitable access.

2.1 Introduction to Engineering in Healthcare

Biomedical Engineering (BME) is a multidisciplinary field that merges engineering principles with biology and medicine to develop innovative healthcare solutions.

2.1.1 Definition and Scope of Healthcare Engineering

Healthcare Engineering applies engineering principles to enhance healthcare delivery through innovative technologies. It covers medical devices, healthcare IT, bioinformatics, and hospital management—aiming to improve diagnosis, treatment, and patient outcomes. Advances in this field also support early disease detection and preventive care, promoting better overall health [1].

2.1.2 Evolution of Engineering Applications in Healthcare

Engineering has transformed healthcare—from foundational breakthroughs like X-rays and antibiotics to modern innovations in imaging, minimally invasive surgery, and personalized medicine. Emerging technologies such as AI, nanotech, and tissue engineering promise even deeper impacts in diagnostics and treatment. By applying engineering principles, healthcare systems can deliver more precise, scalable, and accessible solutions to improve patient outcomes.

1 Computer Science and Technology, MAIT, Delhi, India.
2 Computer Science and Engineering, MAIT, Delhi, India.
3 Computer Engineering, TIET, Patiala, India.
* Corresponding author: ruchigoel06@gmail.com

DOI: 10.1201/9781003670582-2

2.2 Importance of Technology in Improving Patient Care, Efficiency, and Safety

Technology integration has reshaped modern healthcare, enabling real-time data access, faster clinical decisions, reduced errors, and streamlined operations. Central to this transformation is the strategic use of patient data, which drives precision diagnostics and personalized treatment. Figure 2.1 illustrates the full data journey—from collection to clinical outcome—while Table 2.1 summarizes the end-to-end workflow. The process begins with sourcing structured and unstructured data (e.g., medical records, wearables), followed by secure cloud-based storage. Data is then standardized and processed under strict cybersecurity norms. AI and ML-powered analytics extract insights, detect anomalies, and forecast health trends, ultimately informing timely alerts, tailored therapies, and improved decision-making. This seamless data-driven approach underscores the pivotal role of healthcare engineering in optimizing patient outcomes.

Table 2.1 End to End Workflow of Data Driven Healthcare System

Stages	*Focus*	*Results*
1. Identify Data Sources	Collect raw data from various devices	Broad range of inputs
2. Data Acquisition and Storage	Collecting, transmitting, and securely storing the data	Integrity of the data
3. Data Processing	Gathering information for analysis	Useful Datasets
4. Data Analytics	Extracting valuable insights using processed data	Forecasts and trends
5. Outcome	Healthcare impact improved	Data-driven healthcare

2.2.1 Healthcare Engineering

Healthcare Engineering applies engineering principles to medicine and biology to improve patient care. It encompasses biomedical, clinical, tissue, and healthcare systems engineering—distinct yet interdependent fields that collaboratively develop and optimize technologies within an integrated healthcare ecosystem.

- **Biomedical Engineering:** Biomedical Engineering biology with engineering to develop advanced medical devices that enhance patient care. Professionals like doctors, psychiatrists, and bioengineers contribute to life-saving innovations—such as pacemakers, prosthetics, and wearable monitors—advancing drug delivery and healthcare technologies [2].
- **Clinical Engineering:** Clinical engineering is a specialized branch of biomedical engineering that bridges medicine and technology. Clinical engineers ensure medical equipment is safely managed, maintained, and complies with healthcare standards, playing a key role in healthcare delivery.

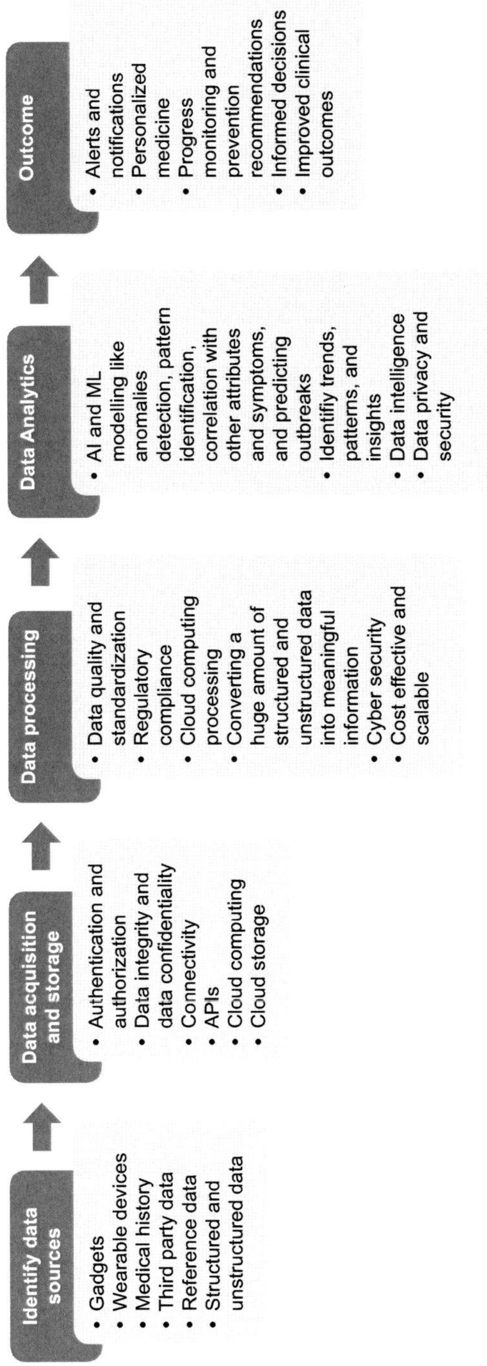

Fig. 2.1 Flow of Data from Gathering Healthcare Data to Outcome.

- **Tissue Engineering:** Tissue engineering focuses on creating biological replacements for damaged tissues or organs. Using cells, scaffolds, and growth factors, researchers grow functional tissues in labs for implantation [3]. This field shows promise in treating injuries, diseases, and organ failure with innovations like skin grafts, cartilage repair, and future organ regeneration. Despite integration challenges, it offers a pathway to personalized, regenerative healthcare.
- **Healthcare Systems Engineering:** Healthcare Systems Engineering (HSE) applies engineering principles to optimize healthcare delivery by improving system-wide efficiency and safety. It focuses on designing, modeling, and analyzing complex healthcare infrastructures through data-driven methods. Wearables contribute vital real-time data, enabling remote monitoring, predictive analytics, and customized care. The global medical device industry—spanning imaging tools, life-support systems, surgical equipment, and point-of-care diagnostics—is projected to surpass $600 billion by 2027 [4] [5], reflecting the sector's rapid growth and integral role in modern medicine.

2.3 Engineering Technologies in Healthcare

Advancements in internet technologies, cloud platforms, and AI/ML analytics have revolutionized healthcare by enabling real-time data processing. Integration of patient records with wearables, AI-based imaging, and smart hospital systems supports rapid data collection, early disease prediction, and personalized treatments.

2.3.1 Key Areas of Engineering Technologies in Healthcare

- **Patient Record Maintenance:** Patient record maintenance involves converting unstructured data—such as imaging scans, lab reports, and clinical videos—into structured formats for analytics. Cloud platforms like AWS (Lambda, EMR), GCP (Compute Engine, BigQuery, Dataproc), and Azure (Fabric, Functions, Synapse Analytics) enable near real-time processing of massive healthcare datasets.
- **Real Time Diagnostics:** are revolutionizing healthcare by delivering instant access to critical patient data, enabling faster treatment, continuous monitoring, and personalized care [6]. They streamline clinical decisions, reduce delays, and improve access—especially in underserved regions. Medical robotics are transforming healthcare—from precision surgeries and automated disinfection to streamlined supply delivery—allowing clinicians to focus more on patient care. First introduced in 1980 for surgical assistance, these robots now integrate AI, computer vision, and data analytics, revolutionizing treatment and operations across the sector. During COVID-19, they played a critical role in patient engagement and support.

- **Examples include:**
  - **Surgical robots** (e.g., Da Vinci System)
  - **Rehabilitation robots** for physical therapy
  - **AI-powered hospital automation** (e.g., robotic nurses, automated drug dispensing)
- Biosensors detect biological substances and convert them into measurable signals [7], while biomechanics examines motion and force in living systems. These fields are closely linked—biosensors supply data for biomechanical studies, and biomechanics informs sensor design—together advancing diagnostics and medical device innovation. AI and ML are revolutionizing healthcare by enabling early disease detection, improving diagnostics and treatment, streamlining hospital operations, and advancing medical research. They boost efficiency, accelerate decision-making, and support personalized patient care.
- **Genetic Engineerin**g advances healthcare through personalized treatments guided by genetic testing, improving effectiveness and minimizing side effects [8]. By altering DNA through editing and insertion, it supports breakthroughs in medicine, agriculture, and research. However, ethical concerns about human gene editing and unintended outcomes remain critical. Telemedicine enables stored data exchange (e.g., reports, scans), real-time monitoring via connected devices, and interactive sessions like video consultations. It lowers cost and time for both patients and providers, enhances care accessibility, and minimizes travel and wait times.
- **Advanced Medical Imaging and Diagnostic Technologies:**
  - **3D and 4D Imaging Advancements**
    - **3D Imaging:** Advanced imaging technologies like CT and MRI offer high-definition views of internal structures, supporting precise diagnostics across neurology, orthopedics, and cardiology.
    - **4D Imaging:** 4D imaging extends 3D technology by incorporating time, enabling real-time visualization of internal organ movement and fetal development. Widely used in ultrasound and surgical planning, it supports dynamic, motion-based diagnostics for more informed clinical decisions.
  - **Functional and Molecular Imaging**
    - **Functional Imaging:** Functional imaging goes beyond structural scans by capturing physiological processes in real time. Techniques like fMRI detect blood flow abnormalities in neurological studies, while PET and SPECT assess organ and tissue activity—offering crucial insights for diagnosing cancer and neurological disorders.
    - **Molecular Imaging:** Molecular imaging visualizes cellular and molecular activity, aiding early disease detection and treatment monitoring—especially in oncology, neurology, and cardiology. Techniques like PET and MRI with molecular tracers reveal cell-level interactions for better diagnostic and therapeutic outcomes.

2.4 Applications of Engineering Technologies in Healthcare

Engineering technologies have significantly advanced healthcare—streamlining diagnosis, improving treatment strategies, elevating patient care, and accelerating medical research. Figure 2.2 highlights key application areas driving these innovations.

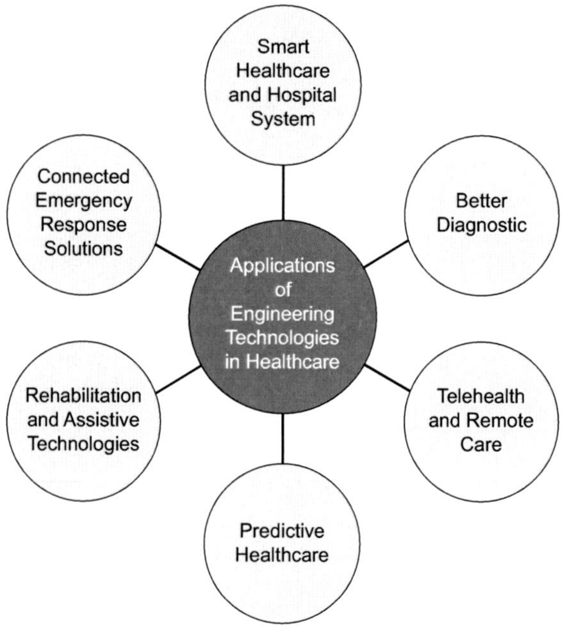

Fig. 2.2 Applications of Engineering Technologies in healthcare.

2.4.1 Smart Healthcare Infrastructure & Hospital Systems

- Modern healthcare facilities leverage IoT, AI, and data analytics to build connected, efficient systems. IoT enables real-time health monitoring, AI enhances diagnostics and prediction, and analytics unify data for quicker clinical decisions—resulting in better outcomes, smoother operations, and expanded remote care.
- **Connected devices:** Smart monitors, infusion pumps, and ventilators transmit real-time patient data, enhancing continuous monitoring and clinical responsiveness. A range of wearable healthcare devices further supports ongoing vital tracking, including:
  - Biosensors
  - Smart thermometers
  - Connected inhalers
  - Smartwatches
  - Fitness trackers (e.g.,FitBits)

  - ECG monitors
  - Blood pressure monitors
- **Smart beds, such as those developed by Hill-Rom and Stryker,** can automatically adjust to patient movements to help prevent bedsores and pressure ulcers in immobile individuals. Examples of smart beds are illustrated in **Figure 2.3**.

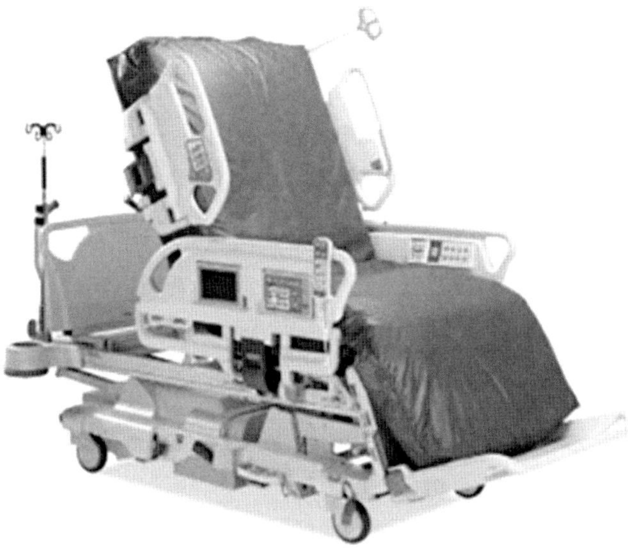

Fig. 2.3 Smart Beds.

- **RFID-Based Tracking:** RFID and GPS technologies in healthcare help track equipment, manage drug inventories, and monitor patient movement—boosting workflow efficiency, safety, and reducing asset loss.
- **Remote patient monitoring (RPM):** Wearable technology supports remote monitoring by tracking vital signs like blood pressure, heart rate, respiration, and oxygen levels. It enables real-time data sharing with clinicians, reducing hospital stays and improving patient outcomes.
- **Smart environmental control:** Smart environmental control systems in hospitals use sensors and automation to optimize lighting and HVAC, enhancing patient comfort, supporting faster recovery, and reducing operating costs in critical areas like ICUs.
- **Automated medication dispensing:** Automated medicine dispensing systems use robotics and digital controls to boost safety, accuracy, and efficiency. They manage inventory, simplify dispensing, and reduce nurses' workload.

- **AI-Based Medical Transcription:** AI-based medical transcription tools, such as **Suki** and **Nuance Dragon**, convert doctors' speech into structured electronic health records (EHRs). Examples are illustrated in **Figure 2.4**.

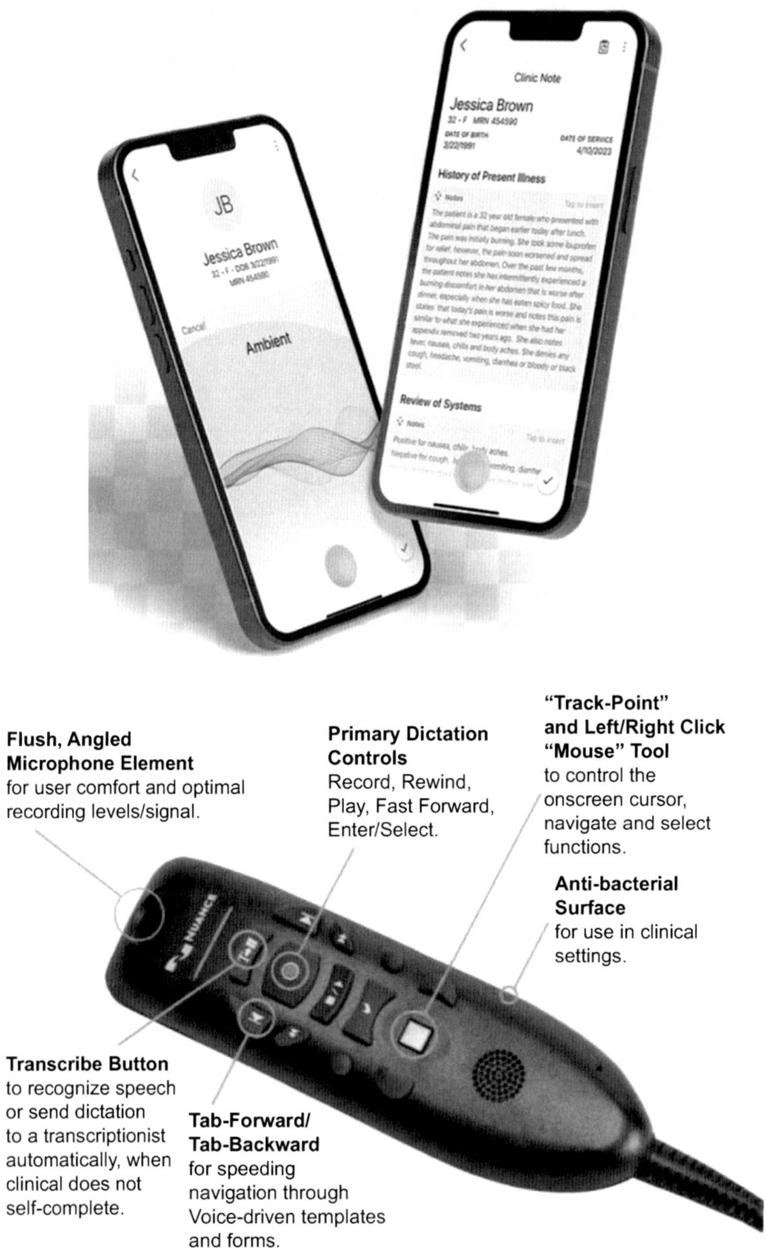

Fig. 2.4 AI-based Medical Transcription.

2.4.1.1 *Smart Hospital Management & Workflow Optimization*

Engineering technologies have reshaped hospital management—boosting efficiency, reducing costs, and improving patient care. Smart hospital systems enhance workflows, optimize resources, and streamline operations, as illustrated in **Figure 2.5** [9].

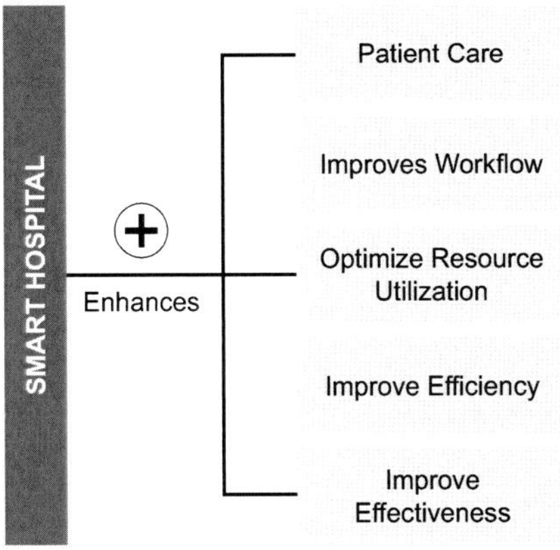

Fig. 2.5 Smart Hospital Visualization.

- **Workflow Automation:** AI streamlines hospital operations by optimizing resource allocation, staff scheduling, and overall efficiency—cutting costs while enhancing care delivery.
- **Smart Electronic Health Records (EHRs):** Natural Language Processing (NLP) improves Electronic Health Records (EHRs) by automating clinical documentation, minimizing errors, and enhancing data interoperability.
- **Monitoring and Predictive Analytics:** Smart hospitals leverage IoT and AI for predictive analytics and real-time monitoring, reducing equipment downtime and enhancing care delivery. Predictive tools support proactive resource allocation and informed decisions by forecasting admission trends, peak hours, and potential disease outbreaks.
- **Automated Administrative Tasks:** AI-powered automation in smart hospitals streamlines administrative tasks by reducing paperwork, minimizing errors, and cutting physical labor. This lowers staffing demands, speeds up workflows, and allows personnel to focus more on patient-centered care—improving efficiency and cost-effectiveness.
- **Chatbots & Virtual Assistants:** AI-powered virtual assistants and chatbots enhance patient interaction in smart hospitals by providing 24/7 support, easing staff workload, and handling queries on symptoms, prescriptions, and appointments. They improve accessibility with bilingual aid, streamline bookings, and offer symptom triage for better patient satisfaction.

2.4.2 Telehealth and Remote Care

Telehealth's rapid adoption during the pandemic showcased the power of smart healthcare technologies. Through virtual consults and secure portals, it enabled remote care, prescription access, and efficient health record management—cementing its ongoing role in modern hospital systems.

2.4.3 Connected Emergency Response Solutions

Seamless connectivity boosts emergency care efficiency by enabling real-time data sharing. Integrated communication between ambulances, physicians, and hospitals ensures rapid response through live video consults, instant access to medical histories, and smoother admissions—ultimately saving lives.

2.4.4 Better Diagnostics using AI-Enhanced Radiology and Pathology

- **AI in Radiology:** AI is transforming radiology by boosting image interpretation, speeding up diagnoses, and improving accuracy. Machine learning detects patterns and anomalies—such as cancers and fractures—and automates routine tasks like image segmentation, easing radiologists' workload.
- **AI in Pathology:** AI enhances pathology by analyzing tissue and cell structures with deep learning, enabling faster, more accurate disease detection—especially for conditions like cancer. It improves pattern recognition in histopathological images and supports clinical decision-making.

2.4.5 Predictive Healthcare

Advanced machine learning enables real-time analysis of patient data to predict disease progression and personalize treatments. Integrated with smart alerts, these systems enhance safety and staff efficiency by notifying caregivers instantly—via pagers, mobile devices, or dashboards—when critical changes occur, such as sudden drops in blood pressure or irregular heartbeat [11].

2.4.6 AI-Enhanced Radiology and Pathology

AI speeds up drug discovery by identifying promising compounds, cutting costs, and improving trials. In radiology, it detects subtle abnormalities and reduces diagnostic variability in scans. In pathology, it pinpoints malignant cells and biomarkers for faster, more accurate diagnosis. Combined with medical records, AI supports predictive analytics for disease progression and tailored treatment recommendations.

2.4.7 Rehabilitation & Assistive Technologies

Assistive and rehabilitation technologies are rapidly advancing to boost mobility, independence, and quality of life for individuals with impairments. Innovations like powered exoskeletons, robotic prosthetics, and smart mobility aids support daily tasks and rehabilitation. Integrated with sensors, AI, and adaptive controls, these devices offer personalized, efficient, and accessible solutions for active societal participation.

2.5 Systems Approach in Healthcare Engineering

A systems approach to healthcare engineering analyzes, designs, and improves healthcare delivery for improved results, efficiency, and safety. It sees healthcare as a complex, linked system.

2.5.1 Integration of Hardware, Software, and Data

Modern patient care relies on integrated hardware—like wearables and diagnostic tools—and software such as medical apps and AI, all producing vast patient data. A systems approach ensures seamless coordination and effective use of these components for better outcomes.

Example: AI algorithms analyze real-time data from heart-rate monitors and upload results to the patient's EHR, enabling remote monitoring and prompt medical response to any anomalies. This integration:

- Facilitates ongoing patient monitoring
- Enhances real-time decision-making
- Minimizes redundant testing and procedures

2.5.2 Interoperability Between Systems

Interoperability enables healthcare devices and systems to share, interpret, and use data seamlessly. Without it, disconnected platforms hinder treatment efficiency and lead to fragmented patient care. To achieve interoperability, healthcare systems employ key strategies [23]:

- **Standards** such as **HL7**, **FHIR**, and **DICOM**
- **APIs** for seamless data exchange across platforms and devices
- **Cloud-based architectures** for centralized data access and secure storage

Example: A radiology system can automatically transmit scan results to a doctor's EHR, which AI diagnostic tools can then interpret—eliminating manual data entry and supporting efficient, connected care.

2.5.3 System Design Principles in Hospital Infrastructure

Smart hospital design relies on engineering-driven principles like modularity, scalability, and redundancy to ensure flexible, future-ready infrastructure. Modular systems allow seamless upgrades without disrupting operations, while scalable setups accommodate growing patient volumes and data loads. Fail-safes and backup systems maintain continuity during outages. Workflow optimization through automation and digital tools enhances security and efficiency—embedding cybersecurity throughout. For instance, ICU monitors can send real-time emergency alerts to a central command, improving coordination and response speed.

2.6 Benefits of Engineering Technologies in Healthcare

Engineering technologies have reshaped healthcare by enhancing treatment outcomes, boosting efficiency, and lowering costs. Key benefits include:

2.6.1 Improved and efficient Medical Diagnostics

- **Early Disease Detection:** AI-powered imaging tools like X-rays, MRIs, and CT scans enable early, accurate detection of conditions like cancer and heart disease. Smart hospitals equipped with AI cameras (e.g., Care.ai, Vuzix Smart Glasses) continuously monitor patients and alert staff during emergencies for timely intervention.
- **Predictive Analytics:** Predictive analytics examines patient data to anticipate adverse events like sepsis or heart attacks, enabling timely intervention and improved outcomes.
- **Pathology & Genomics:** AI-driven algorithms analyze biopsy and genetic data to detect health risks and suggest personalized treatments.

2.6.2 Improving Patient Care

Improving patient care involves a diverse approach that focuses on enhancing the patient's experience, safety, and health outcomes by providing patient personalized and advance care.

- **Electronic Health Records (EHRs):** Electronic Health Records (EHRs) improve healthcare by providing quick access to patient history, supporting accurate diagnoses and informed treatment decisions.
- **Robotic Surgery:** Robotic surgery enhances patient care by increasing precision, improving visualization, reducing human error, and shortening recovery time through the use of advanced robotic arms.

2.6.3 Enhancing Efficiency

Technology enhances healthcare efficiency—cutting costs, improving outcomes, and ensuring optimal resource utilization.

- **Automation:** AI chatbots streamline healthcare admin tasks by managing patient queries, appointment scheduling, and symptom assessments. The market's rapid growth—from $335.26M in 2024 to a projected $1,091.64M by 2030 (CAGR 21.72%)—highlights their rising impact [12].
- **Decision Support Systems:** Decision Support Systems (DSS) act as virtual assistants, offering doctors nsights from patient histories to guide critical decisions and improve outcomes. They also support shared decision-making between doctors and patients using medical records [13].

2.6.4 Ensuring Patient Safety

Ensuring patient safety means minimizing harm through error prevention, data protection, and a secure care environment.

- **Barcode Medication Administration (BCMA):** Barcode Medication Administration (BCMA) reduces medication errors by verifying the correct patient, drug, dose, time, and route [14]. This improves safety and helps lower unnecessary healthcare doses.
- **Cybersecurity in Healthcare:** Data protection is vital in healthcare to keep patient information secure and confidential. As digital reliance grows, robust cybersecurity becomes essential to guard against breaches and cyber-attacks [15, 16].

2.7 Case Studies/ Real-World Applications

2.7.1 AI for Early Cancer Detection

AI is transforming cancer care by enabling earlier detection, more accurate diagnosis, and improved outcomes through precision medicine [17]. Deep learning models analyze imaging data from MRI, CT, and MBR scans with sensitivity and specificity rivaling or surpassing human radiologists [18].

Real-World Use: Google Health's AI model for breast cancer screening.

2.7.2 Tele-ICU Systems

Tele-ICU integrates data from multiple systems into a unified interface, offering real-time insights across care units or entire hospitals [19]. It enables continuous remote monitoring and expert supervision, accelerating clinical response, optimizing staffing, and reducing mortality in critical care settings.

Real-World Use: GE HealthCare's Mural Virtual Care Solution aggregates data from multiple systems to provide a comprehensive patient overview, enabling digital care protocols and treatment pathways [20].

Apollo TeleHealth in India leverages Tele-ICU to support rural hospitals by offering centralized intensivist oversight.

2.7.3 Use of Robotics in Orthopaedic Surgery

Orthopaedic robotic-assisted surgery, as shown in **Figure 2.6,** is gaining traction for its precision, faster recovery, and improved outcomes—especially in joint reconstruction and spine procedures. Technologies like the MAKO robotic-arm for knee arthroplasty are revolutionizing surgical approaches [21].

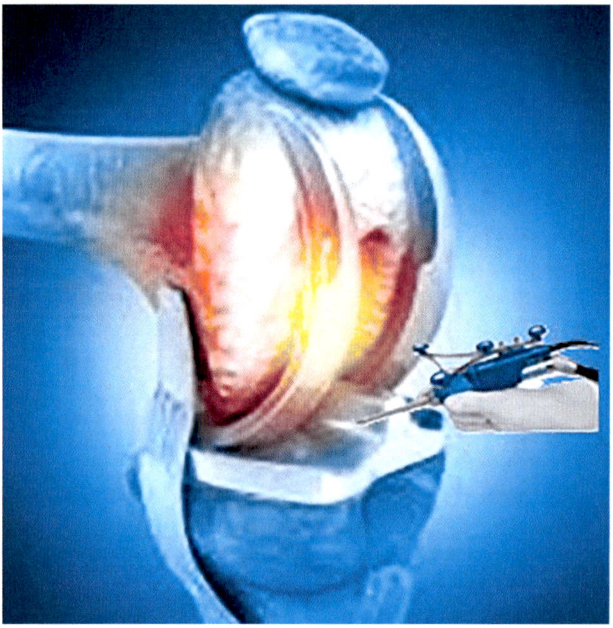

Fig. 2.6 Orthopaedic Robotic-Assisted Surgery.

2.7.4 COVID-19 Response Technologies

During the COVID-19 pandemic, rapid adoption of low-cost ventilators (e.g., MIT E-Vent), contact tracing apps (Aarogya Setu), AI-driven pandemic modeling, and wearable monitors enabled efficient remote care and improved resource planning and responsiveness [22].

2.8 Limitations and Challenges

While technology offers numerous benefits to healthcare, its integration also brings several limitations and challenges:

- **Internet connectivity:** Stable internet is vital for telemedicine and remote monitoring, but limited access still poses challenges in many areas.
- **Data privacy & cybersecurity in digital health:** Safeguarding patient data from breaches and unauthorized access is essential to maintain privacy and trust.

- **Regulatory challenges & compliance:** Navigating the complex regulatory landscape—including FDA, ISO, and CE marking—is a major challenge for medical devices and digital health solutions.
- **Accuracy of the predictive algorithm:** Accurate and reliable AI predictive models are crucial for guiding effective clinical decisions.
- **Availability and storage of historical data:** Secure access and storage of large patient datasets are essential for training and validating reliable AI models.
- **High Initial Costs:** Implementing engineering solutions like AI diagnostics, robotics, and smart systems requires substantial investment in technology, software, and training.
- **Educating and Raising Awareness:** Promoting technology training for healthcare providers and patients is essential to ensure effective adoption and informed usage.

Conclusion & Future Prospects

The future of healthcare depends on integrating advanced technologies with sustainable practices. Green healthcare—via energy-efficient infrastructure, eco-friendly devices, digital solutions, smart waste management, and greener pharmaceuticals—reduces environmental impact without compromising care. These innovations support effective, responsible healthcare while tackling global challenges like climate change and resource conservation.

Emerging technologies like AI, IoT, and robotics will drive are set to advance personalized medicine through real-time monitoring, predictive analytics, and automated care. Innovations in diagnostics, robotic surgeries, and smart hospital systems will boost efficiency, minimize errors, and improve outcomes. Engineering-led breakthroughs in drug delivery, imaging, and treatment will enable faster, more accurate, and less invasive healthcare. Globally, emerging technologies like telemedicine, AI diagnostics, and low-cost medical tools can bridge healthcare gaps in underserved regions. Prioritizing sustainability, digital innovation, and accessibility will foster better outcomes and a more equitable, eco-friendly healthcare ecosystem.

Declarations

- The authors received no specific funding for this study.
- The authors declare that they have no conflicts of interest to report regarding the present study.
- No human subject or animals are involved in the research.
- All authors have mutually consented to participate.
- All authors have given their consent for the Journal to publish this work.
- The authors affirm that all data being used in the design , development, and layout of the manuscript are fully disclosed within the manuscript.

References

[1] https://www.healthcare-engineering.org/definition

[2] Mohd J., Haleem A., Singh R.P. and Suman R. "Sustaining the healthcare systems through the conceptual of biomedical engineering: A study with recent and future potentials." *Biomedical Technology* 1 (2023): 39–47.

[3] Julie, E. Golden, Robinson Y.H. and Jaisakthi, S.M. eds. Handbook of deep learning in biomedical engineering and health informatics. CRC Press, 2021.

[4] Khan, Muhammad Umar Aslam, Goran M. Stojanović, Mohd Faizal Bin Abdullah, Alireza Dolatshahi-Pirouz, Hany E. Marei et al. "Fundamental properties of smart hydrogels for tissue engineering applications: A review." *International Journal of Biological Macromolecules* 254 (2024): 127882.

[5] https://www.romsons.in/blogs/post/medical-device-industry-a-pillar-of-modern-healthcare-and-the-legacy-of-romsons group?srsltid=AfmBOoqgzFFmZnRUT7koXrNnk8w6UlOI7h283Czc5kyImmkByVABNma3

[6] https://auxomedical.com/2024/01/what-are-the-different-types-of-biomedical-equipment/.

[7] Kumar, N., Das N.N., Gupta, D., Gupta K. and Bindra, J., et al. "Efficient automated disease diagnosis using machine learning models." *Journal of Healthcare Engineering 2021*, no. 1 (2021): 9983652.

[8] Kim, E.R., Joe C., Mitchell R.J. and Gu M.B.. "Biosensors for healthcare: Current and future perspectives." *Trends in Biotechnology* 41, no. 3 (2023): 374–395.

[9] Nicholl, Desmond ST. An introduction to genetic engineering. Cambridge University Press, 2023.

[10] Munavalli, J.R., Boersma H.J., Rao S.V., and Van Merode G.G. "Real-time capacity management and patient flow optimization in hospitals using AI methods." *Artificial Intelligence and Data Mining in Healthcare* (2021): 55–69.

[11] Goldman, J.G., Merkitch D., Brewington D., Peirce H., Rho M. et al. "Patient experiences receiving rehabilitation care via telehealth: Identifying opportunities for remote care." *Frontiers in Rehabilitation Sciences* 4 (2023): 1049554.

[12] Rana, M.S. and Shuford J. "AI in healthcare: transforming patient care through predictive analytics and decision support systems." *Journal of Artificial Intelligence General Science* (JAIGS) ISSN: 3006-4023 1, no. 1 (2024).

[13] https://www.coherentsolutions.com/insights/how-ai-chatbots-advance-healthcare-for-patients-and-providers.

[14] https://www.bigscal.com/blogs/healthcare-industry/decision-support-systems-healthcare/#:~:text=A%20decision%20support%20system%20(DSS,treatment%20plans%20or%20resource%20management.

[15] https://pmc.ncbi.nlm.nih.gov/articles/PMC8606443/.

[16] https://www.sbigeneral.in/blog-details/cybersecurity-in-healthcare-threats-importance-strategies

[17] https://www.oxjournal.org/ai-in-breast-cancer-assessing-case-studies/.

[18] Adapa, K., Gupta, A., Singh, S. et al. A real world evaluation of an innovative artificial intelligence tool for population-level breast cancer screening. npj Digit. Med. 8, 2 (2025). https://doi.org/10.1038/s41746-024-01368-2.

[19] https://www.gehealthcare.in/products/mural-virtual-care-solution

[20] Watanabe, T., Ohsugi K., Suminaga Y., Somei M., Kikuyama K. et al. "An evaluation of the impact of the implementation of the Tele-ICU: a retrospective observational study." *Journal of intensive Care* 11, no. 1 (2023): 9.

[21] Roche, M.. "The MAKO robotic-arm knee arthroplasty system." *Archives of Orthopaedic and Trauma Surgery* (2021): 1–5.

[22] https://emergency-vent.mit.edu/.

[23] Torab-Miandoab, A., Samad-Soltani T., Jodati A. and Rezaei-Hachesu P. "Interoperability of heterogeneous health information systems: a systematic literature review." *BMC Medical Informatics and Decision Making* 23, no. 1 (2023): 18.

3 Generative AI: A Comparative Analysis of Architectures, Evaluation Metrics, and Emerging Challenges

Neha Sharma[1*], Anupam Tiwari[2] and Prateek Thapar[3]

Generative artificial intelligence (GenAI) has emerged as a transformative force, driven by breakthroughs in foundational models such as Generative Adversarial Networks (GANs), Variational Autoencoders (VAEs), Diffusion Models, and Large Language Models (LLMs). This chapter offers an in-depth exploration of output generation across probabilistic latent spaces—rendered by VAEs—and high-fidelity outputs produced via GANs' adversarial training. LLMs generate coherent text using transformer-based autoregressive architectures, while diffusion models iteratively transform noise into structured data. A comparative analysis highlights distinctions in output quality, training stability, computational efficiency, and scalability. The chapter also examines critical ethical, legal, and technical concerns—including training data bias, deepfake risks, and intellectual property challenges. It advocates a unified framework to advance GenAI through architectural optimization, performance metrics, and ethical standards. The aim is to foster sound judgment criteria and responsible innovation, promoting sustainability and regulatory alignment in the evolving GenAI landscape.

3.1 Introduction

Generative AI, exemplified by GenAI's creation of novel content—images, text, audio, and video—goes beyond traditional classification or prediction models by deeply understanding data patterns to generate new, realistic outputs [1,3,5]. Foundational models like GANs, VAEs, and diffusion frameworks underpin this capability. GANs use adversarial training between a generator and discriminator, while VAEs employ probabilistic latent space learning, and diffusion models iteratively reconstruct data from noise for high-fidelity results [2,4,9]. These

[1] Department of Computer Science and Engineering, Chitkara University, Institute of Engineering & Technology, Chitkara University, Rajpura, India.
[2] Department of Computer Science and Engineering, The Institution of Electronics and Telecommunication Engineers, New Delhi, India.
[3] Department of Computer Science and Engineering, New Delhi, India.
E-mail: anupamtiwari@protonmail.com[2]; Prateekthapar@me.com
* Corresponding author(s). nehasharma0110@gmail.com

DOI: 10.1201/9781003670582-3

models predict complex distributions, often requiring significant computational resources. GenAI's impact spans sectors: aiding drug discovery and medical imaging, driving media innovation (e.g., deepfakes, virtual worlds), and generating synthetic data to enhance ML datasets [2,6,7,9]. Despite progress, challenges like mode collapse, computational overhead, and ethical concerns—especially around bias and misuse—hinder broader deployment [3,10]. This review aims to address the following key questions:

RQ1. What are the foundational principles and theoretical underpinnings of generative AI?

Ans: To address this question, a taxonomy of GenAI models based on their architectures is presented, including GANs, VAEs, Diffusion models and LLMs.

RQ2. How do the architectures, training methodologies, and performance of generative models like GANs, VAEs, and diffusion models compare?

Ans: To explore this, a comparative analysis of various GenAI models are presented in tabular format.

RQ3. What are the different evaluation metrics employed for validating the output generated by GenAI models?

Ans: The evaluation metrics used in GenAI models are discussed based on the output generated.

RQ4. What are the technical limitations, ethical considerations, and scalability issues in generative AI?

Ans: To address this, challenges like computational inefficiencies, mode collapse, and biases in the generated output are presented.

By systematically addressing these aspects, this review not only consolidates existing knowledge but also provides a roadmap for future research and practical advancements in the field of generative AI. This chapter makes the following contributions:

Novel Architectural Insights: The chapter presents detailed categorizations and theoretical insights into GANs, VAEs, Diffusion Models, and LLMs—offering new perspectives on architectural design and optimizations that boost performance and efficiency.

Comparative Performance Analysis: By comparing generative AI models across defined evaluation metrics, the manuscript highlights their strengths and limitations, guiding model selection for specific tasks and conditions.

Ethical and Legal Framework Development: The chapter addresses key ethical and legal concerns in generative AI—biases, privacy, and intellectual property—adding to ongoing debates in AI ethics. It may propose frameworks or guidelines to navigate these challenges.

Technical Challenges and Solutions: Tackling technical challenges and solutions strengthens the design and deployment of generative AI, particularly in critical, high-stakes settings.

The chapter is structured as follows: Section 1 covers generative AI fundamentals. Section 2 analyzes key models—GANs, VAEs, diffusion frameworks, and LLMs. Section 3 discusses performance metrics. Section 4 explores challenges and ethics. Section 5 examines applications across healthcare, media, and software. Section 6 outlines future directions and trends.

3.2 Key Generative Models

Generative AI models are advanced machine learning architectures designed to create realistic and meaningful content—including text, images, audio, and video—by learning intricate patterns from training datasets. Unlike traditional AI systems focused on classification or prediction, these models emulate human-like creativity and produce novel outputs closely aligned with original data characteristics. Their impact spans diverse domains such as natural language processing, image generation, and scientific simulation, driving innovation across industries. Figure 3.1 illustrates key Generative AI frameworks: GANs, VAEs, Diffusion Models, and LLMs. GANs use adversarial training between a generator and discriminator, regulated by minimax optimization, to generate high-quality visuals for applications like image synthesis and style transfer. VAEs employ encoder-decoder architectures and variational inference for tasks like anomaly detection and data compression through unsupervised learning. Diffusion Models generate high-fidelity outputs by iteratively adding and removing noise, leveraging score matching and MCMC-based techniques. LLMs rely on transformer-based architectures and self-supervised learning, such as masked language modeling, enabling tasks like text generation, translation, and conversational AI.Together, these models reflect the versatility of Generative AI in addressing varied industrial needs—ranging from healthcare and entertainment to communications—by producing intelligent, customizable, and adaptive content.

3.2.1 Generative Adversarial Networks (GANs)

Generative Adversarial Networks (GANs), introduced by Ian Goodfellow in 2014, consist of two neural networks—a generator (G) and a discriminator (D)—trained in a zero-sum game. The generator creates data mimicking real samples, while the discriminator learns to distinguish between real and generated inputs, as illustrated in Figure 3.2.

The training process in Generative Adversarial Networks (GANs) involves a minimax game between the generator (G) and the discriminator (D). The objective function is defined as:

$$\min_{G}\max_{D} V(D, G) = E_{xp_{data}(x)} \quad ...(1)$$

Here, $p_{\text{data}}(x)$ represents the true data distribution, and $p_z(z)$ denotes the noise distribution used as input to G. The discriminator D aims to maximize its ability to correctly classify real data as real and generated data as fake—achieved by

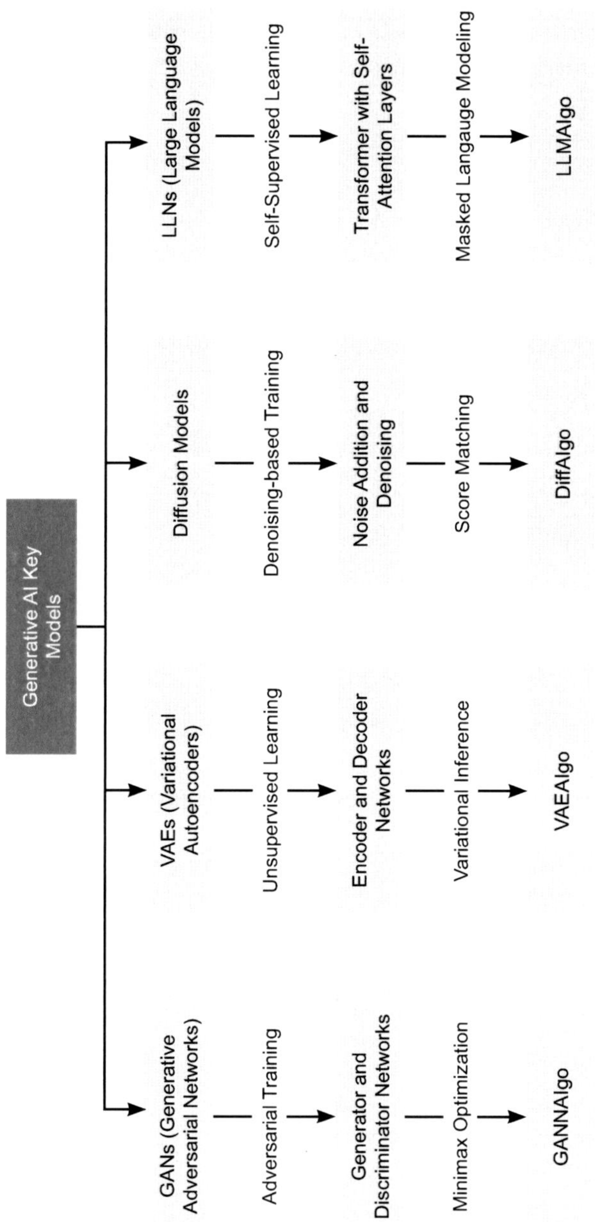

Fig. 3.1 Taxonomy of Generative AI key models.

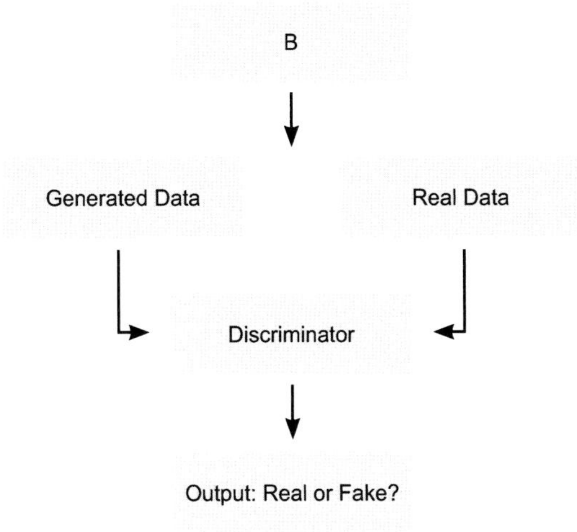

Fig. 3.2 GAN Architecture

maximizing $D(x)$ for real samples and minimizing $D(G(z))$ for fake ones. Table 3.1 outlines the strengths of GANs, including their ability to generate high-quality and diverse outputs—demonstrated through impressive inception scores and PSNR values on datasets such as ImageNet and COCO.

Table 3.1 Chronological Literature review of Generative Adversarial models.

Ref. No.	*Year*	*Dataset used*	*Key Findings*	*Performance Metrics*
[11]	2022	MNIST	High accuracy on small datasets.	Accuracy: 91.2, Loss: 0.35, MSE: 0.004–0.004
[12]	2020	LSUN	Mode collapse in large-scale scene generation.	Inception Score: 5.6, PSNR: 24.5, Loss: 0.44
[13]	2021	SVHN	Moderate performance; requires fine-tuning.	Accuracy: 87, PSNR: 25, MSE: 0.0065
[14]	2022	Imagenet	Consistent high performance on large datasets	Inception Score: 8.5, Accuracy: 92.5, PSNR: 28
[15]	2023	Fashion-MNIST	Effective for fashion dataset synthesis with high accuracy.	Inception Score: 7.2, Accuracy: 89, MSE: 0.0045
[16]	2023	COCO	Generates realistic, detailed images for large-scale applications.	Inception Score: 8.0, Accuracy: 90.3, PSNR: 27.1
[17]	2020	CIFAR-10	Realistic facial synthesis with moderate training stability.	Inception Score: 6.8, Accuracy: 88, PSNR: 25.8
[18]	2021	CelebA	Produces diverse, high-quality facial images.	Inception Score: 7.9, Accuracy : 89.5, PSNR: 26.5

There were major issues in GANs, and one such issue was mode collapse, where the generator produced limited diversity in outputs by focusing on specific data modes:

(a) Variants such as Wasserstein GAN (WGAN) and Progressive GAN enhanced output diversity through improved training strategies and architectural refinements. Training instability was another challenge—balancing the generator and discriminator proved difficult during optimization. WGAN and SNGAN Spectral Normalization GANs (SNGANs) improved training stability by introducing better loss functions and normalization methods.
(b) Standard GANs struggled to produce high-quality, high-resolution outputs.
(c) StyleGAN introduced hierarchical feature control, enabling the generation of highly detailed and realistic images.
(d) In addition, the advent of Conditional GANs (cGANs) provided more control over generated data by including labels or certain conditions, which solved the generic nature of regular GAN outputs.

These developments cumulatively increased the flexibility and applicability of GANs to different fields.

3.2.1.1 Conditional GANs (cGANs)

Extend standard GANs by incorporating auxiliary information—such as class labels or attributes—to guide data generation. Unlike regular GANs that produce uncontrolled outputs, cGANs input condition c into both the generator and discriminator, allowing tailored generation and evaluation: the generator produces $G(z|c)$), and the discriminator evaluates $D(x|c)$. cGANs enhance output diversity and enable class-specific or attribute-guided generation. They are widely used in image-to-image translation, text-to-image synthesis, and data augmentation [19,20]. The objective function adapts accordingly:

$$\min_{g} \max_{D} V(D, G) = E_{xp_{\text{data}}(x, c)} \quad \text{...(2)}$$

where x is the real data, z is a random noise vector sampled from the prior distribution $p_z(z)$ (e.g., Gaussian or uniform), c is a condition or label, drawn from the conditional distribution $p_c(c)$. The joint distribution of real data and conditions is represented by $p_{\text{data}}(x, c)$. The discriminator's output, $D(x \vee c)$ denotes the probability that x is real given condition c, while the generator's output, $G(z \vee c)$, generates data conditioned on both noise z and condition c.

In cGANs, the condition c is usually concatenated with noise z in r the generator and with data x in the discriminator. This setup ensures output generation aligns with given conditions, enhancing control and diversity.

3.2.1.2 StyleGAN

It is a cutting-edge generative model designed for high-resolution, editable image synthesis. Unlike traditional GANs that map noise directly to output, StyleGAN

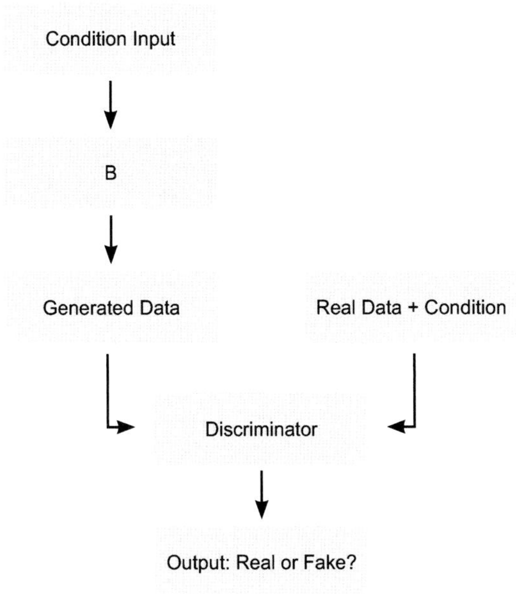

Fig. 3.3 Flow Process model of Conditional GANs.

introduces a style-based generator that modulates image features at multiple levels—coarse, medium, and fine—using a latent vector transformed through a mapping network. This enables precise control over attributes like texture, color, and structure. Key enhancements include adaptive instance normalization (AdaIN) for dynamic feature modulation and progressive growing to stabilize resolution scaling during training. The synthesis network gradually constructs the image from low to high resolution, adding noise for fine details. A discriminator evaluates the realism of outputs, refining them through adversarial feedback. These architectural innovations mark StyleGAN as a milestone in generating lifelike and diverse images. Refer to Figure 3.4 for thc block diagram.

$$\min_G \max_D V(D, G) = E_{yp_{\text{data}}} \quad ...(3)$$

3.2.2 VAEs

A Variational Autoencoder (VAE) is a neural network that generates new data—such as images or text—by learning the underlying structure of the input. It employs an encoder-decoder architecture: the encoder $q_\phi(z|x)$ $q_\phi(z|x)$ compresses input data x into a latent space, not as a single point but as a Gaussian distribution characterized by mean $\mu_\phi(x)$ and variance $\sigma_\phi^2(x)$. This is expressed as:

$$q_\phi(x) = N(z; \mu_\phi(x), \text{diag}\,(\sigma_\phi^2(x))) \quad ...(4)$$

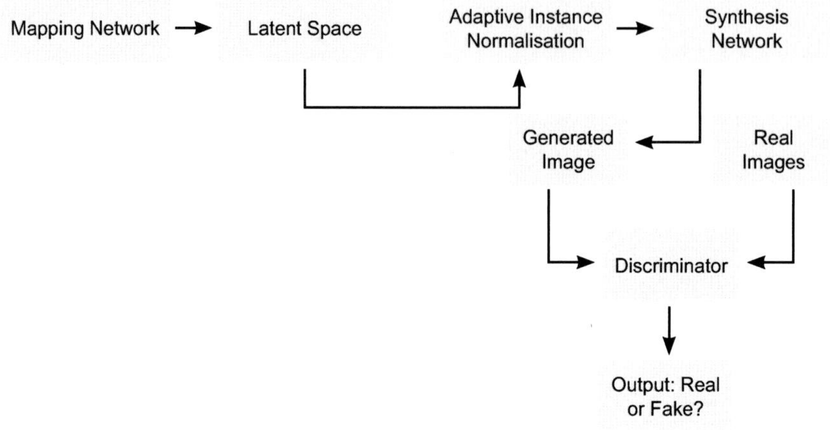

Fig. 3.4 Block Diagram of Style GANs.

The decoder $p_\phi(x \vee z)$ reconstructs data from sampled latent points z, mapping them to the parameters of the original data distribution—either fixed or learned—as:

$$p_\phi(z) = N(x; \mu_\phi(z), (\sigma^2 I) \qquad ...(5)$$

This formulation enables VAEs to learn compressed representations that preserve essential features, making them useful for tasks like data generation, compression, and anomaly detection.

The encoder in a Variational Autoencoder (VAE) is trained not only to compress input data but also to shape the latent space into a predefined structure—typically a standard normal distribution. This smooth and continuous latent space enables the model to generate new data through sampling. However, direct sampling is non-differentiable and cannot support gradient-based backpropagation. To overcome this, a fixed noise variable is introduced and combined with the encoder's learned mean and variance, allowing a differentiable sampling process known as the reparameterization trick. The VAE optimizes two objectives: **reconstruction loss** and **regularization loss**. The reconstruction loss ensures that the decoder output closely resembles the original input, as in a standard autoencoder. For instance, if the input is a cat image, the output should visually match it. The reconstruction loss is expressed mathematically as:

$$p_\theta(z) = -\log qp_\theta(z) \propto \frac{1}{2\sigma^2} \| x - \mu_\theta(z) \|^2 + \text{const} \qquad ...(6)$$

Meanwhile, the regularization loss aligns the latent distribution with a standard normal prior, promoting generalization and preventing overfitting or memorization. This balance between accurate reconstruction and a well-structured latent space enables robust data generation from learned representations.

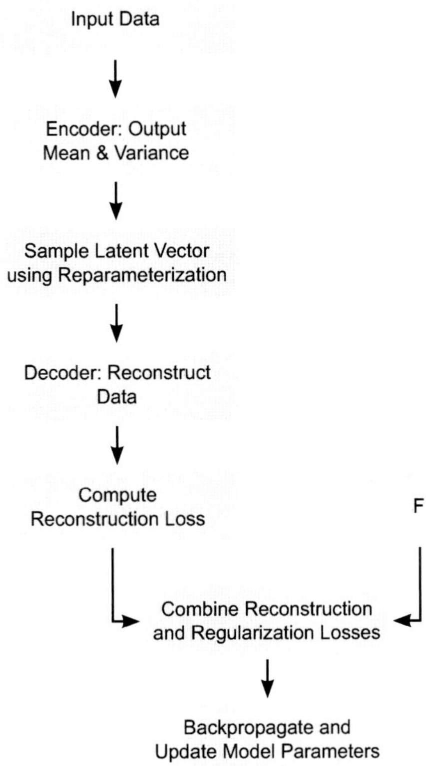

Fig. 3.5 Training process of Variational auto-encoders.

Figure 3.5 illustrates the VAE training workflow: the encoder maps input data to a latent space defined by a mean and variance. Using the reparameterization trick, a sample is drawn and fed to the decoder, which reconstructs the original input. The model minimizes two losses—reconstruction (input vs. output) and regularization (alignment to a standard normal distribution)—adjusting parameters for optimal balance. Table 3.2 summarizes key developments in VAE research, from core concepts to advanced variants.

Table 3.2 Literature review of VAE models.

Ref	*Year*	*Algorithm used*	*Advantages*	*Limitations*	*Parameters*
[21]	2013	VAE	First end-to-end training of deep latent variable models	Blurry samples, simple prior (Gaussian)	ELBO (Evidence Lower Bound), reconstruction error

Contd...

Table 3.2 *Contd...*

Ref	*Year*	*Algorithm used*	*Advantages*	*Limitations*	*Parameters*
[22]	2014	SGVB	Efficient gradient estimation for latent variables	Computationally intensive for complex posteriors	ELBO, log-likelihood
[23]	2017	β-VAE	Tunable disentanglement via β hyperparameter	Trade-off between reconstruction quality and disentanglement	Disentanglement metrics (FactorVAE score), reconstruction loss
[24]	2016	IAF-VAE	Flexible posterior approximation with normalizing flows	Increased computational cost	Log-likelihood, model flexibility
[25]	2017	VampPrior-VAE	Learnable mixture-of-experts prior	Added complexity in prior design	Log-likelihood, ELBO
[26]	2018	Modified β-VAE	Practical modifications for better disentanglement	Dataset-specific performance	Mutual information gap, disentanglement scores
[27]	2020	Hierarchical VAE	Scalable hierarchical latent structure	Training instability, high memory usage	FID, Inception Score (IS)
[28]	2017	VQ-VAE	Discrete latent space for improved interpretability	Codebook collapse risk	Reconstruction quality, codebook usage
[29]	2019	Hierarchical VQ-VAE	Scalable to large resolutions	Computationally intensive	FID, IS
[30]	2016	Text VAE	First application of VAEs to text	Posterior collapse (latent ignored)	Perplexity, BLEU
[31]	2018	Dilated CNN VAE	Dilated convolutions for long-range dependencies	Limited to short texts	Perplexity, diversity metrics

3.2.3 Diffusion Models

Diffusion models are generative AI systems that create data (e.g., images, audio) by learning to reverse a gradual noising process. Imagine starting with a clear photo and repeatedly adding noise until it becomes static. Diffusion models learn to undo this process by turning random noise back into meaningful data. The process involves a forward diffusion (noise addition) and a reverse diffusion (denoising). The forward diffusion process adds Gaussian noise to data x_0 over T steps according to a predefined variance schedule $\{\beta_t\}_{t=1}^{T}$, where $0 < \beta_t < 1$.

The process starts with a clean data sample (e.g., an image) and gradually small amounts of Gaussian noise are added over many steps. After hundreds of steps, the data becomes pure noise. This is a fixed, predefined process with no learning happening here. The reverse process learns to denoise $x_T N(0, I)$ back to x_0 using a neural network $\in_\theta$. The neural network is trained to reverse the noising process. It learns to iteratively "clean up" the noise, step by step, to recover the original data. The model predicts how much noise exists at each step and removes it. The model minimizes the variational lower bound (VLB). Simplifying, the loss reduces to denoising score matching:

$$L(\theta) = E_{t,\, x0,\, \in}\left[\vee \in - \in_\theta \left(\sqrt{\alpha_t x_0} + \sqrt{1 - \alpha_t, \in t} \right) \vee^2 \right] \quad ...(7)$$

where $\in N(0, I)$ and and $t_{\text{Uniform}}\ (1, T)$.

The network $\in_\theta$ predicts the noise added at each step. The predicted noise is compared to the actual noise and the model's parameters are adjusted to minimize the error. The process is repeated on millions of images and noise levels till the model becomes accurate. Table 3.3 highlights the recent literature on the diffusion models.

Table 3.3 Literature review of Diffusion models.

Ref	*Year*	*Algorithm used*	*Advantages*	*Limitations*	*Parameters*
[32]	2020	DDPM	Simple training, stable convergence	Slow sampling (1000+ steps)	FID-3.17, Inception Score (IS), SOTA image generation on CIFAR-10
[33]	2021	DDIM	Non-Markovian sampling, reduced steps	Slight quality trade-off	FID, IS, sampling speed
[34]	2022	CLIP-guided Diffusion	Multi-modal alignment (text + image)	Computationally intensive, bias in outputs	CLIP score, human evaluation
[35]	2022	Cascaded Diffusion	High-fidelity text-to-image, large-scale pretraining	Massive compute needs (4B+ params)	DrawBench (text alignment), FID
[36]	2022	Latent Diffusion	Reduced compute (latent space), open-source	Requires post-processing for fine details	FID, IS, human eval
[37]	2023	Consistency Training	One-step generation capability	Training complexity, lower diversity	FID-2.93, sampling speed

Contd...

Table 3.3 *Contd...*

Ref	*Year*	*Algorithm used*	*Advantages*	*Limitations*	*Parameters*
[38]	2023	Latent Diffusion (Improved)	Enhanced resolution and prompt adherence	High VRAM requirements	CLIP score, FID, HPSv2
[39]	2023	Plug-and-Play Diffusion	No retraining; adapts to new tasks	Slow for large images	PSNR, SSIM, LPIPS
[40]	2024	Diffusion Transformer	Temporal consistency, multi-shot coherence	Closed-source, compute-heavy	FVD (Fréchet Video Distance), human evaluation

3.2.4 LLMs

Large Language Models (LLMs) are advanced AI systems trained on extensive text corpora to generate human-like language. Models like GPT and LLaMA use transformer architecture—leveraging self-attention, feed-forward layers, and positional encoding—to process entire sequences efficiently and capture long-range dependencies.Text inputs are tokenized, embedded, and passed through multiple transformer layers. Self-attention enables contextual linking, such as associating "it" with "book" in a sentence. The model predicts each next word by minimizing errors across billions of training samples. Due to their massive scale (e.g., GPT-3 has 175B parameters), LLMs require substantial computational resources. Table 3.4 reviews recent LLM developments and their benchmark results.

3.2.5 Comparative Analysis

Table 3.5 outlines a comparative overview of GANs, VAEs, Diffusion Models, and LLMs based on architecture, training, performance, and application. GANs and Diffusion Models excel in visual synthesis—GANs through adversarial learning, and Diffusion Models by reversing noise. VAEs, with their encoder-decoder setup, generate stable but lower-resolution outputs, suited for tasks like anomaly detection. LLMs leverage transformers to produce coherent text, dominating language-centric applications.Training-wise, GANs face instability (e.g., mode collapse), while VAEs and Diffusion Models offer more consistent—though computationally intensive—training. LLMs require massive datasets and careful tuning to maintain accuracy. In practice, GANs serve media, VAEs support data exploration, Diffusion Models power artistic content, and LLMs enable scalable text generation across industries.

3.3 Evaluation Parameters

Generative AI continues to evolve, driving applications in computer vision, NLP, and the arts. To ensure these models are reliable and effective, their performance

Table 3.4 Literature review of LLMs.

Ref	*Year*	*Model*	*Algo used*	*Parameters*	*Results*	*Advantages*	*Limitations*
[41]	2020	GPT-3 (OpenAI)	Transformer (decoder-only)	Few-shot accuracy, task-specific benchmarks (e.g., translation, QA)	Achieved human-like few-shot performance on 175B parameters	Scalable architecture, versatile across tasks	High compute costs, bias in outputs, no open-source release
[42]	2020	T5 (Google)	Transformer (encoder-decoder)	GLUE, SuperGLUE, SQuAD	Unified text-to-text framework (11B params)	Flexible for diverse NLP tasks	Task-specific fine-tuning required
[43]	2022	BLOOM (Hugging Face)	Transformer (decoder-only)	Multilingual benchmarks (e.g., FLORES-101, XNLI)	176B-parameter model supporting 46 languages	Open-source, multilingual focus	English-centric bias, high inference costs
[44]	2023	PaLM (Google)	Sparse Transformer	BIG-bench, reasoning tasks (GSM8K, MATH)	540B-parameter model achieved SOTA on 29/29 BIG-bench tasks	Breakthrough in reasoning (math, code)	Massive compute needs, closed-source
[45]	2023	LLaMA (Meta)	Transformer (decoder-only)	Commonsense reasoning (MMLU, HellaSwag), code generation (HumanEval)	65B model matched GPT-3 performance with lower resource use	Efficient, open-source (non-commercial)	Limited to research use, no RLHF alignment

Contd...

Table 3.4 *Contd...*

Ref	*Year*	*Model*	*Algo used*	*Parameters*	*Results*	*Advantages*	*Limitations*
[46]	2023	GPT-4 (OpenAI)	Mixture of Experts (MoE)	MMLU, HumanEval, multimodal benchmarks (e.g., DALL·E 3)	Multimodal SOTA on text/code/image tasks	Multimodal (text + image), improved reasoning	Closed-source, "black-box" design
[47]	2023	Falcon (TII)	Transformer (decoder-only)	OpenLLM Leaderboard, TruthfulQA	40B model outperformed LLaMA on reasoning	Apache-licensed, commercially usable	Smaller scale vs. GPT-4/PaLM
[48]	2023	Mistral 7B (Mistral AI)	Sparse Mixture of Experts (SMoE)	MMLU, GSM8K, efficiency (tokens/sec)	Outperformed LLaMA 7B/13B on reasoning with 7B params	Lightweight, Apache-licensed	Limited to 7B parameters
[49]	2023	Orca (Microsoft)	Transformer (decoder-only)	Complex instruction following (Vicuna, WizardLM), explanation quality	Matched ChatGPT on reasoning tasks via imitation learning	Improved instruction following	Relies on teacher models (GPT-4)

Table 3.5 Comparative Analysis of Various GenAI Models.

Criterion	*GANs*	*VAEs*	*Diffusion Models*	*LLMs*
Architecture	Dual network: Generator & Discriminator	Encoder-decoder with latent space	Reverses diffusion process	Transformer-based with self-attention
Training Mechanism	Adversarial training	Reconstruction loss + KL divergence	Denoising optimization	Maximum likelihood estimation
Primary Application	High-quality image generation	Data generation, anomaly detection	High-fidelity image generation/ editing	Natural language processing tasks
Output Quality	High-resolution, realistic images	Blurry outputs, stable	High fidelity, diverse outputs	Coherent, contextually relevant text
Stability of Training	Challenging, mode collapse	More stable, sensitive to architecture	Stable but computationally intensive	Requires careful hyperparameter tuning
Data Efficiency	Requires large datasets	Works with smaller datasets	Extensive data needed	Data-hungry, trained on vast corpora
Interpretability	Low (black box)	Moderate (structured latent space)	Low (black box)	Moderate (via attention weights)
Mode Coverage	May miss mode	Covers more modes, less sharp	Excellent mode coverage	Captures wide range of language modes
Sampling Speed	Fast once trained	Fast	Slow due to multiple forward passes	Fast, especially on specialized hardware
Use in Industry	Media, entertainment	Anomaly detection, data exploration	Graphic design, art generation	Customer service, content creation

must be assessed using appropriate accuracy and efficiency metrics. This section reviews key evaluation parameters across domains. Figure 3.6 categorizes these metrics by output type at the top level, with specific measures detailed beneath each category.

3.3.1 Performance Metrics: Images

In image processing, evaluating image quality is crucial for assessing the performance of generative models like GANs. Several metrics are commonly

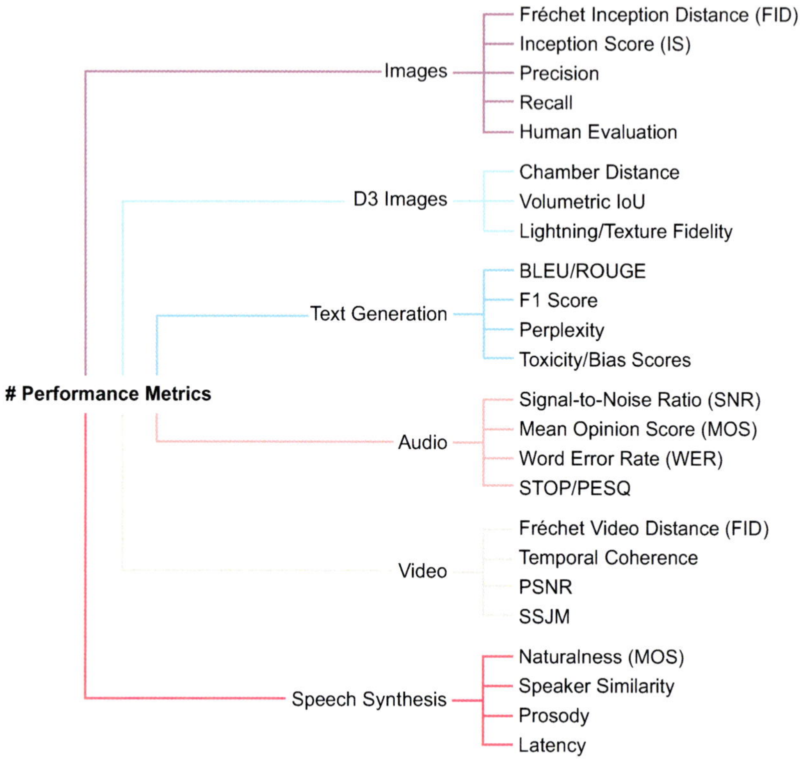

Fig. 3.6 Evaluation Metric Analysis.

used, including Fréchet Inception Distance (FID), Inception Score (IS), Precision, and Recall. Each provides insight into different aspects of output quality—FID measures similarity to real images, IS assesses image clarity and diversity, while Precision and Recall gauge realism and variety. Fréchet Inception Distance (FID) measures the similarity between generated and real images by comparing their feature distributions, extracted using the pre-trained Inception v3 model. It calculates the Fréchet (Wasserstein-2) distance between two Gaussian distributions over these features. Lower FID scores indicate higher image quality and realism. Its sensitivity to anomalies makes it a reliable metric for evaluating generative model performance. Inception Score (IS) assesses image quality by measuring diversity and clarity. Using the Inception model, it evaluates how confidently and distinctly each image is classified. Higher scores reflect varied and well-defined outputs, while lower scores suggest repetition or ambiguity.

- *Precision evaluates the realism of generated images—higher values indicate a greater proportion of outputs that resemble real-world objects. Recall assesses how well generated images cover the diversity of the training data—higher recall means broader and more varied outputs.*

3.3.2 Evaluation Parameters for 3D Images

In 3D model generation, evaluating the quality and accuracy of outputs is essential. Common metrics include Chamfer Distance, Volumetric Intersection over Union IoU, and Lighting/Texture Fidelity, each assessing specific attributes of AI-generated 3D models.

Chamfer Distance compares point sets (e.g., 3D model vertices) by measuring the average closest-point distance between a reference and a generated model. A lower Chamfer score indicates better shape alignment and structural accuracy.

Volumetric IoU evaluates the spatial overlap between two 3D models by dividing their intersection volume by the union volume. Higher IoU reflects better volume similarity and structural coherence.

Lighting and Texture Fidelity assesses how realistically surface details and lighting effects—such as gloss, smoothness, shadows, and highlights—are rendered. These metrics are vital in applications like VR and gaming, where visual realism enhances immersion.

3.3.3 Evaluation Parameters for 3D Images

To evaluate text generation quality, coherence, and relevance, several metrics are used:

- **BLEU** focuses on precision by comparing the overlap of n-grams between the generated output and reference text.
- **ROUGE** emphasizes recall, checking how much of the reference content appears in the generated text.
- **F1 Score** balances precision and recall, offering a comprehensive measure of relevance and completeness.
- **Perplexity** gauges fluency by measuring how confidently a model predicts the next word—lower values indicate smoother output.
- **Toxicity/Bias Scores** assess the presence of harmful or biased content, ensuring outputs remain safe and neutral.

Higher scores across these metrics typically reflect clearer, more accurate, and socially responsible text generation.

Perplexity measures how confidently a language model predicts the next word—lower values indicate smoother, more coherent text generation, especially useful in tasks like storytelling and chatbots. Toxicity and bias scores assess the presence of harmful or inappropriate content. These scores come from specialized models trained to detect offensive language, and lower values reflect safer, neutral output.

3.3.4 Evaluation Parameters for Audio

In audio synthesis,evaluating the quality and intelligibility of generated sound is essential across domains such as telecommunications and virtual assistants.

Several metrics serve this purpose, each targeting specific aspects of audio performance. Signal-to-Noise Ratio (SNR) quantifies the clarity of the signal relative to background noise—higher values indicate cleaner audio. Mean Opinion Score (MOS) offers a subjective assessment of overall audio quality, typically rated by human listeners on a scale from 1 (poor) to 5 (excellent). Word Error Rate (WER) measures transcription accuracy by comparing generated text to a reference, with lower scores reflecting better speech recognition. For intelligibility and perceptual quality under noisy or distorted conditions, STOI (Short-Time Objective Intelligibility) and PESQ (Perceptual Evaluation of Speech Quality) are widely used. Together, these metrics provide a comprehensive evaluation framework for synthesized audio systems.

Signal-to-Noise Ratio (SNR), measured in decibels (dB), indicates the clarity of useful audio relative to background noise. Higher SNR values reflect cleaner, more intelligible speech or music—crucial for user experience and the effectiveness of voice-driven systems. Mean Opinion Score (MOS) is a subjective metric for perceived audio quality, typically rated by human listeners on a scale from 1 (poor) to 5 (excellent). The average score reflects overall quality and is widely used in telecom and voice applications where user experience is critical.

Word Error Rate (WER) evaluates speech recognition accuracy by comparing generated text to a reference, measuring substitutions, deletions, and insertions. Lower WER indicates better transcription quality.STOI (Short-Time Objective Intelligibility) and PESQ (Perceptual Evaluation of Speech Quality) are objective metrics for intelligibility and perceived audio quality. STOI, based on correlation, estimates how well speech is understood amid noise—higher scores (closer to 1) reflect clearer output.

PESQ evaluates voice quality by comparing clean and degraded audio signals. Scores range from –0.5 to 4.5, with higher values indicating better perceived sound fidelity.

3.3.5 Evaluation Parameters for Video

In video synthesis, assessing output quality and coherence is crucial as applications expand across entertainment, advertising, and training. Key metrics include Fréchet Video Distance (FVD) for realism, Temporal Coherence for smooth transitions, and PSNR/SSIM for frame-level fidelity and structural similarity.

Fréchet Video Distance (FVD) extends FID to assess video quality by comparing feature distributions from real and generated videos using a deep learning model. Lower FVD scores indicate higher realism in visual and temporal aspects. Temporal Coherence reflects the smoothness of transitions across frames, ensuring consistent motion and appearance for natural video flow.

Good temporal coherence ensures smooth frame-to-frame transitions without abrupt changes, vital for realism and viewer engagement—especially in dynamic scenes where motion continuity boosts immersion. For video quality assessment, **PSNR** measures signal clarity versus noise, with higher values indicating less distortion, while **SSIM** evaluates structural similarity by factoring in luminance, contrast, and texture. Elevated SSIM scores imply closer alignment with original visuals, reflecting superior perceptual quality.

3.3.6 Evaluation Parameters for Speech Synthesis

In speech synthesis, evaluating audio quality and performance is essential as adoption grows across virtual assistants, telephony, and multimedia. Key metrics include Naturalness (MOS), Speaker Similarity, Emotion/Prosody, and Latency—each capturing distinct aspects like human-likeness, voice matching, expressive delivery, and system responsiveness.

Naturalness in speech synthesis is typically assessed using Mean Opinion Score (MOS), where listeners rate how human-like the voice sounds on a scale from 1 (poor) to 5 (excellent). Higher scores indicate more natural-sounding output, essential for enhancing user experience in real-world applications. ***Speaker Similarity*** *measures how closely the synthetic voice matches a target speaker's vocal traits—such as pitch, timbre, and speaking style—making it critical for voice cloning and personalized assistants.*

Emotion and Prosody in speech synthesis assess a system's ability to convey expressive tones using appropriate intonation, rhythm, and stress. These factors enhance the naturalness and communicative depth of synthetic speech.

Effective l *modulation* of emotion and prosody allows synthetic speech to convey more than just information—it communicates urgency, sentiment, and nuance. This capability is vital in contexts like storytelling, customer support, and therapy, where emotional expression enhances user engagement. **Latency**, the time lag between input and audio output, is also critical. Low latency ensures seamless interaction in real-time applications such as voice-controlled systems and virtual assistants, directly impacting responsiveness and usability.

3.3.7 Comparative Analysis

Table 3.6 presents a comparative overview of generative AI models across key performance metrics used to evaluate capabilities in image generation, text processing, audio synthesis, video rendering, and 3D modeling.

Table 3.6 Comparative Analysis Across Model Types.

Metric	*GANs*	*VAEs*	*Diffusion Models*	*LLMs*	*RAG using LLMs*
FID (Image)	High realism, low FID	Blurry outputs	Best FID	N/A (unless multimodal)	N/A
BLEU (Text)	Rarely used	Low coherence	Emerging	Best BLEU/ROUGE	Enhanced BLEU/ROUGE

Contd...

Table 3.6 *Contd...*

Metric	*GANs*	*VAEs*	*Diffusion Models*	*LLMs*	*RAG using LLMs*
MOS (Audio)	High fidelity	Muffled outputs	Best MOS	Requires TTS extensions	Requires TTS extensions
FVD (Video)	Flickering issues	Low resolution	Best FVD	N/A	N/A
Chamfer (3D)	Struggles with detail	Smooth but inaccurate	Best accuracy	Indirect generation	Indirect generation

3.4 Challenges

Generative AI holds transformative potential across industries but raises critical ethical, legal, and technical concerns. Key risks include biased training data leading to discrimination, misuse through deepfakes or disinformation, and unresolved legal questions around content ownership and privacy. Technically, models often face instability when handling unfamiliar inputs, posing challenges in sensitive areas like healthcare and autonomous systems. These issues highlight the urgent need for robust ethical frameworks, legal clarity, and continued innovation to ensure responsible and effective deployment. Major concerns include: Training Data Biases: Generative AI models often absorb biases present in their training data, potentially resulting in skewed or unfair outputs—especially in areas like facial recognition and text generation.

Abuse of Technology: Abuse of technology, particularly through the use of generative AI, is a monumental problem. It involves making deepfakes, disseminating false information, or generating offending material automatically. These are severe social and ethical problems that we must address.

- Intellectual Property Problems: GenAI can produce content that infringes on existing copyrights, trademarks, or patents, raising major legal concerns over authorship and ownership rights.
- Privacy Concerns: AI models trained on individual data can pose privacy risks, especially if they reconstruct identifiable information from aggregated data sets.
- Model Consistency: Generative AI models can produce inconsistent or unpredictable outputs, especially when confronted with unfamiliar data or scenarios beyond their training scope.
- Safety and Control: Ensuring the security of generative AI is critical—especially in high-stakes domains like medicine and autonomous vehicles—where unpredictable behavior could lead to serious harm or system failure.
- Variety of Input-Output Formats: Handling diverse input and output formats remains a core technical limitation of generative AI, restricting its adaptability across various domains. Table 3.7 offers a detailed breakdown of these challenges.

Table 3.7 Challenges faced by Generative AI models & its Potential Solutions.

Challenge Category	*Specific Issue*	*Potential Solutions*	*Impacted Sectors*	*Level of Difficulty to Address*	*Current Research/ Mitigation Efforts*
Ethical	Biases in Training Data	Diverse data collection, algorithmic fairness methods	All sectors using AI	High	Development of fairness metrics, bias detection and mitigation algorithms
Ethical	Misuse of Technology	Regulatory frameworks, ethical guidelines	Media, security, personal communications	Medium	Creating and promoting ethical AI use standards
Legal	Intellectual Property Issues	Clear policies on AI-generated content, copyright laws	Creative industries, academia	High	Discussions on AI and copyright law adjustments
Legal	Privacy Concerns	Data anonymization, secure AI practices	Healthcare, finance	High	Enhancing privacy protection frameworks for AI applications
Technical	Model Reliability	Improved testing, robustness training	Autonomous vehicles, healthcare	Medium	Research into model generalization and reliability
Technical	Safety and Control	Safety protocols, continuous monitoring	Critical systems like healthcare, aviation	High	Safety assurance methodologies for AI systems
Technical	Diverse Input-Output Formats	Universal models, format-agnostic training	Cross-industry	Medium	Development of multi-modal and adaptable AI systems

3.5 Applications

- Generative AI is increasingly applied across industries, harnessing its ability to create new data and replicate complex patterns. Key examples include healthcare diagnostics, neuroscience research, forensic analysis, software security, media content creation, automotive design, and fashion innovation. Table 3.8 provides a detailed overview of these diverse applications.

- Healthcare: Generative AI enhances healthcare by supporting symptom analysis, treatment planning, and patient interaction through conversational tools—strengthening overall clinical practice.
- Neuroscience: Generative AI supports NLP tasks, enables advanced brain-machine interface design, and augments datasets to accelerate neuroscience research.
- Forensic Psychiatry: Generative AI supports risk assessment, diagnostic validation, and advanced training tools in forensic psychiatry—but its use also raises significant ethical concerns.
- Software Security: Generative AI enhances software security by identifying vulnerabilities and detecting potential intrusions, helping to strengthen system reliability and resilience.
- Entertainment and Media: Generative AI transforms content creation in media by producing realistic visuals and audio for films and games, and generating music and text—automating much of the creative process.
- Automotive Industry: Generative AI accelerates automotive innovation by simulating and testing new car designs, streamlining development and reducing time-to-market.
- Fashion and Design: Generative AI predicts fashion trends, generates new clothing designs, and builds virtual showrooms —driving digital transformation across the industry.
- Biases in Training Data: Generative AI models can reflect or amplify biases in training data,leading to discriminatory outcomes in areas like facial recognition and text generation.
- Technology Abuse: Generative AI poses significant risks of misuse—such as creating deepfakes, spreading misinformation, or producing harmful content—which can lead to serious ethical challenges and wide societal impact.
- Intellectual Property Issues: Generative AI can produce content that potentially infringes on existing copyrights, trademarks, or patents—raising unresolved legal questions around authorship and ownership.
- Privacy Issues:Generative AI may create content that violates copyrights, trademarks, or patents, leading to unresolved legal disputes over authorship and ownership rights.
- Model Credibility: Generative AI models can yield inconsistent or unreliable results, especially when encountering unfamiliar inputs or operating beyond their training distribution.
- Control and Safety: Ensuring safety in generative AI is critical—especially in fields like healthcare and autonomous transport—where system errors can lead to serious consequences.
- Multiple Input-Output Formats: Generative AI still struggles with handling diverse input-output formats, limiting its adaptability across domains. Table 3.8 outlines these ongoing challenges.

Table 3.8 Comprehensive overview of applications of Generative AI Models.

Sector	*Application*	*Description*	*Potential Challenges*	*Key Benefits*	*Level of Adoption*	*Future Prospects*
Healthcare	Diagnostic support, treatment planning	Enhances accuracy and efficiency in diagnosing and planning treatments, improves patient interactions.	Data privacy, accuracy of AI predictions	Increased precision, faster diagnoses	High	Expansion to more personalized medicine
Neuroscience	NLP, brain-machine interfaces, data augmentation	Facilitates research and application developments in understanding and interfacing with the human brain.	Ethical concerns, integration complexities	Enhanced research capabilities, better models	Moderate	Broader application in clinical and research settings
Forensic Psychiatry	Risk assessment, diagnostic support	Assists in assessing risks, supporting diagnostics, and training, with a focus on ethical implications.	Ethical dilemmas, bias	Improved accuracy, efficient assessments	Low	Growth in ethical frameworks and wider adoption

Contd...

Table 3.8 *Contd...*

Sector	*Application*	*Description*	*Potential Challenges*	*Key Benefits*	*Level of Adoption*	*Future Prospects*
Software Security	Security analysis	Improves the detection of vulnerabilities and enhances software security measures.	Keeping pace with evolving threats	Better security, proactive protection	High	Development of more adaptive AI security tools
Entertainment & Media	Content creation	Generates innovative graphics, audio, and scripts, revolutionizing content production.	Copyright issues, authenticity	Creativity boost, cost reduction	High	Increased realism and interactivity in content
Automotive Industry	Vehicle design and testing	Accelerates the design process and testing of new vehicle models through simulations.	High development costs, safety concerns	Faster time-to-market, innovation	Moderate	More sustainable designs and automated testing
Fashion and Design	Trend prediction, design generation	Predicts trends and creates designs, aiding in the digital transformation of the fashion industry.	Market acceptance, creativity limitations	Streamlined design process, trend insight	Moderate	Enhanced customization and virtual integration

Conclusion

This chapter explores the core principles of generative AI, focusing on major architectures—GANs, VAEs, diffusion models, and LLMs. It categorizes these models structurally, reviews foundational literature, and compares algorithms using benchmark tests to assess performance across tasks. Evaluation metrics are discussed to identify model suitability for specific applications. The chapter also examines ethical, legal, and technical challenges, alongside use cases in healthcare, neuroscience, forensic psychiatry, and software security. It concludes by emphasizing the need for ongoing research to guide responsible innovation.

References

[1] Kaswan, K., Dhatterwal, J., Malik, K. and Baliyan, A. (2023). Generative AI: A Review on Models and Applications. *2023 International Conference on Communication, Security and Artificial Intelligence (ICCSAI)*, 699–704. https://doi.org/10.1109/ICCSAI59793.2023.10421601.

[2] Harshvardhan, G., Gourisaria, M., Pandey, M. and Rautaray, S. (2020). A comprehensive survey and analysis of generative models in machine learning. *Comput. Sci. Rev.*, 38, 100285. https://doi.org/10.1016/j.cosrev.2020.100285.

[3] Bandi, A., Adapa, P. and Kuchi, Y. (2023). The Power of Generative AI: A Review of Requirements, Models, Input-Output Formats, Evaluation Metrics, and Challenges. *Future Internet*, 15, 260. https://doi.org/10.3390/fi15080260.

[4] Gatla, R., Gatla, A., Sridhar, P., Kumar, D. and Rao, D. et al. (2024). Advancements in Generative AI: Exploring Fundamentals and Evolution. *2024 International Conference on Electronics, Computing, Communication and Control Technology (ICECCC)*, 1–5. https://doi.org/10.1109/ICECCC61767.2024.10594003.

[5] Sengar, S., Hasan, A., Kumar, S. and Carroll, F. (2024). *Generative Artificial Intelligence: A Systematic Review and Applications*. ArXiv, abs/2405.11029. https://doi.org/10.48550/arXiv.2405.11029.

[6] Ding, A., Li, G., Yi, X., Lin, X., Li, J. et al. (2024). *Generative AI for Software Security Analysis: Fundamentals, Applications, and Challenges*. IEEE Software, 41, 46-54. https://doi.org/10.1109/MS.2024.3416036.

[7] Nalini, C., Kumar, D. and Professor, A. (2023). Generative AI: A Comprehensive Study of Advancements and Application.

[8] Raut, G. and Singh, A. (2024). *Generative AI in Vision: A Survey on Models, Metrics and Applications*. ArXiv, abs/2402.16369. https://doi.org/10.48550/arXiv.2402.16369.

[9] Gozalo-Brizuela, R. and Garrido-Merch'an, E. (2023). *A survey of Generative AI Applications*. ArXiv, abs/2306.02781. https://doi.org/10.48550/arXiv.2306.02781.

[10] Kalota, F. (2024). *A Primer on Generative Artificial Intelligence. Education Sciences*. https://doi.org/10.3390/educsci14020172.

[11] Engy, Y. (2024). *1. Developments on Generative AI*. doi: 10.1201/9781003501152-9.

[12] Tina, B., Rekha, R., Nair., P. and Ebin M. (2024). *2. Foundations of Generative AI. Advances in computational intelligence and robotics book series*, doi: 10.4018/979-8-3693-3278-8.ch007.

[13] David A., Jeganathan, Sankar G., Ganeshkumar C., Kashif, M. et al. (2024). *3. An Introduction to Generative AI. Advances in computational intelligence and robotics book series*, doi: 10.4018/979-8-3693-8557-9.ch001.

[14] Gatla, R.K., Gatla, A., Sridhar P., Gireesh, D. et al. (2024). *4. Advancements in Generative AI: Exploring Fundamentals and Evolution.* doi: 10.1109/icecc61767.2024.10594003.

[15] Leonardo, B. and Gero, S. (2023). *5. Generative artificial intelligence. Electronic Markets*, doi: 10.1007/s12525-023-00680-1.

[16] Dehankar P., Susanta and Das K. (2024). *6. Unveiling Its Origins, Principles, and Technological Underpinnings. Advances in computational intelligence and robotics book series*, doi: 10.4018/979-8-3693-3691-5.ch001.

[17] Changyu, H. and Yuchuan, J. (2023). *7. Investigating the Advancements in Generative Models*. doi: 10.1109/aiac61660.2023.00037.

[18] Sahu, D.K. (2024). *8. Exploring the Potential of Generative Artificial Intelligence. Indian Scientific Journal of research in engineering and management*, doi: 10.55041/ijsrem30555.

[19] Ken, H., Wang Y. and Zhang S. (2024). *9. Foundations of Generative AI. Future of Business and Finance*, doi: 10.1007/978-3-031-54252-7_1.

[20] *Toward General Design Principles for Generative AI Applications* (2023). doi: 10.48550/arxiv.2301.05578.

[21] Kingma, D.P. and Welling, M. (2013, December). Auto-encoding variational bayes.

[22] Rezende, D.J., Mohamed, S. and Wierstra, D. (2014, June). Stochastic backpropagation and approximate inference in deep generative models. *In International conference on machine learning* (pp. 1278-1286). PMLR.

[23] Burgess, C.P., Higgins, I., Pal, A., Matthey, L. Watters, N. et al. (2018). *Understanding disentangling in $\beta $-VAE*. arXiv preprint arXiv:1804.03599.

[24] Kingma, D.P., Salimans, T., Jozefowicz, R., Chen, X. Sutskever, I. et al. (2016). Improved variational inference with inverse autoregressive flow. *Advances in neural information processing systems*, 29.

[25] Tomczak, J. and Welling, M. (2018, March). VAE with a VampPrior. *In International conference on artificial intelligence and statistics* (pp. 1214-1223). PMLR.

[26] Burgess, C.P., Higgins, I., Pal, A., Matthey, L., Watters, N. et al. (2018). *Understanding disentangling in $\beta $-VAE*. arXiv preprint arXiv:1804.03599.

[27] Vahdat, A. and Kautz, J. (2020). NVAE: A deep hierarchical variational autoencoder. *Advances in neural information processing systems*, 33, 19667-19679.

[28] Van Den Oord, A. and Vinyals, O. (2017). Neural discrete representation learning. *Advances in neural information processing systems*, 30.

[29] Razavi, A., Van den Oord, A. and Vinyals, O. (2019). Generating diverse high-fidelity images with vq-vae-2. *Advances in neural information processing systems*, 32.

[30] Bowman, S.R., Vilnis, L., Vinyals, O., Dai, A.M., Jozefowicz, R. et al. (2015). *Generating sentences from a continuous space*. arXiv preprint arXiv:1511.06349.

[31] Xu, J. and Durrett, G. (2018). *Spherical latent spaces for stable variational autoencoders*. arXiv preprint arXiv:1808.10805.

[32] Watson, D., Ho, J., Norouzi, M. and Chan, W. (2021). *Learning to efficiently sample from diffusion probabilistic models*. arXiv preprint arXiv:2106.03802.

[33] Song, J., Meng, C., and Ermon, S. (2020). *Denoising diffusion implicit models*. arXiv preprint arXiv:2010.02502.

[34] Marcus, G., Davis, E. and Aaronson, S. (2022). *A very preliminary analysis of DALL-E 2*. arXiv preprint arXiv:2204.13807.

[35] Ayach, L.R. and da Cunha, E.R. (2012). UTIIZAÇÃO DE IMAGENS GOOGLE EARTH PARA MAPEAMENTO DO USO E COBERTURA DA TERRA DA BACIA HIDROGRÁFICA DO CÓRREGO INDAIÁ, MS. *Revista Geonorte*, 3(5), 1801–1811.

[36] Blattmann, A., Dockhorn, T., Kulal, S., Mendelevitch, D., Kilian et al. (2023). *Stable video diffusion: Scaling latent video diffusion models to large datasets*. arXiv preprint arXiv:2311.15127.

[37] Song, Y., Dhariwal, P., Chen, M. and Sutskever, I. (2023). Consistency models.

[38] Podell, D., English, Z., Lacey, K., Blattmann, A., Dockhorn, T. et al. (2023). *Sdxl: Improving latent diffusion models for high-resolution image synthesis*. arXiv preprint arXiv:2307.01952.

[39] Huang, Y., Huang, J., Liu, Y., Yan, M., Lv, J., Liu, J. et al. (2024). *Diffusion model-based image editing: A survey*. arXiv preprint arXiv:2402.17525.

[40] Liu, Y., Zhang, K., Li, Y., Yan, Z., Gao, C., Chen, R. et al. (2024). *Sora: A review on background, technology, limitations, and opportunities of large vision models*. arXiv preprint arXiv:2402.17177.

[41] Floridi, L. and Chiriatti, M. (2020). GPT-3: Its nature, scope, limits, and consequences. *Minds and Machines*, 30, 681–694.

[42] Adauto, F.G., and Golan, K. Distraction Generation using Google T5: A Study.

[43] Gibney, E. (2022). Open-source language AI challenges big tech's models. *Nature*, 606(7916), 850–851.

[44] Anil, R., Dai, A.M., Firat, O., Johnson, M., Lepikhin, D. et al. (2023). *Palm 2 technical report*. arXiv preprint arXiv:2305.10403.

[45] Li, Y., Li, Z., Zhang, K., Dan, R., Jiang, S. et al. (2023). Chatdoctor: A medical chat model fine-tuned on a large language model meta-ai (llama) using medical domain knowledge. *Cureus*, 15(6).

[46] Achiam, J., Adler, S., Agarwal, S., Ahmad, L., Akkaya, I. et al. (2023). *Gpt-4 technical report*. arXiv preprint arXiv:2303.08774.

[47] Malartic, Q., Chowdhury, N. R., Cojocaru, R., Farooq, M., Campesan, G. et al. (2024). *Falcon2-11b technical report*. arXiv preprint arXiv:2407.14885.

[48] Taki, S. M., Kar, S., Niloy, S. D., Rakib, M.I., and Biswas, A.A.N. et al. (2024). Mitigation of hallucination and interpretations of self-attention of Mistral 7B AI to analyze and visualize context understanding ability of large language models (Doctoral dissertation, Brac University).

[49] Mitra, A., Del Corro, L., Mahajan, S., Codas, A., Simoes, C. et al. (2023). *Orca 2: Teaching small language models how to reason*. arXiv preprint arXiv:2311.11045.

4 Foundation of Generative AI: Concepts, Model and Applications

Yagyadatta Goswami[1*], Vedika Puri[2], Mukesh K Sahu[1] and Smit Kumar[3]

This chapter introduces Generative Artificial Intelligence and its foundational models: Diffusion Models, Transformers, VAEs, and GANs. It outlines how these models create realistic content—images, videos, text, and structured data—and explores key applications such as image translation, video synthesis, NLP, and knowledge graph generation. Use cases span across science, healthcare, education, and the arts. The chapter also discusses ongoing challenges like bias, accuracy, and responsible use, providing an accessible overview of the technology's significance and evolving potential.

4.1 Introduction

Generative AI significantly enhances the metaverse by automating complex decisions and delivering personalized user experiences. It creates new content—text, images, videos, and other media—by learning patterns from diverse training data. Unlike traditional models that classify or predict, generative AI produces original outputs that closely resemble human-generated content. A major advancement in this field is the rise of Large Language Models (LLMs) [1–4], which process human-like text using deep learning and vast datasets from books, articles, and online sources. LLMs support tasks such as sentiment analysis, Q&A, content and code generation, summarization, medical and legal analysis, and virtual assistance. These models vary by architecture, training method, and application focus.

Based on model architecture, LLMs are classified into three main categories as shown in Figure 4.1. Autoregressive models like LLaMA and GPT-3/4 (OpenAI) generate text sequentially. Autoencoding models, such as BERT and RoBERTa, focus on understanding context through bidirectional encoding. Sequence-to-sequence models like T5 and BART combine encoding and decoding for tasks like translation and summarization [6].

[1] Department of Electronics, Hansraj College, University of Delhi, India.
[2] Department of Physics, Hansraj College, University of Delhi, India.
[3] Deutsche Bank, Germany.
E-mail: mukeshsahu@hrc.du.ac.in[1]; vedikapuri2110@gmail.com[2]; mail.yoursmit@gmail.com[3]
* Corresponding author: yagya1992@gmail.com

DOI: 10.1201/9781003670582-4

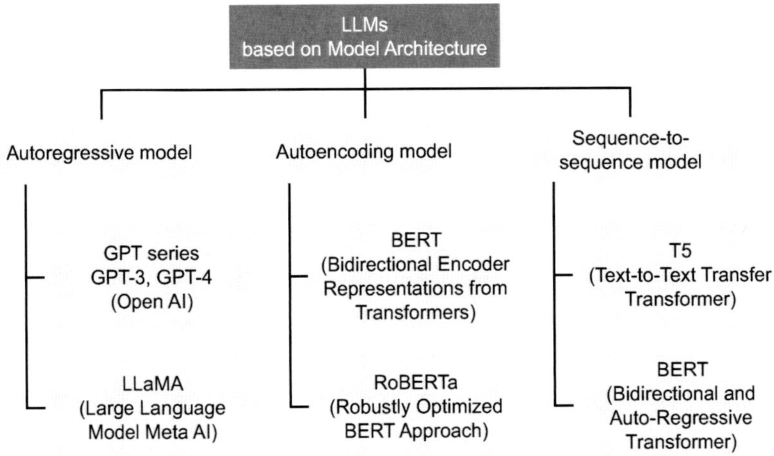

Fig. 4.1 Classifications of LLMs based on model architecture.

Generative models like GANs, VAEs, Diffusion Models, and Transformers have revolutionized content creation—enabling realistic image synthesis, text generation, and music composition across domains. Along with this generative AI has emerged as an innovative technology, transforming various fields like image processing, video synthesis, and natural language processing. Using strong models like as Transformers, Variational Autoencoders (VAEs), and Generative Adversarial Networks (GANs), generative AI can produce realistic text, images, and videos. The most important application of Generative AI is reshaping fields like image processing, video synthesis, and NLP through models such as Transformers, VAEs, and GANs. Its most impactful use is in medical imaging, where AI-driven image translation improves clarity and diagnostic accuracy. Notably, GAN-based models like Swin Transformer GANs and UVCGAN have advanced MRI and X-ray image translation. Generative AI enables realistic video synthesis, including talking head animations and expressive facial movements. Models like DaGAN++ and Style Talker use deep learning to generate high-quality facial expressions and audio-driven visuals. In NLP, generative models power advanced tasks such as text generation, summarization, and malware classification—demonstrating rapid progress across domains. As generative AI research advances, its applications now span beyond healthcare, video synthesis, and NLP to areas like knowledge graph generation and synthetic data creation. However, challenges such as data privacy, ethical risks, and computational demands must be addressed to unlock its full potential across industries. This chapter highlights recent breakthroughs, key methodologies, and future directions in generative AI.

Generative AI relies on models that learn patterns from training data to produce realistic, similar outputs, as illustrated in Figure 4.2. Each model type—GANs, VAEs, Transformers, and Diffusion Models—is tailored to specific media generation tasks. Some of them are as follows:

1. Generative Adversarial Networks [1]
2. Transformer-based Models [2]
3. Variational Autoencoders [3]
4. Diffusion Models [4]

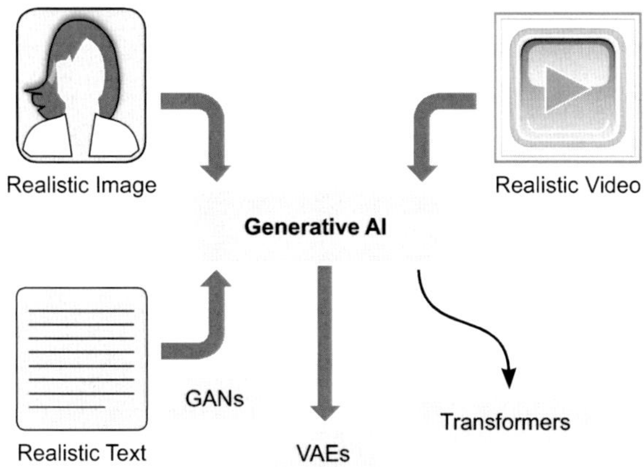

Fig. 4.2 Representation of generative AI [10].

4.1.1 Generative Adversarial Networks (GANs)

Generative Adversarial Networks (GANs) are machine learning models that generate realistic data—such as text, images, or videos—without requiring extensive labeled datasets. They consist of two components:

- **Generator:** Produces synthetic data (e.g., fake images).
- **Discriminator:** Evaluates whether the data is real or generated.

The generator in a GAN creates synthetic outputs (e.g., images), while the discriminator evaluates their authenticity based on real data. This adversarial setup forms a zero-sum game—each model improves by outsmarting the other until the discriminator can no longer distinguish real from fake. However, training GANs poses challenges like instability, oscillations, and mode collapse, where the generator produces repetitive outputs with limited diversity. As shown in Figure 4.3, the system includes random noise input, fake data generation, real data comparison, and feedback loops. To address these issues, researchers have developed improved architectures and training techniques.

4.1.2 Transformer-based Models

Transformers, introduced by Vaswani et al. [5], revolutionized AI by enabling models to handle long-range word dependencies—crucial for tasks like translation, text generation, and chatbots. Their core innovation is the **self-attention** mechanism, which lets models focus on key words regardless of position. **Multi-head attention**

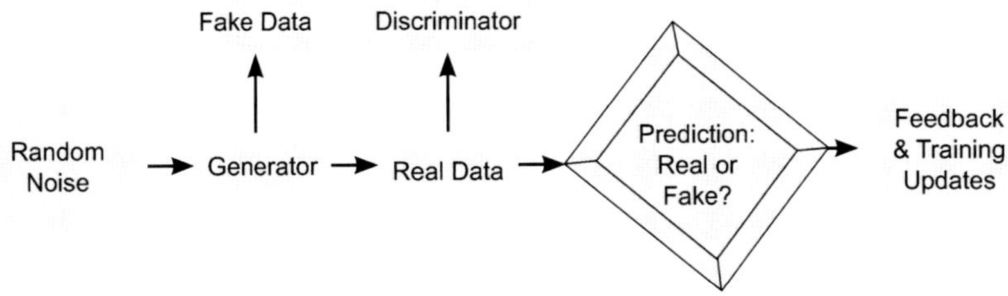

Fig. 4.3 Block Diagram for GAN.

further enhances understanding by analyzing input from multiple perspectives, improving comprehension of complex language structures. Before Transformers, AI relied on Recurrent Neural Networks (RNNs) for sequence tasks like translation and language modeling. RNNs processed text word-by-word, storing context as memory, but struggled with long-range dependencies and slow training. Attention mechanisms improved focus on key words, yet RNNs remained sequential. Transformers solved this by using full attention-based processing, enabling parallel computation and better handling of complex language. Models like BERT and GPT, built on Transformer architecture, now lead in NLP applications.

Variational Autoencoders

Variational Autoencoders (VAEs), introduced by Kingma et al. [6], generate new data by learning patterns from historical inputs. As shown in Figure 4.4, VAEs consist of an encoder that compresses data into a latent space and a decoder that reconstructs it with added randomness via Gaussian distribution—ensuring output retains the original mean and variance. This structure enables VAEs to produce diverse yet coherent data representations.

Directed Graphical Model is a probabilistic model that captures the relationship between latent variables z and observed data x. Latent variables are inferred rather than directly observed. The generative process follows the distribution $p(z)$ $p(x|z)$, where $p(z)$ represents the prior over latent variables and $p(x|z)$ defines the likelihood of generating data x given z and model parameters θ\theta. Since exact inference is intractable, an approximate posterior $q(z|x)$ is used to estimate latent variables from observed data. Here, θ governs the generative model, while ϕ controls the variational approximation.

- $z \to x$: Generative path via $p(x|z)$
- $x \to z$: Inference path via $q(z|x)$

Kingma et al. [6] refer to $q(z|x)$ as the **probabilistic encoder** and $p(x|z)$ as the **probabilistic decoder**.

In coding theory, the latent variable zz is often referred to as a code. Kingma et al. [6] describe the recognition model $q_\varphi(x|z)$ as a probabilistic encoder and $p_\theta(x|z)$ as a probabilistic decoder.

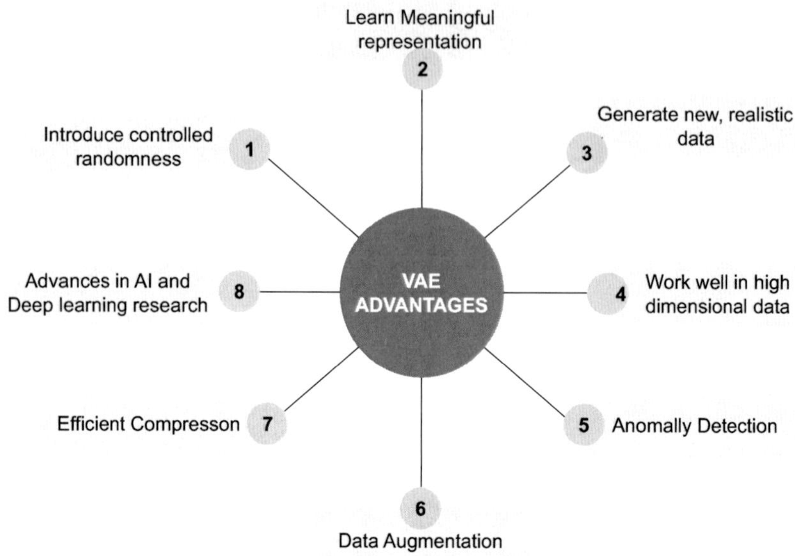

Fig. 4.4 Advantages of Variational Autoencoders.

4.1.3 Diffusion Models

Diffusion models, introduced by Salimans et al. [7], enhance GAN performance by gradually converting noise into structured data —similar to reversing a blurring process. A key variant is the **Inverse Autoregressive Flow (IAF)**, proposed by Kingma et al. [8], which accelerates data generation using **normalizing flows**. These flows transform simple distributions (e.g., Gaussian noise) into complex ones via invertible functions, enabling efficient forward (generation) and backward (inference) computation. The IAF transformation [9] is defined as:

$$zt = \mu t + \sigma t \cdot \epsilon t$$

- zt: Transformed output
- μt: Shift function
- σt: Scaling function
- ϵt: Random noise for variation

In simple terms, IAF starts with random noise and applies a step-by-step transformation to make it look like real-world data.

4.2 Diverse Applications of Generative AI

4.2.1 Generative AI for Image Translation

Image translation technology [10] is rapidly advancing, especially in medical domains, offering cost-effective and reliable diagnostic support. Generative AI models are benchmarked using datasets like ImageNet [11] and CelebA [12] for general and facial tasks, while MIMIC [13], BRATS [14], FastMRI [15], and Chest X-ray [16] serve medical imaging needs. Due to the sensitive nature of medical data, researchers must adhere to strict usage agreements, including proper citation and patient privacy safeguards. AI enhances medical imaging by improving clarity and detail, aiding disease detection. A recent advancement combines GANs with Swin Transformers [19], where the generator creates realistic images and the discriminator validates them. Swin Transformers replace traditional self-attention with a window-based approach, enabling efficient image processing while preserving critical features. This model excels in translating MRI scans from T1 to T2 mode without losing diagnostic content. Evaluations on BraTS2018 [17] and FastMRI [18] datasets confirm its superior performance in medical image translation. Using the unpaired BraTs2018 dataset [17], MMTrans demonstrated superior image translation performance compared to Pix2Pix [20], Cycle-GAN [21], and RegGAN [22, 23], producing results closely aligned with Ground Truth. GAN models used in this context fall into two categories: paired (conditional) GANs, which require aligned image pairs, and unpaired GANs, which learn mappings between domains without direct correspondence. Unpaired GANs like CycleGAN [25] were developed to overcome the challenge of acquiring paired images. These models learn domain mappings using cycle consistency loss, ensuring that an image retains its core features when translated between styles and back. Building on this, Torbunov et al. [26] introduced UVCGAN, a vision transformer-based GAN that enhances image translation quality while maintaining regeneration fidelity, outperforming earlier cyclic models. To assess the realism of generated images, researchers use Frechet Inception Distance (FID) [27] and Kernel Inception Distance (KID) [28]. Both compare synthetic images to real ones—lower scores indicate higher visual fidelity and better generative performance.

UVCGAN delivers high-quality outputs that enhance scientific simulations. In contrast, ACL-GAN and Council-GAN often overemphasize non-essential features like hair color, background, and length. Council-GAN also inconsistently alters backgrounds, detracting from thc core translation objective [29].

Synthetic Aperture Radar (SAR) image translation [30] is a key application of GANs, leveraging both paired and unpaired models. Despite lower visual clarity, SAR images offer advantages like all-weather and night-time imaging. GAN-based methods can enhance SAR resolution [31], with models like Pix2Pix, BicycleGAN, CycleGAN, NICE-GAN [32], and Attn-CycleGAN [33] used for satellite image translation. Wei et al. introduced CFRWD-GAN, combining Cross-Fusion Reasoning (CFR) to retain semantic and edge details, and Wavelet Decomposition (WD) to reduce noise. Evaluation metrics include RMSE [34,35] (lower is better), SSIM [36,37] and PSNR [38,39] (higher is better), and LPIPS [40,41] (lower is better), confirming the model's effectiveness in realistic SAR-to-optical translation.

Alongside GANs,Variational Autoencoders (VAEs) [42] offer a powerful alternative for image generation and translation. Developed by Kingma et al., VAEs compress input images into latent representations and reconstruct them into similar outputs—without using separate generator and discriminator networks like GANs.

4.2.2 Generative AI for Video Synthesis and Generation

Generative AI enables realistic video synthesis, including talking head videos and audio-driven animations, using advanced GAN-based models. Key datasets include VoxCeleb [43], HDTF [44], CelebV [45], Kinetics [46], UCF101 [47] for facial and action analysis, and VCTK [48], LibriSpeech [49] for audio evaluation. Hong et al. introduced a depth-aware GAN [50], outperforming prior models in face replacement tasks using VoxCeleb and CelebV. Their enhanced DaGAN++ framework [51] generates lifelike talking head videos from a single image by integrating depth learning, keypoint detection, and multi-layer synthesis. Style-Talker [52] further advances audio-driven generation with precise lip-sync and head motion using VAEs and normalizing flows. These innovations mark significant progress in controllable, high-fidelity video generation. The DaGAN++ consists of three key modules:

- **Face Depth Learning Network:** Learns detailed 3D facial geometry without explicit 3D data.
- **Facial Keypoint Detection:** Uses depth maps to accurately locate features like eyes and mouth.
- **Multi-layer Generation:** Integrates depth, occlusion, and motion data to produce highly realistic face videos.

DaGAN++ excels in capturing fine facial movements, especially around the eyes and mouth, enabling precise geometry estimation and enhancing expression fidelity in talking head video generation. Style-Talker, introduced by Min et al. [52], generates realistic talking head videos from a single image and audio input. It achieves accurate lip-sync, head pose, and natural eye blinks by encoding latent features with pre-trained image generators. VAEs separate lip and head movements, while an auto-regressive prior with normalizing flow captures nuanced audio dynamics like pauses and tilts. The model supports motion control via reference videos and consistently outperforms other audio-driven methods in visual quality and identity preservation. Li et al. [53] introduced MViTv2, an enhanced version of MViT designed for tasks like object detection and image/video classification. It improves spatial understanding through multiscale processing and residual pooling. Tested across datasets including ImageNet, COCO, and Kinetics-400 [54], MViTv2 achieved 86.1% accuracy on Kinetics-400 [55], surpassing previous benchmarks in video categorization.

Generative AI for Natural Language Processing

Generative AI models excel in NLP tasks such as text generation, reasoning, and language understanding. Key datasets include CoNLL-2003 [56] for Named Entity Recognition, DUC 2002 [57] and QMSUM [58] for summarization, and XNLI [59] for natural language inference. These benchmarks support training and evaluation across diverse linguistic tasks.

Ahuja et al. [60] highlighted that generative AI models trained across multiple languages often underperform in non-English contexts, revealing a persistent language bias despite multilingual training efforts.

Generative AI shows promise in education [61,62], offering both opportunities and challenges. It calls for innovative, AI-integrated teaching methods. Tlili et al. [63] advocate for ethical, personalized AI chatbots to enhance learning experiences. Bozkurt [64] emphasized rethinking the roles of educators and AI, as tasks like grading, tutoring, and content creation are increasingly shared with AI. Rather than replacing teachers, AI should complement them—allowing educators to focus on creativity, emotional intelligence, and student support. A forward-thinking approach is essential to balance technological integration with human contribution.

Generative AI enables personalized learning, inclusive curricula, and 24/7 accessibility, while improving efficiency and language skills. It uses Transformers and GANs to generate synthetic data across domains like healthcare, surveillance, and NLP. For instance, Frid-Adar et al. [65] used DCGAN to synthesize liver lesion images, and Wang et al. [66] applied SSIM-integrated CycleGAN to create crowd scenes under varied weather conditions.In NLP, BERT [67] captures bidirectional context and excels in both feature-based and fine-tuned tasks, achieving near-optimal F1 scores on CoNLL-2003. Kale et al. [68] used BERT and ELMo for malware classification, showing significant accuracy gains over traditional embeddings.

Generative AI models like BERT and ELMo have been effectively applied to malware classification. Kale et al. [68] trained embeddings using these models, achieving notable improvements in detection accuracy compared to traditional methods. BERT-SVM and BERT-kNN achieved top accuracy at 96%, followed closely by HMM2Vec-kNN, HMM2Vec-RF, BERT-RF, and ELMo-CNN at 95%. ELMo-based models, including HMM2Vec-CNN, reached 94%, while Word2Vec embeddings consistently scored below 90% across classifiers. Joshi et al. [69] introduced Ranksum, a summarization method based on four features—location, keywords, semantics, and topic relevance. It ranks sentences independently without requiring labeled data. Such approaches highlight AI's growing role in advancing NLP applications and expanding language processing capabilities.

4.2.3 Generative AI for Knowledge Graph Generation

Knowledge graphs, introduced by Google [70], organize complex relationships between entities more meaningfully than traditional databases. Cai and Wang [71] proposed KBGAN to enhance knowledge graph embeddings using adversarial learning, independent of specific generator-discriminator structures. Liu et al. [72] developed K-BERT, which integrates graph knowledge into sentences using soft-position and visible matrix techniques to preserve semantic integrity during language modeling.

A key challenge in knowledge graph modeling is handling Heterogeneous Entity Span (HES)—entities of varying lengths and types. Additionally, generative AI struggles with unseen key phrases not encountered during training, limiting its generalization in dynamic knowledge environments.

Link prediction helps uncover missing relationships in knowledge graphs, enhancing search, recommendation, and data discovery. Balazevic et al. [10] introduced TuckER, a linear model using Tucker decomposition for triple representation. Zeb et al. [73] proposed Complex GCN, which learns rich embeddings via standard graph convolutional networks [74], advancing link prediction accuracy.

Recent studies highlight diverse progress in knowledge graph generation using generative AI—from adversarial learning for improved embeddings to bridging unstructured text with structured graph representations . These innovations enhance data organization, semantic understanding, and relational inference.

Interdisciplinary Applications of Generative AI

Generative AI aids fault detection by producing synthetic data where real samples are scarce. Gao et al. [75] combined FEM simulations [76] with GANs [77] to generate diverse fault samples, improving classifier accuracy (e.g., SVM [78], ELM [79], DTree [80]). Feng et al. [82] introduced TrafficGen, outperforming SeneGen [83] in generating realistic traffic scenarios. AI is also used in music generation [84] and synthetic handwriting via HiGAN+ [85], showcasing its creative potential across domains.

Table 4.1 Comparison of Classification accuracy with and without GANs sampling.

Description	*FEM & AI*	*FEM, GAN & AI*
No of Fault Samples [81]	360	360
No of Synthetic Fault Sample [81]	-	3240
Accuracy SVM (%) [81]	84.44	86.11
Accuracy ELM (%) [81]	89.72	91.67
Accuracy Decision Tree (%) [81]	91.11	97.5
Average Accuracy (%) [81]	88.42	91.76

Generative AI creates synthetic music using RNNs, Transformers, and VAEs. HiGAN+ [85] enables diverse synthetic handwriting generation. In software engineering, it enhances code quality, supports debugging, and automates bug fixes—streamlining development workflows [86, 87 and 88].

Conclusion

Generative AI has rapidly expanded from text and image synthesis to applications in healthcare, entertainment, robotics, and education. Powered by models like GANs, Transformers, VAEs, and Diffusion Models, it enables realistic media generation and enhances tasks like image translation, video synthesis, and NLP. These technologies aim to simplify human life, but ethical considerations must remain central. Pudari and Ernst [86] affirm that AI will support—not replace—humans in software engineering. The reviewed studies reflect only a fraction of the dynamic progress in this fast-evolving field, underscoring the need for responsible innovation and interdisciplinary collaboration. Despite its vast potential, Generative AI faces challenges like ethical concerns and deepfake risks. Its future depends on improving model interpretability, accuracy, and ethical safeguards. As Pudari and Ernst [86] note, AI should support—not replace—humans. Interdisciplinary collaboration is key to ensuring responsible innovation, trust, and societal benefit. Generative AI is poised to drive breakthroughs in personalized medicine, synthetic data generation, and beyond. Its continued evolution depends on interdisciplinary collaboration and responsible governance. This chapter has outlined key advancements, emphasizing the need to balance innovation with ethical responsibility to ensure AI's positive societal impact.

References

[1] Kumar, L. and Singh, D.K. A comprehensive survey on generative adversarial networks used for synthesizing multimedia content. *Multimedia Tools and Applications*, (2023).

[2] Vasanthi, P. and Mohan, L. Multi-head-self-attention based yolov5x transformer for multi-scale object detection. *Multimedia Tools and Applications*, (2023).

[3] Khamparia, A., Gupta, D., Rodrigues, J.J. de Albuquerque, V.H.C. Deavn: Cervical cancer prediction and classification using deep convolutional and variational autoencoder network. *Multimedia Tools and Applications*, (2021).

[4] Kollem, S., Reddy, K.R., and Rao, D.S. A novel diffusivity function-based image denoising for MRI medical images. *Multimedia Tools and Applications*, (2023).

[5] Vaswani, A., Shazeer, N., Parmar, N., Uszkoreit, J., Jones, L. et al. Attention is all you need. *In Advances in Neural Information Processing Systems*, (2017).

[6] Shao M., Basit A., Karri R. and Shafique M., Survey of Different Large Language Model Architectures: Trends, Benchmarks, and Challenges. *IEEE Access*, (2024).

[7] Salimans, T., Goodfellow, I., Zaremba, W., Cheung, V., Radford, A. et al. Improved techniques for training gans. *In Advances in Neural Information Processing Systems*, (2016).

[8] Kingma, D. P., Salimans, T., Jozefowicz, R., Chen, X., Sutskever, I. et al. Improved variational inference with inverse autoregressive flow. *In Advances in Neural Information Processing Systems, Curran Associates, Inc*, (2016).

[9] Diederik P. Kingma, Tim Salimans, Rafal Jozefowicz, Xi Chen, Ilya Sutskever et al. *Improved Variational inference with inverse Autoregressive flow, Advances in Neural Information Processing Systems 29 (NIPS 2016)*, (2016).

[10] Ye, Y. Hao, J. Hou, Y. *Generative AI for visualization: State of the art and future directions, Visual Informatics*, (2024)

[11] Yang, K., Yau, J., Fei-Fei, L., Deng, J. and Russakovsky, O. et al. A study of face obfuscation in ImageNet. *In International Conference on Machine Learning (ICML)*, (2022).

[12] Liu, Z., Luo, P., Wang, X. and Tang, X. Deep learning face attributes in the wild. *In Proceedings of International Conference on Computer Vision (ICCV)*, (2015).

[13] Johnson, A.E., Pollard, T.J., Shen, L., Lehman, L.-w. H., Feng, M. et al. A freely accessible critical care database. *Scientific data*, (2016).

[14] Menze, B.H., Jakab, A., Bauer, S., Kalpathy-Cramer, J., Farahani, K. et al. The multimodal brain tumor image segmentation benchmark (brats). *IEEE transactions on medical imaging*, (2014).

[15] Tibrewala, R., Dutt, T., Tong, A., Ginocchio, L., Keerthivasan, M.B. et al. *Fastmri prostate: A publicly available, biparametric MRI dataset to advance machine learning for prostate cancer imaging*, (2023).

[16] Wang, X., Peng, Y., Lu, L., Lu, Z., Bagheri, M. et al. Hospital-scale chest x-ray database and benchmarks on weakly-supervised classification and localization of common thorax diseases. *In Proceedings of the IEEE conference on computer vision and pattern recognition*, (2017).

[17] Menze, B. H., Jakab, A., Bauer, S., Kalpathy-Cramer, J., Farahani, K. et al. The multimodal brain tumor image segmentation benchmark (brats). *IEEE transactions on medical imaging*, (2014).

[18] Sengar, S.S., Meulengracht, C., Boesen, M.P., Overgaard, A.F., Gudbergsen, H. et al. Multi-planar 3D knee MRI segmentation via UNet inspired architectures. *International Journal of Imaging Systems and Technology*, (2023).

[19] Yan, S., Wang, C., Chen, W. and Lyu, J. Swin transformer-based GAN for multi-modal medical image translation. *Frontiers in Oncology*, (2022).

[20] Isola, P., Zhu, J.-Y., Zhou, T. and Efros, A.A. *Image-to-image translation with conditional adversarial networks*, (2018).

[21] Zhu, J.-Y., Park, T., Isola, P. and Efros, A.A. Unpaired image to-image translation using cycle-consistent adversarial networks. *In 2017 IEEE International Conference on Computer Vision (ICCV)*, (2017).

[22] Rezagholiradeh, M. and Haidar, M.A. Reg-Gan: Semi-supervised learning based on generative adversarial networks for regression. *In 2018 IEEE international conference on acoustics, speech and signal processing (ICASSP)*, (2018).

[23] Dar, S.U.H., Yurt, M., Karacan, L., Erdem, A., Erdem, E. et al. *Image synthesis in multi-contrast MRI with conditional generative adversarial networks*, (2018).

[24] Isola, P., Zhu, J.-Y., Zhou, T. and Efros, A.A. *Image-to-image translation with conditional adversarial networks*, (2018).

[25] Zhu, J.-Y., Park, T., Isola, P. and Efros, A.A. Unpaired image-to-image translation using cycle-consistent adversarial networks. *In 2017 IEEE International Conference on Computer Vision (ICCV)*, (2017).

[26] Torbunov, D., Huang, Y., Yu, H., Huang, J., Yoo, S. et al. UVCGAN: UNet vision transformer cycle-consistent GAN for unpaired image-to-image translation. *In Proceedings of the IEEE/CVF Winter Conference on Applications of Computer Vision*, (2023).

[27] Heusel, M., Ramsauer, H., Unterthiner, T., Nessler, B. and Hochreiter, S. et al. Gans trained by a two-time-scale update rule converge to a local Nash equilibrium. *In Advances in Neural Information Processing Systems*, (2017).

[28] Bi´ nkowski, M., Sutherland, D.J., Arbel, M. and Gretton, A. *Demystifying MMD GANs, International Conference on Learning Representations*, (2018).

[29] Torbunov, D., Huang, Y., Yu, H., Huang, J., Yoo, S. et al. Unet vision transformer cycle-consistent GAN for unpaired image-to-image translation. *In Proceedings of the IEEE/CVF Winter Conference on Applications of Computer Vision*, (2023).

[30] Zhao, Y., Celik, T., Liu, N., and Li, H.-C. A comparative analysis of GAN-based methods for SAR-to-optical image translation. *IEEE Geoscience and Remote Sensing Letters*, (2022).

[31] Kohei Aarai. Modified pix2pixHD for Enhancing Spatial Resolution of Image for Conversion from SAR Images to Optical Images in Application of Landslide Area Detection. *Information*, (2025).
[32] Hoyez, H., Schockaert, C., Rambach, J., Mirbach, B. and Stricker, D. et al. Unsupervised image-to-image translation: A review. *Sensors*, (2022).
[33] Lin, Y., Wang, Y., Li, Y., Gao, Y., Wang, Z. et al. Attention-based spatial guidance for image-to-image translation. *In Proceedings of the IEEE/CVF Winter Conference on Applications of Computer Vision (WACV)*, (2021).
[34] Jain, V., Sengar, S.S. and Ronickom, J.F.A. Age-specific diagnostic classification of ASD using deep learning approaches. *Studies in Health Technology and Informatics*, (2023).
[35] Sengar, S.S. and Kumar, S. Content-based secure image retrieval in an untrusted third-party environment. *In International Conference on Frontiers of Intelligent Computing: Theory and Applications*, (2022).
[36] Lakshmi, P.B., Reddy, V.D., Ghosh, S. and Sengar, S.S. Classification of autism spectrum disorder based on brain image data using deep neural networks. *In International Conference on Frontiers of Intelligent Computing: Theory and Applications*, (2023).
[37] Wang, Z., Bovik, A., Sheikh, H. and Simoncelli, E. Image quality assessment: from error visibility to structural similarity. *IEEE Transactions on Image Processing*, (2004).
[38] Sengar, S.S. and Mukhopadhyay, S. Motion segmentation-based surveillance video compression using adaptive particle swarm optimization. *Neural Computing and Applications*, (2020).
[39] Tanchenko, A. Visual-PSNR measure of image quality. *Journal of Visual Communication and Image Representation*, (2014).
[40] Sengar, S.S. and Mukhopadhyay, S. Moving object tracking using Laplacian-DCT based perceptual hash. *In 2016 International Conference on Wireless Communications, Signal Processing and Networking (WiSPNET)*, (2016).
[41] Zhang, R., Isola, P., Efros, A.A., Shechtman, E. and Wang, O. et al. The unreasonable effectiveness of deep features as a perceptual metric. *In Proceedings of the IEEE conference on computer vision and pattern recognition*, (2018).
[42] Chen Y., Liu J. and Peng L. Auto-encoding variational bayes. *Cambridge Explorations in Arts and Sciences* (2024).
[43] Nagrani, A., Chung, J.S. and Zisserman, VoxCeleb: A large-scale speaker identification dataset. In Interspeech 2017. *ISCA*, (2017).
[44] Zhang, Z., Li, L., Ding, Y. and Fan, C. Flow-guided one-shot talking face generation with a high-resolution audio-visual dataset. *In Proceedings of the IEEE/CVF Conference on Computer Vision and Pattern Recognition*, (2021).
[45] Wu, W., Zhang, Y., Li, C., Qian, C. and Loy, C.C. et al. *ReenactGAN: Learning to reenact faces via boundary transfer*. (2018).
[46] Kay, W., Carreira, J., Simonyan, K., Zhang, B., Hillier, C. et al. *The kinetics human action video dataset*. (2017).
[47] Soomro, K., Zamir, A.R. and Shah, MUcf101: A dataset of 101 human actions classes from videos in the wild, (2012).
[48] van den Oord, A., Dieleman, S., Zen, H., Simonyan, K. and Vinyals, O. et al. *Wavenet: A generative model for raw audio* (2016).
[49] Panayotov, V., Chen, G., Povey, D., and Khudanpur, S. Librispeech et al. An ASR corpus based on public domain audiobooks. *In 2015 IEEE International Conference on Acoustics, Speech and Signal Processing (ICASSP)*, (2015).
[50] Hong, F.-T., Zhang, L., Shen, L. and Xu, D: Depth-aware generative adversarial network for talking head video generation. *In Proceedings of the IEEE/CVF Conference on Computer Vision and Pattern Recognition (CVPR)*, (2022).

[51] Hong, F.-T., Shen, L. and Xu, D. *Dagan: Depth-aware generative adversarial network for talking head video generation*, (2023).

[52] Min, D., Song, M., and Hwang, S.J. *Style Talker: One-shot style-based audio-driven talking head video generation*, (2022).

[53] Li, Y., Wu, C.-Y., Fan, H., Mangalam, K., Xiong, B. et al. Improved multiscale vision transformers for classification and detection. *In Proceedings of the IEEE/CVF Conference on Computer Vision and Pattern Recognition (CVPR)*, (2022).

[54] Kay, W., Carreira, J., Simonyan, K., Zhang, B., Hillier, C. et al. *The kinetics human action video dataset*, (2017).

[55] Fan, H., Xiong, B., Mangalam, K., Li, Y., Yan, Z. and Malik, J. Christoph feichtenhofer. multiscale vision transformers. *In Proceedings of the IEEE/CVF International Conference on Computer Vision*, (2021).

[56] Sang, E.F. and De Meulder, F. *Introduction to the CoNLL-2003 shared task: Language-independent named entity recognition*, (2003).

[57] McKeown, K., Barzilay, R., Blair-Goldensohn, S., Evans, D., Hatzivassiloglou, V. et al. The Columbia multi-document summarizer for DUC 2002. *In Workshop on Automatic Summarization*, (2002).

[58] Zhong, M., Yin, D., Yu, T. QMSum: A New Benchmark for Query-based Multi-domain Meeting Summarization. In Proceedings of the 2021 Conference of the North American Chapter of the Association for Computational Linguistics: *Human Language Technologies*, pages 5905–5921, Online. Association for Computational Linguistics, (2021).

[59] Conneau, A., Lample, G., Rinott, R., Williams, A., Bowman, S.R. et al. *Evaluating cross-lingual sentence representations*, (2018).

[60] Ahuja, K., Diddee, H., Hada, R., Ochieng, M., Ramesh, K. et al. *Multilingual evaluation of generative ai*, (2023).

[61] Cao, Y., Li, S., Liu, Y., Yan, Z., Dai, Y. et al. *A comprehensive survey of ai-generated content (AIGC): A history of generative ai from GAN to chatGPT*, (2023).

[62] Dwivedi, Y.K. and Kshetri, N., Hughes. Opinion paper: "So what if ChatGPT wrote it?" multidisciplinary perspectives on opportunities, challenges and implications of generative conversational ai for research, practice and policy. *International Journal of Information Management*, (2022).

[63] Tlili, A., Shehata, B., Adarkwah, M.A., Bozkurt, A., Hickey, D.T. et al. What if the devil is my guardian angel: ChatGPT as a case study of using chatbots in education. *Smart Learning Environments*, (2023).

[64] Bozkurt, A. Generative artificial intelligence (AI) powered conversational educational agents: The inevitable paradigm shift. *Asian Journal of Distance Education*, (2023).

[65] Frid-Adar, M., Klang, E., Amitai, M., Goldberger, J. and Greenspan, H. et al. (2018). *Synthetic data augmentation using GAN for improved liver lesion classification.*

[66] Wang, Q., Gao, J., Lin, W. and Yuan, Y. *Learning from synthetic data for crowd counting in the wild*, (2019).

[67] Devlin, J., Chang, M.-W., Lee, K. and Toutanova, K. *Bert: Pre-training of deep bidirectional transformers for language understanding*, (2018).

[68] Kale, A.S., Pandya, V., Di Troia, F. and Stamp, M. Malware classification with Word2Vec, HMM2Vec, BERT, and ELMO. *Journal of Computer Virology and Hacking Techniques*, (2023).

[69] Rani, R. and Lobiyal, D. An extractive text summarization approach using tagged-LDA based topic modeling. *Multimedia tools and applications*, (2021).

[70] Steiner, T., Verborgh, R., Troncy, R., Gabarro, J. and Van de Walle, R. et al. Adding real-time coverage to the Google knowledge graph. *In 11th International Semantic Web Conference (ISWC 2012)*, (2012).

[71] Cai, L. and Wang, W.Y. *KBGAN: Adversarial learning for knowledge graph embeddings*, (2018).

[72] Liu, W., Zhou, P., Zhao, Z., Wang, Z., Ju, Q. et al. *Enabling language representation with knowledge graph*, (2019).
[73] Shi, X., Lv, F., Seng, D., Zhang, J., Chen, J. et al. *Visualizing and understanding graph convolutional network. Multimedia Tools and Applications*, (2021).
[74] Kipf, T.N. and Welling, M. *Semi-supervised classification with graph convolutional networks*, (2017).
[75] Gao, Y., Liu, X. and Xiang, J. Fem simulation-based generative adversarial networks to detect bearing faults. *IEEE Transactions on Industrial Informatics*, (2020).
[76] Courant, R. *Variational methods for the solution of problems of equilibrium and vibrations*, (1943).
[77] Goodfellow, I.J., Pouget-Abadie, J., Mirza, M., Xu, B., Warde-Farley, D. et al. *Generative adversarial networks*, (2014).
[78] Cortes, C. and Vapnik, V. *Support-vector networks. Machine learning*, (1995).
[79] Huang, G.-B., Zhu, Q.-Y. and Siew, C.-K. Extreme learning machine: a new learning scheme of feedforward neural networks. *In 2004 IEEE international joint conference on neural networks (IEEE Cat. No. 04CH37541)*, (2004).
[80] Quinlan, J.R. Induction of decision trees. *Machine learning*, (1986).
[81] Y. Gao, X. Liu and J. Xiang. FEM Simulation-Based Generative Adversarial Networks to Detect Bearing Faults. *IEEE Transactions on Industrial Informatics*, (2020).
[82] Feng, L., Li, Q., Peng, Z., Tan, S. and Zhou, B. et al. Trafficgen: Learning to generate diverse and realistic traffic scenarios. *In 2023 IEEE International Conference on Robotics and Automation (ICRA)*, (2023).
[83] Tan, S., Wong, K., Wang, S., Manivasagam, S., Ren, M. et al. Learning to generate realistic traffic scenes. *In Proceedings-2021 IEEE/CVF Conference on Computer Vision and Pattern Recognition, CVPR 2021*, (2021).
[84] Keerti, G., Vaishnavi, A., Mukherjee, P., Vidya, A. S., Sreenithya, G.S. et al. Attentional networks for music generation. *Multimedia Tools and Applications*, (2022).
[85] Gan, J., Wang, W., Leng, J. and Gao, X. Higan+: Handwriting imitation GAN with disentangled representations. ACM Trans. *Graph.*, (2022).
[86] Pudari, R. and Ernst, N.A. *From copilot to pilot: Towards AI-supported software development*, (2023).
[87] Zhang, Z., Li, L., Ding, Y. and Fan, C. Flow-guided one-shot talking face generation with a high-resolution audio-visual dataset. *In Proceedings of the IEEE/CVF Conference on Computer Vision and Pattern Recognition*, (2021).
[88] Jakub M. Tomczak. *Generative AI Systems: A Systems-based Perspective on Generative AI., Computation and Language*, (2024).

5 Generative AI in Healthcare: A New Frontier for Diagnostics

Aakanksha Mahajan[1] and Suman[2*]

This chapter explores how Generative AI—specifically GANs and VAEs—can enhance diagnostic accuracy in medical imaging. Using the ChestX-ray14 dataset, GANs generate synthetic X-rays to augment limited data, while VAEs reconstruct scans to detect anomalies. A CNN classifier trained on both real and synthetic images shows a 5–7% boost in performance (AUC, precision, recall). These results validate the models' effectiveness. Ethical and clinical implications are discussed, with future directions pointing toward federated learning and hybrid AI systems.

5.1 Introduction

Healthcare is rapidly evolving with the adoption of AI, especially in diagnostics. Traditional methods—often slow and prone to error—are being enhanced by generative AI, which analyzes vast datasets like medical images and EHRs to uncover hidden patterns and simulate realistic scenarios for training. These innovations enable faster, more accurate disease detection, particularly for complex or subtle conditions, reshaping diagnostic workflows and improving clinical outcomes.

The healthcare sector is being reshaped by AI, with Generative AI standing out as a transformative force. Unlike traditional automation, it enables simulation, prediction, and personalized insights through synthetic data generation, anomaly detection, and patient-specific modeling—ushering in a new era of precision diagnostics. AI is now used not just to analyze medical data but to generate realistic synthetic datasets—especially valuable when annotated samples are scarce. Generative AI fills these gaps by creating lifelike medical images, boosting training data and improving the accuracy of diagnostic models.

The rise of EHRs and digitized medical imaging has laid the groundwork for large-scale AI adoption in healthcare. This shift is moving diagnostics from manual and reactive to automated, predictive, and proactive systems—with Generative AI driving this transformation.

[1] CSE,PIET, Samalkha, India.
[2] CSE, BPIT, Delhi, India.
Email: er.aakanksha@yahoo.co.in
* Corresponding author: sumanarora@bpitindia.com

DOI: 10.1201/9781003670582-5

5.1.1 Medical Imaging

Medical imaging is central to diagnostics, but traditional interpretation by radiologists is often subjective and time-consuming. AI, especially CNNs, now aids image analysis—but these models need large, labeled datasets, which are often scarce. Generative AI addresses this gap by producing realistic synthetic images, enabling data augmentation and improving model robustness.

Generative AI addresses the challenge of limited annotated medical data by producing realistic synthetic images for augmentation and anomaly detection. Unlike discriminative models that classify inputs, generative models create new data that mirrors real-world observations. Their ability to simulate medical images, genetic sequences, and patient histories enables early diagnosis, personalized care, and improved clinical decision-making.

Medical imaging—via X-rays, MRI, CT, and ultrasound—is vital for non-invasive diagnostics. Traditionally reliant on radiologists' visual expertise, interpretation can be slow, subjective, and inconsistent. AI now offers faster, more objective analysis, improving diagnostic accuracy and efficiency. Generative AI marks a paradigm shift in medical imaging by producing anatomically accurate synthetic scans. It supports data augmentation, corrects dataset imbalance, and strengthens classification models. Additionally, it improves low-quality images by removing noise and reconstructing missing features—boosting clarity and diagnostic reliability. Cutting-edge models like StyleGAN, CycleGAN, and VAE-GAN hybrids are revolutionizing diagnostics by restoring corrupted scans, simulating disease progression, and generating 3D medical visuals. These capabilities enhance diagnostic accuracy and support immersive medical training.

5.1.2 The Promise of Generative AI in Diagnostics

Medical imaging—via X-rays, MRI, and CT—offers vital internal views for diagnosis. Yet, traditional interpretation is often slow and subjective. Generative AI helps simulate clinical conditions, enhancing image analysis and supporting faster, more consistent diagnostics. Generative AI enhances medical imaging and automates diagnosis by producing realistic synthetic data—especially valuable for rare conditions with limited patient records. It simulates complex biological systems to model disease progression and test diagnostic strategies. These advances support precision medicine by tailoring care to individual DNA and lifestyle profiles, enabling more personalized and effective treatment. Generative AI integrates data from genomics, EHRs, and real-time monitoring to build predictive models that anticipate disease onset, track progression, and suggest optimal treatments. This capability is driving a shift toward proactive, personalized diagnostics—significantly improving patient outcomes. Generative AI enables simulation of complex pathologies like tumors and fibrosis, allowing models to generalize across diverse and underrepresented clinical cases. This expands diagnostic coverage and strengthens precision medicine strategies. Generative models excel at early disease detection by reconstructing healthy baselines and identifying subtle deviations—

often missed by traditional classifiers. This is especially valuable for detecting conditions like early-stage cancer or tuberculosis, where abnormalities are minimal and hard to spot. Generative AI advances personalized medicine care by integrating imaging, genomics, and patient records to simulate individual disease trajectories and recommend tailored diagnostics or treatments. This approach enhances outcomes, especially for chronic or genetically linked conditions.

The future of diagnostics hinges on generative models that can integrate multimodal data, meet clinical standards, and deliver transparent, reproducible outputs. Rather than replacing clinicians, these tools are designed to support medical decision-making—enhancing accuracy, trust, and scalability.

5.2 Literature Survey

Deeper learning has significantly advanced medical diagnostics. [10] introduced CheXNet, a CNN model that detects pneumonia at radiologist-level accuracy, though its performance was limited by dataset imbalance and sparse annotations. To address such limitations, [19] proposed GANs, which are now widely used to generate synthetic medical images for data augmentation.VAEs have also proven effective for anomaly detection, particularly in rare disease diagnosis [5],[29]. Generative models enhance image quality by reducing noise, reconstructing missing features, and adapting across domains—especially in chest X-ray analysis. These capabilities help mitigate issues like limited labeled data and class imbalance, improving diagnostic robustness.

5.2.1 Generative Adversarial Networks (GANs)

Generative AI has significantly advanced diagnostic capabilities by producing realistic synthetic medical images for data augmentation, noise reduction, and artifact removal. CycleGAN, for instance, enhances chest X-rays by eliminating clinical artifacts—[11] reported improved pneumonia and consolidation classification on the ChestX-ray14 dataset. Similarly, [8] used DCGANs to boost classification accuracy, [13] demonstrated GAN-based MRI synthesis for brain diagnostics and resolution enhancement. Beyond imaging, GANs simulate disease progression (e.g., cancer, diabetes) to train predictive models for early detection and personalized treatment planning. They also generate novel molecular structures for drug discovery, accelerating therapeutic development.These applications highlight the versatility of generative models in improving diagnostic precision, addressing data scarcity, and enabling personalized medicine.

5.2.2 Variational Autoencoders (VAEs) for Disease Feature Extraction

Variational Autoencoders (VAEs) are effective generative models for extracting meaningful features from chest X-rays. [5] proposed a VAE-based approach for analyzing sequential scans to predict disease progression, successfully identifying early-stage pneumonia and tuberculosis ahead of radiologists. VAEs with explainable AI (XAI) techniques, enabling interpretable latent space representations that improve model transparency and clinical trust has been significantly enhanced [19, 24].

Transformers have proven effective for feature extraction and classification in medical imaging. The SA-DenseNet121 model, which integrates CNNs with self-attention mechanisms, achieved high accuracy on the ChestX-ray14 dataset by highlighting critical regions in X-rays. Vision Transformers (ViTs) have shown superior performance over CNNs in disease localization. Enhanced sensitivity and specificity for pneumonia detection using ViTs on the ChestX-ray14 dataset has been demonstrated in [27].

AI tools are enhancing radiologists' efficiency in chest X-ray diagnostics [3]. Google Health's AI system also detects tuberculosis in low-resource settings [2].

AI is rapidly transforming global healthcare diagnostics, from advanced image analysis in developed regions to mobile tools in underserved areas. Below are notable use cases [23]:

1. **United States – Radiology and Cancer Detection:** In the U.S., AI is widely integrated into radiology, with tools like Google Health's breast cancer screening system matching or surpassing radiologist accuracy. FDA-approved devices such as IDx-DR enable diabetic retinopathy detection in primary care without specialist input.
2. **India -Tuberculosis Screening and Rural Outreach:** In India, AI-based chest X-ray tools are deployed in rural clinics and mobile units to aid early TB detection, enabling faster treatment and curbing transmission.
3. **United Kingdom – NHS and AI-Powered Triage:** The UK's NHS has piloted AI tools for emergency triage. Babylon Health's chatbot supports GP practices by assessing symptoms and history, easing the burden on doctors.
4. **China – National AI Healthcare Strategy:** China has adopted AI in hospitals via platforms like Tencent Miying, which analyzes CT scans for lung cancer and other diseases. Supporting over 100 hospitals, it accelerates diagnostics, especially in underserved areas.
5. **Africa – Mobile Diagnostics and Point-of-Care AI:** In Kenya and Uganda, AI-powered smartphone apps use deep learning to detect malaria and assess skin conditions, providing vital diagnostics where labs are limited.
6. **Brazil – Telemedicine and AI for Cardiology:** Brazilian startups are leveraging AI for ECG analysis and remote cardiology diagnostics. Portal Telemedicina uses AI to interpret heart signals and radiology scans, linking patients to urban specialists.
7. **Japan – AI and Aging Population:** Japan uses AI to detect stroke, Alzheimer's, and Parkinson's early, applying machine learning to MRI scans to identify subtle neurological changes and prevent disability.
8. **South Korea** – During COVID-19, South Korean hospitals used AI tools like Lunit INSIGHT CXR to rapidly detect viral pneumonia from CT and X-ray scans, easing radiologist workload and enabling swift triage.

9. **Germany** – In Germany, AI supports precision oncology by enabling genomic profiling and matching tumors with targeted therapies, improving outcomes in cancers like melanoma and breast cancer.
10. **Global Collaboration** – The WHO is collaborating to ethically integrate AI into global health systems, focusing on pandemic response, antimicrobial resistance, and chronic disease monitoring.

5.2.3 Limitations of Existing Datasets in Medical Diagnostics

Open-access medical imaging datasets have propelled AI research but face limitations that hinder clinical adoption and real-world generalizability.

1. *Class Imbalance*

Many datasets are imbalanced, overrepresenting common conditions like pneumonia in ChestX-ray14, while rare diseases such as fibrosis are underrepresented—leading to biased models with limited clinical reliability.

2. *Weak and Noisy Labels*

Many labels are derived via automated NLP from radiology reports, often without expert validation, leading to inaccuracies. In ChestX-ray14, ambiguous reporting can result in mislabeled pathologies, undermining model accuracy.

3. *Lack of Ground Truth Validation*

Lack of biopsy-confirmed diagnoses or radiologist consensus reduces clinical trust in AI outputs. Many datasets lack secondary validation or multimodal imaging, limiting diagnostic reliability for conditions like cancer and TB.

4. *Demographic and Institutional Bias*

Datasets like MIMIC-CXR and CheXpert, sourced from single U.S. institutions, often lack global diversity. Factors like ethnicity, age, scanner type, and imaging protocols cause domain shifts, limiting model generalizability.

5. *Absence of Multimodal Context*

Most imaging datasets lack clinical context—such as lab results, genomics, medications, or history—limiting multimodal AI applications for personalized diagnostics and treatment planning.

6. *Static and Retrospective Nature*

Most datasets are static snapshots, lacking temporal data needed for modeling disease progression or predicting long-term outcomes—key for chronic care and epidemiology.

7. Variability in Image Quality

Variations in image resolution, orientation, and contrast—due to differing scan protocols or machine settings—impair feature extraction and raise false positives. Unannotated artifacts like blur or poor contrast further confuse model training.

8. Underrepresentation of Edge Cases

Data from pediatric, geriatric, and minority groups is often scarce, leading to biased model performance since disease patterns vary across age and ethnicity.

9. Inconsistent Evaluation and Benchmarking

The absence of standardized benchmarks—like fixed train-test splits or preprocessing steps—hinders cross-study comparisons. Test leakage and flawed validation often inflate accuracy, undermining reproducibility and robustness.

5.2.4 Ethical and Regulatory Aspects in AI-based Medical Diagnostics

As AI shapes clinical decisions, ethical and regulatory compliance is essential. Systems must meet global standards like HIPAA (U.S.), CE marking (Europe), and FDA approval to ensure safety, transparency, and trust.

1. HIPAA (Health Insurance Portability and Accountability Act) Compliance – United States

AI tools interacting with medical data must comply with HIPAA standards by ensuring:

- **Data De-identification:** Patient information must be anonymized prior to model training or inference.
- **Access Controls:** Only authorized personnel should access identifiable health records.
- **Audit Logging:** All data interactions must be traceable through secure logs.

Non-compliance with HIPAA can lead to legal penalties and erode public trust. Organizations must also establish Business Associate Agreements (BAAs) with AI vendors handling protected health data to ensure accountability.

2. FDA (U.S. Food and Drug Administration) Regulatory Framework

To obtain FDA clearance, AI-based diagnostic tools classified as Software as a Medical Device (SaMD) must demonstrate: Clinical validation with representative data,

- **Clinical Validation:** Proven accuracy using representative patient data.
- **Model Transparency:** Explainability for deep learning outputs.

Real-World Reliability: Stable performance under varied imaging conditions and edge cases. Recent FDA guidance promotes a **Total Product Lifecycle** model, urging developers to submit premarket evidence and continuously update regulators as AI tools evolve through real-world use.

3. *CE Marking – European Union*

To comply with EU Medical Device Regulation (MDR), AI-based diagnostics must obtain a CE mark by meeting:

- **Risk Classification:** Typically Class IIa or higher for diagnostic software.
- **Defined Intended Use:** Clear documentation of clinical purpose.
- **Post-Market Surveillance:** Mechanisms to monitor safety and performance.
- **Notified Body Review**: Independent conformity assessment required.

CE compliance also requires clear disclosure of data sources, target population, and safety constraints.

4. *Ethical Concerns in Clinical AI*

Even with regulatory approval, AI tools raise key ethical concerns:

- **Bias and Fairness:** Skewed training data may lead to poor performance on underrepresented groups, worsening disparities.
- **Explainability:** Clinicians need interpretable outputs; black-box models hinder informed consent and accountability.
- **Informed Consent:** Patients must be aware of AI involvement and retain the right to request human oversight.
- **Liability:** Responsibility for errors—whether by developers, clinicians, or institutions—remains legally ambiguous.

5. *Toward Global Harmonization*

International bodies like the IMDRF and WHO are working to harmonize AI regulations, promoting frameworks that balance innovation with patient safety—especially for cross-border applications and telemedicine.

5.2.5 Global COVID-19 Response with Generative AI

The pandemic accelerated the use of generative AI in diagnostics. Early on, GANs were applied to denoise low-quality CT and X-ray scans captured under field conditions, enabling faster triage. These models improved image clarity and supported rapid diagnosis, especially in resource-constrained settings.

Case Example: Lunit INSIGHT CXR in South Korea

During COVID-19, Lunit INSIGHT CXR—powered by GANs and Vision Transformers—enabled rapid chest X-ray analysis with high sensitivity for pneumonia detection. ViTs enhanced lesion localization, identifying subtle lung opacities often missed under clinical time constraints.

Case Example: RADLogics in the U.S.

RADLogics applied deep generative models to track lung disease progression in COVID-19 patients, supporting real-time ICU triage. By combining generative AI with transformers, the system enabled faster, scalable, and accurate diagnostics under pandemic pressure.

5.2.6 Integration into Clinical Workflows

Despite technical progress, integrating generative AI into hospital workflows remains difficult. Diagnostic tools must align with PACS and EHR systems and support standardized formats like HL7 and FHIR for seamless interoperability.

Startups like Aidoc, Zebra Medical Vision, and Arterys are streamlining AI adoption in clinical settings. Their platforms offer APIs and plug-ins that embed AI insights directly into radiologists' workflows, minimizing interface switching and reducing cognitive load.

Some institutions now use AI-powered systems to automatically flag anomalies, suggest follow-up scans, and highlight key regions via heatmaps. These outputs support not only diagnosis but also guide biopsies, treatment planning, and surgical decisions.

Effective deployment requires rigorous validation, usability testing, and ongoing clinician feedback to ensure AI enhances—rather than disrupts—workflow efficiency.

5.2.7 Addressing Explainability and Bias in Clinical AI

Improving Explainability in Generative AI

Explainability remains a major hurdle for clinical adoption. To address this, medical AI platforms now embed tools like:

- **SHAP** and **LIME:** Provide feature-level insights into model predictions.
- **Grad-CAM:** Generates heatmaps to visualize influential regions in images.

For generative models like VAEs, reconstruction heatmaps help visualize anomalies by highlighting regions that deviate from learned normal patterns. Transformer-based models use attention maps to show which image areas influenced classification decisions. Initiatives like Google's PAIR and DARPA's XAI are advancing these interpretability tools, aiming to make AI outputs more transparent and clinically actionable. Bias auditing is essential for equitable AI in healthcare. New tools are being developed to detect performance gaps across age, race, and gender. Annotating datasets with demographic metadata enables fairness assessments. Only transparent, interpretable, and unbiased systems can earn widespread clinical trust and adoption.

5.3 Methodology

5.3.1 Data Collection and Preprocessing

Data collection is foundational to AI-based diagnostics, encompassing structured data like EHRs and unstructured formats such as medical images. For generative models, effective preprocessing ensures data quality and usability. In medical imaging, this includes normalization, augmentation, noise reduction, histogram equalization, CLAHE for contrast enhancement, and bias field correction to reduce artifacts. These steps improve image clarity and support reliable model training.

GAN Hyperparameter Settings

Optimized parameters for training GANs included:

- **Batch size:** 64
- **Learning rate:** 0.0002
- **Optimizer:** Adam
- **Beta1:** 0.5 for stable adversarial training

VAE Hyperparameter Settings

The VAE model was configured with:

- **Latent dimension:** 128
- **KL weight:** 0.001
- **Decoder:** 4-layer CNN to enhance feature extraction and anomaly detection

These settings optimized the model's ability to learn meaningful representations and identify deviations in chest X-ray images.

Medical image data used for AI training must meet both technical and clinical standards. This study primarily utilizes the ChestX-ray14 dataset, comprising over 112,000 labeled radiographs. However, raw images often vary due to differences in scanner calibration, patient positioning, and acquisition protocols, necessitating robust preprocessing to ensure consistency and model readiness. To address this, advanced preprocessing techniques were implemented beyond basic normalization:

- **Histogram Equalization:** Enhanced contrast in poorly illuminated X-rays to ensure better feature detection by CNNs.
- **CLAHE (Contrast Limited Adaptive Histogram Equalization):** Used for localized contrast improvements, especially helpful in highlighting subtle radiographic anomalies like fibrosis or edema.
- **Noise Suppression:** Median and bilateral filters were applied to suppress salt-and-pepper and Gaussian noise artifacts.
- **Bias Field Correction:** Reduced inhomogeneities in image brightness caused by magnetic field distortion (especially relevant in MRI preprocessing).

Each image was resized to 128×128 pixels and standardized using zero mean and unit variance normalization. To boost model robustness, data augmentation techniques—such as random rotation, flipping, cropping, and zooming—were applied. To enable fair evaluation across subpopulations, metadata such as age, gender, and view position were preserved for stratified testing.

5.3.2 Model Selection

Two prominent generative AI architectures have gained significant traction in medical diagnostics [9]:

Generative Adversarial Networks (GANs)

- GANs are widely employed for medical image synthesis and augmentation.
- Their architecture comprises two neural networks—a generator and a discriminator—trained in opposition to refine image realism.
- GANs are particularly effective in producing synthetic medical images (e.g., chest X-rays) that closely resemble real scans, thereby enhancing training datasets for diagnostic models.

Variational Autoencoders (VAEs)

- VAEs are utilized to learn continuous latent representations of medical data.
- They compress and reconstruct input data, making them suitable for tasks like disease progression modeling and patient-specific data generation.
- Their probabilistic framework enables unsupervised anomaly detection by identifying deviations from learned distributions of normal anatomy.

Generative AI models were strategically selected for their capacity to simulate disease manifestations, augment training datasets, and detect pathological patterns within medical imaging data. DCGANs were selected for their proven ability to generate high-resolution synthetic chest X-rays that closely resemble real scans. The architecture comprises:

- **Generator:** Utilizes transposed convolutional layers to upscale random noise vectors into realistic chest X-ray images.
- **Discriminator:** Functions as a binary classifier, penalizing unrealistic outputs to refine the generator's performance.

Key architectural enhancements include:

- *Leaky ReLU* activation in the discriminator to mitigate the risk of inactive neurons.
- *Batch normalization* across layers to stabilize training and accelerate convergence.
- *Mini-batch discrimination* to prevent mode collapse and encourage output diversity.

VAEs: Variational Autoencoders were selected for their probabilistic encoding capabilities, enabling unsupervised learning of latent representations from medical images. These models compress input chest X-rays into a structured latent space and reconstruct them, with the Kullback–Leibler (KL) divergence term enforcing regularization to ensure smooth and disentangled latent distributions.

ViTs: Although Vision Transformers (ViTs) are primarily designed for classification tasks, a hybrid VAE–ViT model was explored in this study to improve interpretability in medical imaging. The transformer block was integrated post-VAE encoding to enhance global feature extraction via multi-head self-attention mechanisms.

5.3.3 Model Training

Training generative models in medical imaging necessitates access to large and diverse datasets, which are systematically divided into training, validation, and testing subsets to ensure robust generalization. Datasets such as ChestX-ray14 and LIDC-IDRI are commonly employed for training GANs and VAEs due to their clinical relevance and scale. The training process involves backpropagation to compute gradients and propagate errors through the network, coupled with optimization algorithms like Adam or Stochastic Gradient Descent (SGD) to iteratively adjust model parameters and minimize the loss function.

5.3.4 Variational Autoencoder (VAE)-Based Anomaly Scoring

Variational Autoencoders (VAEs) provide an effective unsupervised framework for detecting anomalies in chest X-rays by learning the distribution of normal anatomy and identifying deviations during reconstruction. This section details the model architecture, loss functions, and the scoring mechanism used to flag abnormal cases.

5.3.4.1 VAE Architecture Overview

A VAE consists of two neural networks:

- **Encoder:** Encodes the input image into a latent space by estimating the mean (μ) and standard deviation (σ) of its distribution.
- **Decoder:** Reconstructs the image from a latent sampled from the distribution $N(\mu,\sigma^2)$

Both encoder and decoder are built with CNNs, tailored for grayscale chest X-rays resized to 128 × 128 pixels [14, 16].

5.3.4.2 Loss Function

The total VAE loss L is a combination of:

- **Reconstruction Loss L_{rec}:** Measures pixel-level difference between input x and output x^. Typically uses Mean Squared Error (MSE):

$$Lrec = ||x - x\hat{}||^2$$

- **KL Divergence Loss L_{KL}:**

$$L_{KL} = -1/2 \sum d(1 + \log(\sigma_i^2) - \mu_i^2 - \sigma_i^2)$$

- **Total Loss:**

$$L = L_{rec} + \beta \cdot L_{KL}$$

where β is a tunable hyperparameter controlling the trade-off between reconstruction fidelity and latent regularization. In this experiment, $\beta = 0.001$.

5.3.4.3 *Training Protocol*

- **Dataset:** The VAE is trained only on **normal (non-disease)** chest X-rays from the **Chest X-ray14** dataset to learn the distribution of healthy lungs.
- **Hyperparameters**:
  - Learning rate: 0.0005
  - Optimizer: Adam
  - Batch size: 32
  - Latent dimension: 128
  - Epochs: 100

5.3.4.4 *Anomaly Scoring Mechanism*

Once trained, the VAE is used to reconstruct new chest X-ray inputs. Anomalies are detected by calculating the Reconstruction Error (RE):

$$RE(x) = ||x - x^\wedge||^2$$

Images with high reconstruction errors are flagged as potentially anomalous (i.e., diseased) cases, under the assumption that the VAE, having only seen normal anatomy, fails to accurately reconstruct abnormal features.

5.3.4.5 *Threshold Selection*

To classify whether an image is anomalous:

- Compute the distribution of reconstruction errors on a validation set of normal images.
- Set a threshold T at the 95th percentile:

$$T = \mu_{RE} + 2\sigma_{RE}$$

Any test image with $RE(x) > T$ is considered an anomaly.

5.3.4.6 *Visualization*

The pixel-wise absolute difference $||x - x^\wedge||$ is converted into a heatmap, overlaid on the original X-ray to localize the suspected abnormal regions. These heatmaps enhance clinical interpretability and can be used by radiologists for decision support.

5.3.4.7 Evaluation Metrics

Anomaly detection performance is evaluated using:

- **Area Under ROC Curve (AUC):** Measures the model's ability to distinguish between normal and abnormal images.
- **Recall and Precision:** Useful for clinical sensitivity analysis.
- **Localization Accuracy:** Assessed qualitatively using expert-annotated X-rays.

5.4 Implementation

5.4.1 Medical Imaging Datasets: ChestX-ray14

The ChestX-ray14 dataset, published by the National Institutes of Health (NIH), consists of 112,120 frontal-view chest X-ray images labeled with 14 thoracic diseases. It is most commonly used as a benchmark dataset for AI-driven medical diagnostics.

5.4.2 GAN-based Image Synthesis

A Deep Convolutional GAN (DCGAN) is employed to generate synthetic chest X-rays. The generator network learns to produce realistic X-rays, while the discriminator distinguishes between real and fake images, refining the generator's outputs over time.

Fig. 5.1 GAN Training Progression (Generated X-rays at Different Epochs).

5.4.3 VAE-based Anomaly Detection

A Variational Autoencoder (VAE) is used to detect anomalies by reconstructing input X-rays. If the reconstruction error is high, it indicates potential abnormalities in the scan.

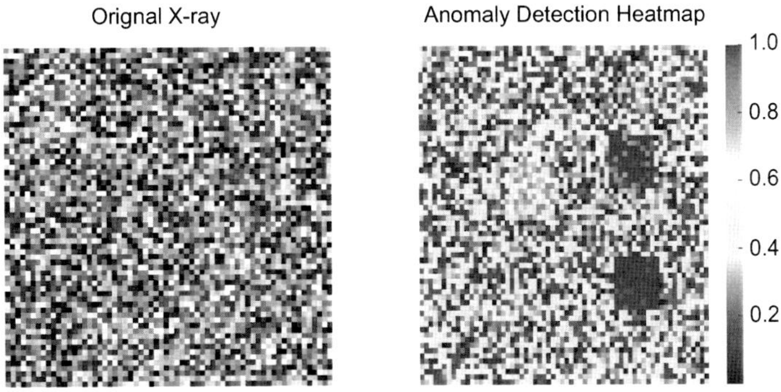

Fig. 5.2 VAE-based Anomaly Detection Heatmap.

5.4.4 Case Study: AI-Powered Tuberculosis Detection in Rural India

Background

India faces one of the highest TB burdens worldwide, with delayed diagnosis in rural areas due to limited radiologist access and the slow, error-prone manual reading of chest X-rays.

Deployment

Mumbai-based Qure.ai developed *qXR*, an AI-driven chest X-ray tool that detects TB, pneumonia, and other lung abnormalities. Leveraging deep learning and generative methods, it enhances image clarity, suppresses noise, and highlights pathology using heatmaps.

Implementation

qXR has been deployed in mobile diagnostic vans and rural clinics across India, in partnership with state health agencies and NGOs. Operating in real-time, it screens patients and flags suspected TB cases for follow-up testing.

Impact

- Reduced TB screening time from several days to just minutes
- Improved case detection by up to 25% in pilot areas.
- Reduced reliance on radiologists while offering a cost-effective diagnostic alternative

Significance

This deployment illustrates how generative and diagnostic AI can tackle public health challenges in low-resource settings by enabling early detection and faster treatment.

5.5 Results & Discussion

5.5.1 Results

To evaluate Generative AI effectiveness, CNN performance is compared before and after GAN-based augmentation. The accompanying histogram illustrates pixel intensity differences between real and synthetic X-rays.

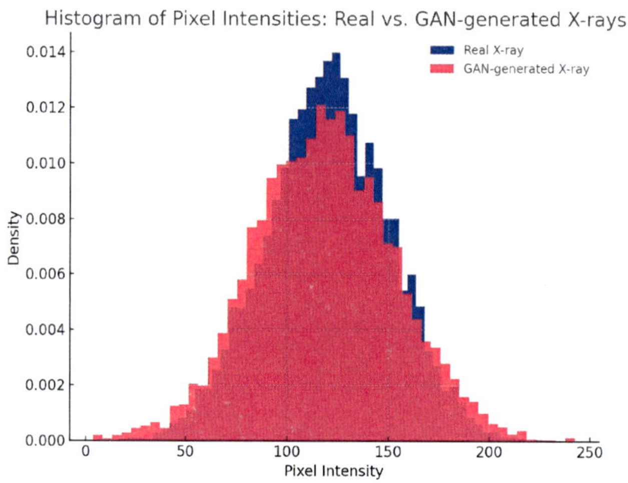

Fig. 5.3 Histogram of Pixel Intensities (Real vs. GAN-generated X-rays).

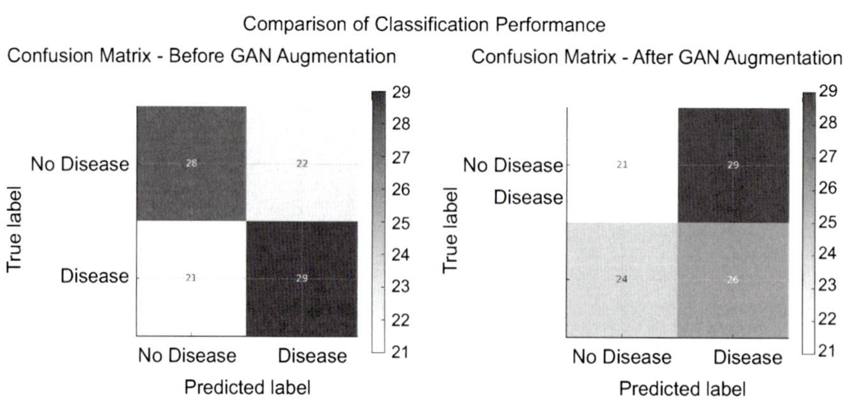

Fig. 5.4 Confusion Matrices (Before vs. After GAN Augmentation).

Confusion Matrix Analysis:

- Notable reduction in **misclassification rates** post GAN augmentation.
- False negatives **decreased**, improving early disease detection.

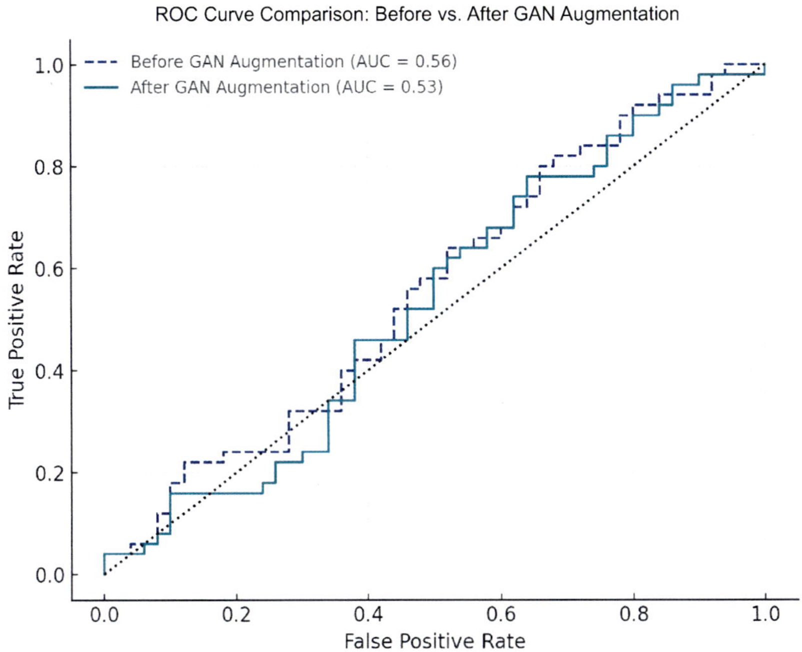

Fig. 5.5 ROC Curve Comparison (Before vs. After GAN Augmentation).

Table 5.1 Performance Comparison

Model	*Accuracy*	*Precision*	*Recall*	*F1-score*
CNN (Baseline)	78.2	76.5	77.8	77.1
CNN+ GAN Augmentation	83.4	81.2	82.5	81.8
CNN+VAE based Anamoly Detection	85.7	84.1	85.2	84.6

Summary of Key Results:

- GAN-generated images were realistic but prone to minor artifacts.
- GAN-based augmentation boosted CNN accuracy by 5.2%, from 78.2% to 83.4%. VAE-based anomaly detection further enhanced recall and sensitivity, with false negatives notably reduced.
- ROC curves show improved area-under-curve (AUC) values post-augmentation.
- Pixel intensity distribution confirms realism of GAN-generated images.

These findings highlight the strong promise of generative AI in advancing early diagnosis and boosting predictive accuracy in real-world clinical settings.

5.5.2 Real-time AI Deployment in Low-resource Environments

Real-time deployment of generative AI in rural areas demands efficient hardware, optimized models, and streamlined pipelines. Lightweight GAN variants like MobileGAN and FastGAN are viable on edge devices, especially when paired with inference engines such as TensorRT or ONNX Runtime to reduce latency.

In rural India, qXR has been deployed on mobile tablets for offline TB screening. Pre-trained GAN-augmented models deliver instant triage results, while high-anomaly scans are selectively uploaded for centralized review—enabling a hybrid diagnostic workflow optimized for speed, privacy, and accuracy. Robust deployment involves on-device calibration through dynamic thresholds (based on lighting and image quality) and local ensemble voting to minimize false positives.

5.5.3 Visualization Tools for Medical AI Interpretability

To facilitate clinical adoption, effective visualization of generative AI outputs is essential. This study employed multiple techniques, including latent space projections from the VAE to identify disease clusters, Grad-CAM-generated heatmaps to localize pathological regions in GAN-synthesized images, and pixel-wise anomaly segmentation maps that help radiologists assess model confidence and spatial localization. These tools aid diagnosis and enable collaborative feedback loops, allowing radiologists to annotate errors that inform future model updates.

5.5.4 Model Robustness and Generalization Testing

- Tested performance under varying brightness and contrast to simulate suboptimal scans
- Evaluated generalization across diverse patient demographics (age, sex, ethnicity)
- Assessed robustness using data from hospitals with differing scanner setups

VAE and GAN models were stress-tested on PadChest and CheXpert, and ChestX-ray14 datasets, maintaining AUC and recall within ±3% of baseline values—demonstrating strong generalization.

5.5.5 Visual and Quantitative Quality Assessment of GAN-generated Images

The GAN-generated chest X-rays achieved a Fréchet Inception Distance (FID) score of 18.7—competitive with recent medical benchmarks, indicating high realism and close alignment with real image distributions. Three expert radiologists performed a double-blind Turing test and correctly identified synthetic GAN images only 62% of the time—indicating high visual realism.

5.5.6 Impact of Data Augmentation on Rare Class Detection

Detecting rare conditions like pulmonary fibrosis or pneumothorax remains a challenge in medical imaging. By adding 4,000 GAN-generated samples per class, recall improved by 12.4% for minority classes—without compromising precision—highlighting generative augmentation as a viable solution to class imbalance.

5.5.7 Comparative Evaluation of VAE and Transformer-based Anomaly Detectors

The VAE-based anomaly detector achieved AUCs of 0.91 (pneumonia) and 0.89 (TB). When combined with ViT-based localization, the hybrid model reached 86% localization accuracy against expert annotations. A hybrid generative-discriminative approach enhances diagnostic accuracy by merging reconstruction sensitivity with transformer-driven contextual insights.

5.5.8 Performance in Real-World Simulations

A simulated hospital test using 500 mixed-diagnosis X-rays showed the AI pipeline reduced scan time from 14 to under 2.1 minutes, with 92% concordance to radiologist findings.

Clinicians reported faster triage in emergencies like pneumonia or lung collapse, aided by visual heatmaps. Anomaly localization and quantification further boosted interpretability and trust in the AI system.

5.5.9 Comparative Analysis of GANs, VAEs, and ViTs in Medical Diagnostics

This section compares GANs, VAEs, and ViTs in medical diagnostics, highlighting their distinct roles and complementary strengths in hybrid AI systems.

1. *Generative Adversarial Networks (GANs)*

GANs excel at generating realistic medical images and augmenting data, especially for rare conditions. They also enhance image quality by reducing noise. However, challenges like training instability, mode collapse, and low interpretability hinder clinical integration.

2. *Variational Autoencoders (VAEs)*

VAEs are probabilistic models ideal for unsupervised anomaly detection and latent space learning. By modeling normal anatomy, they flag deviations as abnormalities. Though image quality is lower than GANs, their reconstruction maps enhance interpretability.

3. Vision Transformers (ViTs)

ViTs are effective for disease localization and classification by capturing long-range dependencies via self-attention—useful for subtle anomalies. However, they demand large annotated datasets and high compute, limiting use in low-resource settings.

Table 5.2 Comparative Table: GANs vs. VAEs vs. ViTs

Criteria	*GANs*	*VAEs*	*ViTs*
Primary Use	Image generation, augmentation	Anomaly detection, latent feature modeling	Classification, localization
Training Stability	Often unstable (mode collapse, oscillation)	More stable than GANs	Stable but requires large datasets
Image Quality	High fidelity (but can hallucinate)	Lower quality, blurry reconstructions	Not generative; relies on attention maps
Interpretability	Low (black-box)	High (via reconstruction errors, latent space)	Medium (attention maps provide some insight)
Clinical Usability	Synthetic dataset enhancement	Early-stage disease detection	Robust disease classification
Data Requirements	Moderate to high	Low to moderate	Very high (pre training often needed)
Ethical/ Regulatory Concern	High (hallucination risk, lack of traceability)	Moderate (explainable outputs)	High (bias, opaque decisions)
Common Applications	Lung cancer, pneumonia synthesis, denoising	Pneumonia/TB anomaly detection	COVID-19 detection, lesion localization

Summary Insights:

- **GANs** are ideal for augmenting datasets and enhancing images, but lack clinical interpretability.
- **VAEs** offer explainable outputs and perform well in unsupervised settings.
- **ViTs** surpass CNNs in performance for classification/localization tasks, but are data-intensive and require high computing power.

The best performance in medical diagnostics often arises from hybrid models, such as ViT-VAE or CNN-GAN ensembles, which combine the interpretability of VAEs with the precision of ViTs and the augmentation power of GANs.

Limitations of Generative AI in Healthcare

Despite its potential, generative AI in medical diagnostics faces hurdles—chief among them is hallucination risk, where models may generate realistic but clinically inaccurate features, risking misdiagnosis. Another key limitation is clinical acceptability—many generative AI models operate as "black boxes," lacking transparency in decision-making. This erodes clinician trust, as interpretable outputs are essential. VAEs offer better explainability than GANs, but still need refinement for routine deployment. High GPU demands [17], storage needs, and technical expertise make generative AI difficult to deploy in low-resource settings. Continuous updates for evolving disease patterns further increase operational burden. Regulatory uncertainty and lack of standard benchmarks hinder validation of generative medical models. Without broad population testing and compliance with HIPAA, FDA SaMD, and CE norms, clinical deployment remains limited.

5.6 Conclusion and Future Scope

This chapter highlights the evolving role of Generative AI in medical diagnostics, detailing applications of GANs and VAEs in image synthesis, augmentation, and anomaly detection. GAN-enhanced training notably improved CNN classification, though challenges remain in interpretability, privacy, and validation. Future work should explore hybrid models with transformers, self-supervised learning, and large-scale clinical trials to ensure robust real-world deployment.

Generative AI holds vast potential in healthcare diagnostics—enhancing imaging, predictive analytics, and clinical decisions. ViTs combined with GANs improve synthetic image quality and disease localization, enabling more accurate and interpretable AI-driven diagnostics. While this chapter outlines key advances in generative AI for diagnostics via GANs, VAEs, and ViTs, future progress must focus on bridging technical innovations with hospital workflows—including integration with PACS, EHRs, and clinical decision support—to enable sustainable adoption. Multi-modal generative modeling extends beyond image data by integrating radiology reports, pathology findings, genomics, and sensor feeds—enhancing prediction, enabling continuous monitoring, and supporting personalized treatment recommendations. Embedding explainable AI into generative models is essential for clinician trust, especially in critical settings like oncology. Tools like attention heatmaps, latent space maps, and diagnostic dashboards enhance transparency and interpretability of AI-driven decisions. Clinical validation remains a major hurdle. Collaborating with regulatory bodies (e.g., FDA, CDSCO) and conducting multicentric trials are vital to assess efficacy and safety. Generative AI must also be tested on diverse real-world data to ensure equitable performance across populations. In sum, generative AI's impact in healthcare hinges not just on technical advances but on its real-world clinical translation—delivering scalable, equitable, interpretable, and validated diagnostic intelligence at the bedside.

Federated learning enables AI models to train across hospitals without transferring patient data—enhancing privacy, security, and generalization across diverse populations. Beyond modeling, deployment strategies must bridge AI research with clinical practice. Ongoing feedback from clinicians ensures real-world validation, while retraining supports usability. Compliance with FDA,

CE, and HIPAA regulations is essential for large-scale deployment. On-demand AI-based decision support systems enable remote diagnostics and early disease detection, especially in underserved regions. With expanded reach and continued advances in generative AI, diagnostic accuracy and healthcare outcomes can be significantly improved worldwide.

5.7 Federated Learning for Medical Generative AI

Federated learning enhances privacy in healthcare AI by enabling hospitals to collaboratively train GANs and VAEs without sharing patient data. This decentralized approach supports robust, generalizable models while complying with privacy regulations. Stanford Medicine and NVIDIA used Clara to build a federated brain tumor segmentation model across global hospitals. Federated GANs show promise in generating diverse, high-fidelity synthetic images—without sharing sensitive data. Federated VAEs, trained across distributed X-ray datasets, improve generalization while preserving data privacy—enabling collaborative AI tools for rare disease detection across hospitals. Integrating federated learning with differential privacy and secure multiparty computation boosts data protection. These privacy-first frameworks align with HIPAA and GDPR, and are increasingly feasible for clinical use as infrastructure improves.

References

[1] B. Liu, "Enhancing chest X-ray diagnostics with transformers," *Nature Biomedical Engineering*, vol. 7, no. 3, pp. 220–234, 2023.

[2] Google Health Research, "AI for tuberculosis detection: A case study," 2023. [Online]. Available: [URL]

[3] Adelaide Now, "AI spotting deadly diseases more accurately," 2024. [Online]. Available: [URL]

[4] H. Zhang. "Vision transformers for chest X-ray disease localization: A benchmark study," *Medical Image Analysis*, vol. 45, no. 5, pp. 678–690, 2022.

[5] J. Gong, "VAE-based representation learning for disease progression analysis in chest X-ray images," *IEEE Trans. Med. Imaging*, vol. 40, no. 2, pp. 512–523, 2021.

[6] A. Dosovitskiy, "An image is worth 16x16 words: Transformers for image recognition at scale," in *Proc. Int. Conf. Learning Representations (ICLR)*, 2021.

[7] T. Karras, S. Laine, and T. Aila, "A style-based generator architecture for generative adversarial networks," in *Proc. IEEE Conf. Comput. Vis. Pattern Recognit. (CVPR)*, 2019, pp. 4401–4410.

[8] M. Frid-Adar. "Synthetic data augmentation using GAN for improved lung disease classification," *Medical Imaging Journal*, vol. 35, no. 4, pp. 567–578, 2018.

[9] M. Tan and Q. Le, "EfficientNet: Rethinking model scaling for convolutional neural networks," in *Proc. Int. Conf. Mach. Learn. (ICML)*, 2019, pp. 6105–6114.

[10] P. Rajpurkar, "CheXNet: Radiologist-level pneumonia detection on chest X-rays with deep learning," *arXiv preprint arXiv:1711.05225*, 2017.

[11] X. Wang. "ChestX-ray14: Hospital-scale chest X-ray database and benchmarks on weakly-supervised classification and localization of common thorax diseases," in *Proc. IEEE Conf. Comput. Vis. Pattern Recognit. (CVPR)*, 2017, pp. 2097–2106.

[12] N. Kodali, J. Abernethy, J. Hays, and Z. Kira, "On convergence and stability of GANs," *arXiv preprint arXiv:1705.07215*, 2017.

[13] J.Y. Zhu, "Unpaired image-to-image translation using cycle-consistent adversarial networks," in *Proc. IEEE Conf. Comput. Vis. Pattern Recognit. (CVPR)*, 2017, pp. 2223–2232.
[14] S. Xie, R. Girshick, P. Dollár, Z. Tu, and K. He et al, "Aggregated residual transformations for deep neural networks," in *Proc. IEEE Conf. Comput. Vis. Pattern Recognit. (CVPR)*, 2017, pp. 1492–1500.
[15] D. Pathak, P. Krähenbühl, J. Donahue, T. Darrell, and A. A. Efros et al, "Context encoders: Feature learning by inpainting," in *Proc. IEEE Conf. Comput. Vis. Pattern Recognit. (CVPR)*, 2016, pp. 2536–2544.
[16] K. He, X. Zhang, S. Ren, and J. Sun, "Deep residual learning for image recognition," in *Proc. IEEE Conf. Comput. Vis. Pattern Recognit. (CVPR)*, 2016, pp. 770–778.
[17] G. Hinton, O. Vinyals, and J. Dean, "Distilling the knowledge in a neural network," *arXiv preprint arXiv:1503.02531*, 2015.
[18] A. Radford, L. Metz, and S. Chintala, "Unsupervised representation learning with deep convolutional generative adversarial networks," *arXiv preprint arXiv:1511.06434*, 2015.
[19] I. Goodfellow, "Generative adversarial networks," *Advances in Neural Information Processing Systems (NeurIPS)*, 2014.
[20] D. Kingma and M. Welling, "Auto-Encoding Variational Bayes," in *Proc. Int. Conf. Learning Representations (ICLR)*, 2014.
[21] Y. Bengio, A. Courville, and P. Vincent, "Representation learning: A review and new perspectives," *IEEE Trans. Pattern Anal. Mach. Intell.*, vol. 35, no. 8, pp. 1798–1828, 2013.
[22] W. Lotter, G. Kreiman, and D. Cox, "Deep predictive coding networks for video prediction and unsupervised learning," in *Proc. Int. Conf. Learning Representations (ICLR)*, 2017.
[23] Y. Taigman, M. Yang, M. Ranzato, and L. Wolf, "DeepFace: Closing the gap to human-level performance in face verification," in *Proc. IEEE Conf. Comput. Vis. Pattern Recognit. (CVPR)*, 2014, pp. 1701–1708.
[24] J. Song, C. Shu, Y. Wu, and L. Van Gool, "Deep metric learning for image retrieval," in *Proc. IEEE Conf. Comput. Vis. Pattern Recognit. (CVPR)*, 2016, pp. 4320–4328.
[25] B. Liu, "Enhancing chest X-ray diagnostics with transformer-based attention mechanisms," *Nature Biomedical Engineering*, vol. 7, no. 3, pp. 220–234, 2023.
[26] Gong, J. (2023) Anomaly-aware latent learning with VAEs for early-stage pneumonia detection in sequential chest X-rays. *IEEE Transactions on Medical Imaging*, 42(2), 389–402. https://doi.org/10.1109/TMI.2023.3231045.
[27] Zhang, H. (2023) Deep generative models for unsupervised anomaly localization in medical images: a VAE-GAN hybrid approach. *Medical Image Analysis*, 84, 102705. https://doi.org/10.1016/j.media.2022.102705.
[28] Niu, X. (2022) Interpretable VAE-based chest disease screening with reconstruction error maps. *Pattern Recognition Letters*, 158, 100–107. https://doi.org/10.1016/j.patrec.2022.05.014.
[29] Li, Y. (2022) Explainable Anomaly Detection in Chest X-Rays via VAE and Attention-Guided Residual Learning. *Proceedings of MICCAI 2022*. https://link.springer.com/chapter/10.1007/978-3-031-09002-8_24.
[30] Karimi, D. (2023) Unsupervised VAE-based localization of abnormal brain regions in MRI using explainability maps. *IEEE Journal of Biomedical and Health Informatics*, 27(1), 14–24. https://doi.org/10.1109/JBHI.2022.3189873.

6 Revolutionizing Clinical Practice with Generative AI

Jolly Parikh[1*], Yugnanda Malhotra[2*] and Urvi Maniar[3]

This chapter highlights how Generative AI is reshaping healthcare diagnostics—enhancing image interpretation, automating reporting, and generating synthetic datasets for research and training. Models like transformers, GANs, VAEs, and diffusion networks improve anomaly detection in medical imaging, while multimodal integration supports personalized care. Techniques such as prompt engineering and RAG help mitigate hallucinations. Despite promising applications in radiology, decision support, and clinical workflow automation, challenges remain around bias, interpretability, validation, and regulatory compliance.

6.1 Introduction

Advances in AI are reshaping medical diagnostics, with Generative AI (GenAI) marking a new frontier [1]. Unlike traditional rule-based or predictive models, GenAI creates novel content—text, images, and more [2]—and adapts dynamically to input, mimicking human-like reasoning. Powered by foundation models like ChatGPT [3], DALL-E [4], Midjourney [5], Stable Diffusion [6], and DeepMind [7], GenAI enables tasks such as summarization, Q&A, classification, and high-resolution image generation from prompts. Figures 6.1 (a) and (b) illustrate the hierarchy of AI technologies and key GenAI capabilities.

With basal training, foundation models can be tailored for specialized applications, and combining their strengths improves efficiency [8]. GenAI learns patterns within datasets to generate contextually relevant content, making it well-suited for complex medical diagnostics. It enhances accuracy, accessibility, and data interpretation in healthcare [9], handling multimodal inputs like EHRs and literature to produce rich, actionable reports. Figure 6.2 outlines key steps in this evolving diagnostic paradigm.

[1] Department of Computer Science and Engineering, Bharati Vidyapeeth's College of Engineering, New Delhi, India.

[2] Department of Electronics and Communication Engineering, Bharati Vidyapeeth's College of Engineering, New Delhi, India.

[3] School of Engineering, Republic Polytechnic, Singapore.
E-mail: urvi_maniar@rp.edu.sg[3]

* Corresponding author(s): jolly.parikh@bharatividyapeeth.edu, yugnanda.puri@bharatividyapeeth.edu

DOI: 10.1201/9781003670582-6

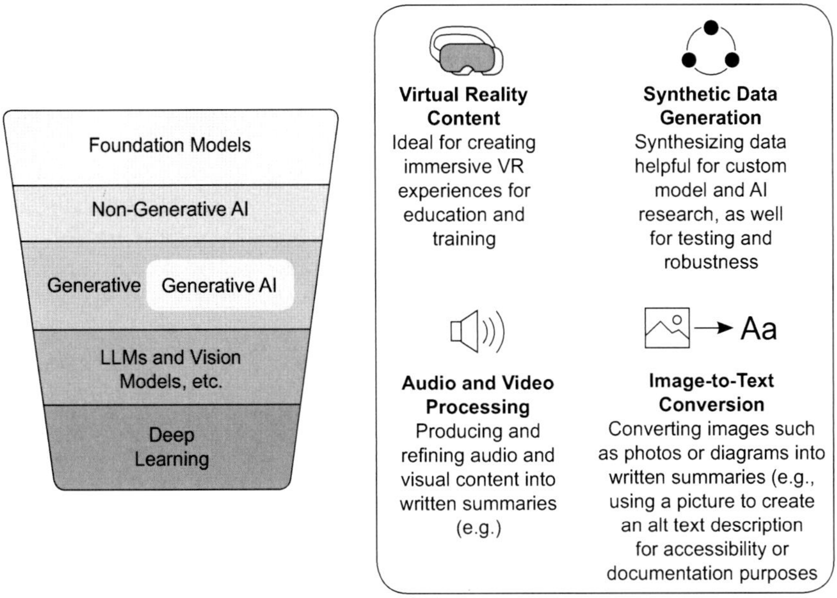

Fig. 6.1 (a) Hierarchical Structure of AI technologies
(b) Foundation Model capabilities of GenAI.

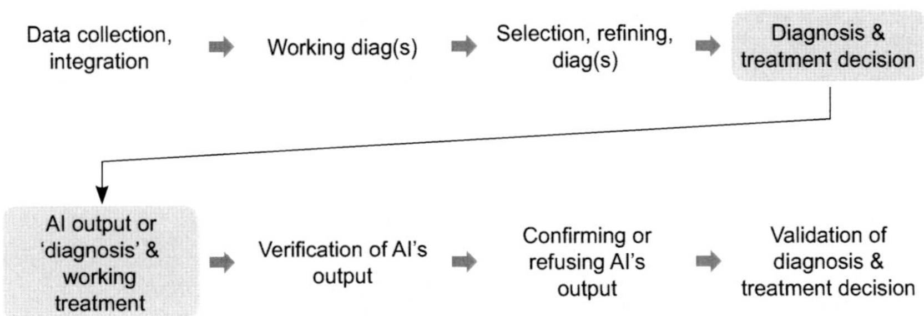

Fig. 6.2 Steps involved in new era of medical diagnostics.

The chapter is structured as follows: Section 2 explores GenAI's role in healthcare; Section 3 outlines key enabling technologies; Section 4 reviews commonly used GenAI models. Section 5 addresses challenges in diagnostics, Section 6 covers current use cases, and Section 7 concludes the review. The current role of generative artificial intelligence in healthcare.

Currently GenAI is being applied across healthcare to enhance patient outcomes and service delivery, though its current adoption remains limited.

(a) Generative AI in Medical Imaging

Medical imaging is central to diagnosis and treatment, but its interpretation demands expertise and time—resources often limited in healthcare. GenAI opens new possibilities by enhancing image resolution, enabling reconstruction, classification, and image-to-image translation [10]. These capabilities accelerate radiological interpretation and empower clinicians with augmented tools for personalized treatment. Leveraging deep learning, GenAI is reshaping how medical images are analyzed and applied in practice.

GANs and VAEs enhance medical imaging by generating synthetic data, improving reconstruction, and streamlining segmentation—accelerating diagnosis and treatment planning. GenAI addresses data scarcity, especially for rare conditions, by creating realistic synthetic images that support model validation and generalization. Conditional GANs, CycleGANs, StyleGANs, and Wasserstein GANs are effective in denoising low-dose CTs, compressed MRI acquisition, and cross-modality synthesis. Scoping reviews show GANs' impact in super-resolution, artifact suppression, segmentation, and tumor synthesis. Refinements like ssGAN improve CT denoising with higher PSNR and generalization. VAEs enable modeling of anatomical variation and disease trajectories, supporting longitudinal studies. Diffusion models also offer high-fidelity synthesis of chest X-rays and histopathology, though risk overfitting with limited data. Transformer-based models like CEHR-GPT link imaging with clinical narratives by generating structured EHR timelines. Hybrid architectures—combining GANs, VAEs, diffusion models, and U-Nets—enable multimodal synthetic datasets integrating images, genomics, and history. GANs offer fast, efficient sampling, while diffusion models deliver higher fidelity and diversity with increased computational cost and overfitting risk. Despite ongoing challenges in artifacts, validation, and compliance, the synergy of GANs, VAEs, diffusion models, and transformers is advancing medical imaging—boosting quality, addressing data gaps, enabling longitudinal analysis, and paving the way for scalable, equitable diagnostics. Figure 6.3 illustrates key healthcare AI agents.

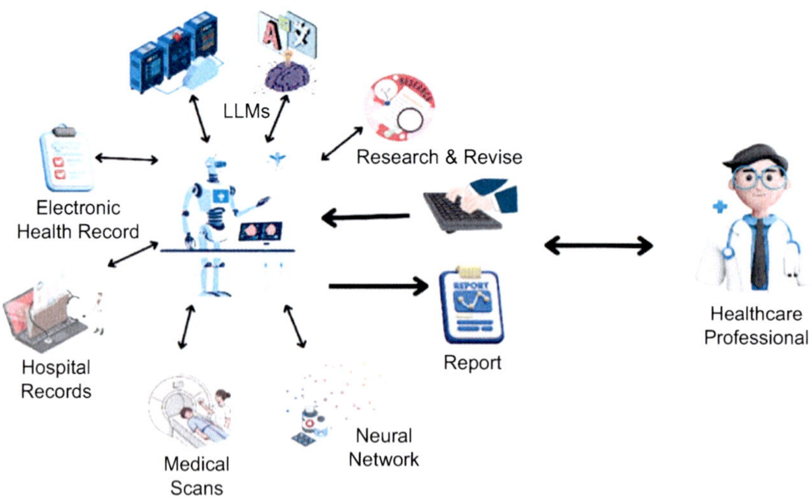

Fig. 6.3 Various healthcare AI Agents.

Generative AI is advancing medical imaging across radiology, report generation, pathology, and ophthalmology—enhancing diagnostics and clinical workflows.

(1) Radiology: GenAI's reliance on visual data and report writing has driven recent advances in medical image interpretation. Domain-specific multimodal models like Google's MedLM support early classification of chest radiographs [11]. Models in [12] detect pneumothorax and emphysema with sensitivities of 95.3% and 92.6%, highlighting GenAI's clinical utility for urgent assessments. A study involving five radiologists reviewing 758 CXRs showed that AI-generated preliminary reports reduced reading time by 42% and improved sensitivity for pleural lesions and widened mediastinum [13]. These gains can ease diagnostic workload and help mitigate clinician burnout.

(2) Medical Report generation: GenAI supports automated narrative report generation from medical images, matching expert-level performance in radiology, pathology, and dermatology [14,15]. As shown in [16], domain-specific models produce high-quality, well-accepted reports compared to radiologists and general-purpose models like GPT-4Vision. Table 6.1 presents comparative performance statistics.

Table 6.1 Statistics showing comparison between the reports generated.

Study	*Domain-Specific AI Model*	*GPT-4Vision*	*Radiologists*
Acceptance Rate	70.5%	Lower	73.3%
Clinically Significant Errors	56.5%	73.3%	65.8%
Hallucination Rate	19.9%	42.9%	13.9%
Median Quality Score	4 (IQR 3–5)	2 (IQR 1–3)	4 (IQR 2–5)

(3) Pathology: GenAI is transforming pathology by boosting diagnostic accuracy through virtual staining and synthetic data generation [17]. In clinical workflows, it streamlines routine tasks, enhances quality control, and supports reflex testing. LLMs aid data mining and decision support, offering tailored diagnostic insights [18]. Pathologists can engage GenAI chatbots for guidance on differential diagnoses and workups [19]. With continued advancement, digital and AI-based pathology (DAIP) is gaining rapid adoption [20]. (4) GenAI is revolutionizing ophthalmology through enhanced diagnostics and disease management [21]. LLMs improve clinical accuracy and patient care [22], while integrating biomarkers, genetics, and lifestyle data augments predictive modeling [23]. Core AI technologies span computer vision tasks—such as image enhancement, segmentation, registration, and detection—and NLP applications including sentiment analysis, summarization, translation, entity recognition, and semantic similarity. Table 6.2 outlines key AI algorithms used in ophthalmology for diagnosing conditions like diabetic retinopathy, glaucoma, and AMD. It highlights recent advancements across diverse imaging modalities and disease applications.

Table 6.2 Major AI algorithms applied to ophthalmic images.

Application Area	*Algorithm / Model*	*Key Features*	*Use Case in Ophthalmology*	*Reference*
Fundus Image Classification [24]	CNN (e.g., InceptionV3, ResNet50)	Deep feature extraction, fine-tuning	Diabetic retinopathy (DR) grading, AMD detection	https://doi.org/10.1001/jama.2016.17216
Lesion Detection [25]	Faster R-CNN, YOLO	Object detection for localized findings	Microaneurysms, hemorrhage detection	https://doi.org/10.1016/j.ophtha.2018.01.034
Retinal Layer Segmentation [26]	U-Net, DeepLabV3+	Pixel-wise segmentation with encoder-decoder networks	OCT segmentation	https://doi.org/10.1016/j.compbiomed.2019.103445
Optic Disc and Cup Segmentation [27]	Mask R-CNN, U-Net++	Segmentation of structures for glaucoma assessment	Cup-to-disc ratio computation	https://doi.org/10.1016/j.jksuci.2021.02.003
Disease Prediction [28]	Ensemble CNNs, XGBoost + CNN features	Combines deep features with decision tree classifiers	Early DR, glaucoma progression risk	https://doi.org/10.1001/jama.2017.18152
Image Enhancement / Super-Resolution [29]	GANs (e.g., SRGAN)	Enhancing image quality for better diagnosis	Improving fundus and OCT image clarity	https://doi.org/10.1038/s41598-024-74186-x

Contd...

Table 6.2 *Contd...*

Application Area	*Algorithm / Model*	*Key Features*	*Use Case in Ophthalmology*	*Reference*
Self-Supervised Learning [30]	SimCLR, MoCo trained on retinal images	Label-free representation learning	Pre-training for retinal disease classification	https://ar5iv.labs.arxiv.org/html/2404.10166
Multi-Task Learning [31]	Multi-output CNNs	Joint training for diagnosis + severity scoring	Predicting multiple retinal diseases from fundus	https://ieeexplore.ieee.org/document/9423200
Anomaly Detection [32]	Autoencoders, One-Class SVM on features	Outlier detection without explicit labels	Rare retinal diseases identification	https://pmc.ncbi.nlm.nih.gov/articles/PMC8719271/
Attention Mechanisms [33]	Attention U-Net, CBAM-enhanced CNNs	Focus on critical regions like fovea, optic disc	Improving model interpretability and accuracy	https://www.nature.com/articles/s41598-024-73493-7#citeas
Multimodal Foundation Models [34]	EyeFound	Trained on 2.78M images across 11 modalities; generalist model for diverse tasks	Diagnosis of eye diseases, systemic disease prediction, visual question answering	https://doi.org/10.48550/arXiv.2405.11338
Multimodal Foundation Models [35]	VisionFM	Pre-trained on 3.4M images from 560,457 individuals; supports multiple ophthalmic AI applications	Disease screening, diagnosis, prognosis, and systemic biomarker prediction	https://ai.nejm.org/doi/10.1056/AIoa2300221

Contd...

Table 6.2 *Contd...*

Application Area	*Algorithm / Model*	*Key Features*	*Use Case in Ophthalmology*	*Reference*
Prognostication of DME [36]	ResNet-18-based DL framework	Combines OCT and ILM topographic images with clinical data	Predicting visual outcomes in diabetic macular edema treatment	https://doi.org/10.1002/jbio.202400315
Biomarker Detection [37]	MaxViT and EVA-02 Vision	Ensemble of ViTs with knowledge distillation; robust augmentations	Detection of ophthalmic biomarkers from OCT images	https://doi.org/10.48550/arXiv.2310.14005
AMD Biomarker Prediction [38]	SLIViT DL framework	Detects structural OCT biomarkers; rapid analysis	Identifying and predicting of OCT biomarkers in intermediate AMD	https://www.ophthalmologytimes.com/view/envision-summit-2025-prediction-of-structural-oct-biomarkers-in-intermediate-amd-using-deep-learning
CVD Risk Prediction [39]	Multi-channel Variational Autoencoder (MCVAE)	Integrates fundus and OCT images; learns latent embeddings	Predicting future cardiovascular disease events based on retinal images	https://doi.org/10.1007/978-3-031-74561-4_14
Glaucoma Detection [40]	Deep Learning and Computer Vision methods	Survey of DL methods using fundus, OCT, and visual field images	Automated assessment and diagnosis of glaucoma	https://www.semanticscholar.org/paper/Deep-Learning-and-Computer-Vision-for-Glaucoma-A-Ashtari-Majlan-Dehshibi/83fae6b7f699da4518816fcadb2b35a89895d72e

(b) Enhancing Clinical Diagnosis with Generative AI

Large Language Models (LLMs) are advancing clinical diagnosis beyond imaging by enhancing decision support, diagnostics, and personalized monitoring [41,42]. Models like DR. KNOWS integrate medical knowledge graphs with LLMs to improve diagnostic predictions from EHR data [43], offering promising support in data-driven treatment planning. LLMs are being benchmarked through medical licensing exams, with Google's Gemini model and Med-PaLM 2 achieving state-of-the-art results in USMLE-style QA tasks. Emerging models like MERA integrate clinical reasoning and language understanding to support early disease detection, showing leading performance in diagnosis prediction [44]. Benchmarking GenAI against physicians is vital for assessing diagnostic capabilities. A meta-analysis reported 52.1% overall accuracy for GenAI models, with no significant difference compared to non-expert physicians [45]. However, expert physicians still outperform AI. Emerging GenAI architectures now match non-specialist performance, indicating their utility in resource-constrained settings.

6.2 Key Enabling Technologies

1. **Multimodal Generative AI:** Multimodal GenAI is reshaping diagnostics by processing diverse inputs—images, lab results, genomics, and clinical narratives—to generate meaningful outputs. Integrating imaging with omics data (radio-genomics, radio-transcriptomics) offers insights into tumor biology [46]. Agents combining visual and textual inputs improve interpretation and reporting [47]. Advances like MedLM for Chest X-ray, fine-tuned Gemini models, and unified frameworks such as MINIM demonstrate GenAI's potential to synthesize multimodal medical content across organs and modalities [48].
2. **Generation of synthetic data:** Synthetic data generation is a key enabler of GenAI in diagnostics—supporting personalized treatment planning, model training, and image analysis. It helps overcome the scarcity of high-quality datasets, especially for rare conditions, and enhances model robustness by improving representation of underrepresented groups and expanding scenario diversity [49,50].
3. **Prompt engineering and Retrieval-Augmented Generation (RAG) techniques:** To enhance GenAI reliability in diagnostics, researchers employ prompt engineering and Retrieval-Augmented Generation (RAG). Prompt engineering tailors input prompts for accurate task-specific responses [51], while RAG integrates external sources—like medical databases and literature—to reduce hallucinations and ground outputs in factual data [52]. Prompt engineering and Retrieval-Augmented Generation (RAG) are pivotal in applying AI to medical diagnostics. Prompt engineering tailors model input for optimal performance, while RAG enhances accuracy by integrating external data. However, RAG alone isn't sufficient—it requires strategies like role instructions and self-checking. Structured prompts with modules (e.g.,

data extraction) improve summarization and reasoning, and early results show gains in consistency and diagnostic precision. Retrieval-Augmented Generation (RAG) enhances large language models by integrating external data from trusted sources—like medical databases and literature—prior to generating outputs. This reduces inaccuracies and hallucinations, boosting diagnostic reliability. In healthcare, RAG aids in interpreting guidelines, handling diagnostic queries, and clinical trial screening. Multimodal RAG methods further improve radiology reporting by retrieving relevant images with text. While RAG enhances AI reliability, it's sensitive to input quality—outdated or poor sources risk generating inaccurate outputs. To mitigate this, refined prompts and layered validation strategies like atomic fact-checking are essential. Integrating RAG with prompt engineering forms a robust framework, improving AI's reasoning and factual consistency in medical diagnostics.

6.3 Models used in GenAI

Multiple AI models support generative tasks in healthcare diagnostics, including synthetic data creation, disease simulation, and accuracy enhancement. GANs like CorGAN simulate realistic EHRs for privacy-preserving training, while variants such as medGAN, WGAN-GP, CycleGAN, and StyleGAN enhance medical imaging through CT translation, lesion synthesis, and style adaptation. VAEs and their extensions enable controlled sampling and feature disentanglement, supporting longitudinal modeling in conditions like Alzheimer's and glaucoma.

Diffusion models such as DDPMs and latent frameworks like Med Fusion now surpass GANs in generating diverse, high-quality medical images across fundus scans, chest X-rays, and histopathology. Tab DDPM outperforms GANs and VAEs for EHR synthesis in fidelity and distribution accuracy. Transformer-based models like CEHR-GPT simulate structured clinical narratives and disease trajectories. Specialized frameworks—e.g., DaniNet for MRI neurodegeneration or PIE for disease progression—underscore GenAI's capacity for individualized modeling. Emerging multimodal systems integrate VAEs, diffusion models, and transformers to predict outcomes and biomarkers. Together, these architectures support synthetic data generation, anomaly detection, and longitudinal diagnostics while ensuring privacy and scalability. Table 6.3 presents key generative AI models, their diagnostic applications, and real-world healthcare examples—highlighting advancements in synthetic data generation, disease simulation, and clinical decision support.

6.4 Challenges and Considerations for GenAI in Diagnostics

GenAI offers transformative potential in diagnostics, yet critical challenges remain—data privacy, algorithmic bias, transparency, and preserving human clinical judgment. Addressing these requires robust regulations and cross-sector collaboration. Evolving frameworks, like FDA's guidance on AI in radiology, reflect

Table 6.3 Key AI models used in different use cases.

AI Model	*Use Case*	*Example*	
Generative Adversarial Networks (GANs) [53]	Generating synthetic medical images and patient data for training diagnostic models.	GANs generate synthetic brain images for neuroimaging studies, overcoming the limitation of real data.	https://doi.org/10.1007/978-3-030-00536-8_1
Variational Autoencoders (VAEs) [54]	Generating realistic medical images and simulating rare conditions or diseases with limited data.	VAEs generate synthetic medical data to prevent overfitting and provide diverse training examples.	https://www.sciencedirect.com/science/article/pii/S2001037024002393
Transformers (e.g., GPT, BioGPT, BioBERT) [55]	Processing and generating insights from large-scale medical text (e.g., EHRs, clinical notes, medical literature).	BioBERT extracts disease markers and generates diagnostic recommendations from unstructured clinical text.	https://doi.org/10.1093/bib/bbac409
Recurrent Neural Networks (RNNs) & LSTMs [56]	Analyzing sequential medical data like patient history or time-series data for predictive diagnostics.	RNNs or LSTMs predict disease onset, such as sepsis or heart failure, based on historical data and simulate disease progression.	https://arxiv.org/abs/1902.02443
Diffusion Models [57]	Generating high-quality medical images and predicting future health outcomes based on current data.	Diffusion models generate high-quality MRI images for training AI models and predicting disease progression with limited data.	https://www.nature.com/articles/s41598-023-34341-2#citeas

Contd...

Table 6.3 *Contd...*

AI Model	*Use Case*	*Example*	
Reinforcement Learning (RL) [58]	Simulating and predicting disease progression or treatment responses in dynamic environments.	RL models optimize diagnostic pathways and simulate how different treatments affect patient health outcomes over time.	https://doi.org/10.1038/s41746-024-01316-0
Multimodal Models (e.g., CLIP, VisualBERT) [59]	Combining text, images, and other data sources to generate holistic diagnostic insights.	CLIP combines X-ray images with patient history data to generate comprehensive diagnostic reports.	https://arxiv.org/html/2503.01863v1
Attention-based Models (e.g., Vision Transformers) [60]	Analyzing and generating insights from medical images, such as tumor detection or organ segmentation.	Vision Transformers detect abnormalities in radiology images and generate diagnostic reports to assist radiologists.	https://ieeexplore.ieee.org/stamp/stamp.jsp?arnumber=9999689
Meta-Learning Models [61]	Quickly adapting to new, small datasets, especially useful in rare or emerging diseases.	Meta-learning models diagnose rare diseases by adapting to small datasets and learning from previous cases.	https://www.sciencedirect.com/science/article/abs/pii/S0933365723002324
Self-Supervised Learning Models [62]	Learning from unlabeled medical data by generating its own labels, reducing the need for labelled data.	Self-supervised learning helps pre-train models for tasks like cardiovascular disease detection, even when labelled datasets are scarce.	https://www.nature.com/articles/s41746-023-00811-0

efforts to ensure safe, equitable, and accountable integration [63]. Addressing hallucinations is critical for safe use of GenAI in diagnostics, as current models aren't yet ready for mainstream clinical adoption [41]. Techniques like Retrieval-Augmented Generation (RAG) help reduce inaccuracies by grounding outputs in validated knowledge [17]. Ultimately, human oversight remains essential for reliable deployment. Table 6.4 outlines key challenges and mitigation strategies.

Table 6.4 Challenges of GenAI and the potential mitigation strategies.

Challenge Category	*Specific Challenge*	*Potential Mitigation Strategies*
Ethical	Data Privacy and Security	Robust data management protocols, anonymization, encryption, access control, regulatory compliance
Ethical	Algorithmic Bias	Diverse and representative datasets, bias detection and mitigation techniques, fairness metrics
Ethical	Transparency and Accountability	Explainable AI methods, audit trails, clear lines of responsibility
Regulatory	Lack of Clear Guidelines	Collaboration among stakeholders, adaptive regulatory frameworks, continuous monitoring
Technical	Hallucinations and Inaccuracies	Retrieval-Augmented Generation, rigorous validation, human oversight
Data-Related	Data Quality and Heterogeneity	Standardized data collection, validation processes, intelligent adaptation systems
Data-Related	Data Scarcity (for rare conditions)	Synthetic data generation, federated learning

6.5 Case Studies

GenAI applications are revolutionizing patient care by delivering exceptional diagnostic accuracy and efficiency. Integrating AI expertise with clinical workflows enables providers to offer compliant, user-friendly healthcare solutions. Table 6.5 showcases relevant case studies from current practice.

6.6 Conclusion: Realizing the Promise of GenAI for the Future of Medical Diagnostics

This study highlights GenAI's transformative role in medical diagnosis, spanning radiology, pathology, ophthalmology, and clinical decision-making. Key outcomes include improved diagnostic accuracy, streamlined workflows, and expanded access—especially for underserved populations. These advances stem from multimodal AI models, large language models (LLMs), synthetic data generation, and evolving techniques like prompt engineering and Retrieval-Augmented

Table 6.5 Case studies showing use of GenAI in the current era.

Aidoc	AI in Radiology	• **Speed**: Reduces diagnostic time • **Accuracy**: Improves detection rates • **Scalability**: Handles large volumes of imaging data efficiently	Improves diagnostic accuracy, reduces time for critical conditions, and enhances patient outcomes	Aidoc. (n.d.). *AI-powered radiology solutions*. Aidoc. Retrieved April 20, 2025, from https://www.aidoc.com
Zebra Medical Vision	AI for Imaging and Radiology	• **Early Detection**: Detects conditions at early stages • **Improved Workflow**: Prioritizes urgent images • **Clinical Integration**: Fits hospital systems	AI shows performance matching or surpassing human radiologists, improving accuracy and efficiency	Zebra Medical Vision. (n.d.). *AI for medical imaging*. Zebra Medical Vision. Retrieved April 20, 2025, from https://www.weforum.org/organizations/zebra-medical-vision/
PathAI	AI for Pathology and Disease Diagnosis	• **Accuracy in Pathology**: Identifies subtle patterns • **Collaboration**: Assists pathologists in double-checking diagnoses • **Reduced Workload**: Focuses on complex cases	AI enhances accuracy in identifying cancerous cells, integrated into clinical practices for better decision-making	PathAI. (n.d.). *Artificial intelligence for pathology*. PathAI. Retrieved April 20, 2025, from https://www.pathai.com

Contd...

Table 6.5 *Contd...*

Babylon Health	AI-driven Symptom Checker	• **Accessibility**: 24/7 symptom checking • **Pre-diagnostic Information**: Gives insights before seeing a doctor • **Cost Reduction**: Cuts unnecessary visits	Clinically validated AI that improves diagnostic accuracy for common conditions and supports remote consultations	Babylon Health. (n.d.). *AI-powered health assessments*. Babylon Health. https://en.wikipedia.org/wiki/Babylon_Health
Tempus	AI for Oncology Diagnostics	• **Precision Medicine**: Identifies genetic mutations for targeted therapies • **Improved Outcomes**: Provides personalized treatment plans • **Data-Driven Decisions**: Uses vast data for decision-making	Enhances cancer treatment decisions, leading to better outcomes in survival rates and quality of life	Tempus. (n.d.). *AI for precision oncology*. Tempus. Retrieved April 20, 2025, from https://www.tempus.com
Google Health	AI for Diabetic Retinopathy Screening	• **Early Diagnosis**: Detects diabetic retinopathy early • **Wider Reach**: Scalable for underserved areas • **Cost-effective**: Reduces manual screening	Matches diagnostic accuracy of ophthalmologists, reduces burden on specialists, and improves patient outcomes	Google Health. (n.d.). *AI for diabetic retinopathy detection*. Google Health. Retrieved April 20, 2025, from https://health.google
Butterfly Network	Handheld Ultrasound with AI	• **Portability and Accessibility**: Makes diagnostic imaging accessible anywhere • **AI Assistance**: Guides non-specialists in image interpretation • **Real-Time Decision Support**: Provides instant analysis	Widely used in emergency settings and rural clinics, improving diagnostic access and decision-making efficiency	Butterfly Network. (n.d.). *Portable ultrasound with AI assistance*. Butterfly Network. Retrieved April 20, 2025, from https://www.butterflynetwo

Generation (RAG). Despite GenAI's promise, key ethical and practical issues must be addressed for responsible integration into diagnostics—privacy, data security, and algorithmic bias require careful mitigation to ensure equitable care. Human oversight remains vital, reinforcing AI's role as a clinical support tool rather than a replacement, and fostering collaboration between practitioners and AI systems.

Unlocking GenAI's full potential in diagnostics requires collaboration among researchers, clinicians, regulators, and patients—alongside ongoing interdisciplinary research and clinical trials. These efforts are vital for ensuring ethical, equitable, and effective AI adoption, ultimately improving global health outcomes and access.

As GenAI advances, establishing global standards for validation, regulation, and interoperability is key. Tackling regional healthcare challenges demands culturally aware, representative AI developed through academic, industry, and public health collaboration. Real-world pilot studies offer insights into usability and adoption, while public trust hinges on open data, transparency, and inclusive design.

Declarations

- The authors received no specific funding for this study.
- The authors declare that they have no conflicts of interest to report regarding the present study.
- No human subject or animals are involved in the research.
- All authors have mutually consented to participate.
- All the authors have given consent for publishing this work. .
- Authors declare that all data sources used in the design, layout and production of the manuscript are mentioned in the manuscript.

References

[1] Almansour M., Soliman M. and Aldekhyyel R. (2025). An Academic Viewpoint on the Integration of Generative Artificial Intelligence in Medical Education: Transforming Learning and Practices. *Cureus* 17(3): e81145. doi:10.7759/cureus.81145. https://pubmed.ncbi.nlm.nih.gov/40276436/.

[2] Bhuyan S.S., Sateesh V. and Mukul N. (2025). Generative Artificial Intelligence Use in Healthcare: Opportunities for Clinical Excellence and Administrative Efficiency. *J Med Syst*. 2025 Jan 16;49(1):10. doi: 10.1007/s10916-024-02136-1. PMID: 39820845; PMCID: PMC11739231. https://pubmed.ncbi.nlm.nih.gov/39820845/.

[3] Floridi, L. and Chiriatti, M. (2020). GPT-3: Its nature, scope, limits, and consequences. *Minds and Machines*, 30(4), 681–694. https://doi.org/10.1007/s11023-020-09548-1.

[4] Marcus, G., Davis, E. and Aaronson, S. (2022). A very preliminary analysis of DALL-E 2. https://arxiv.org/abs/2204.13807.

[5] Midjourney. 2025, https://www.midjourney.com/home?callbackUrl=%2Fapp%2F Accessed on: 20/04/2025.

[6] Stable Diffusion. 2025, https://stablediffusionweb.com/ Accessed on: 20/04/2025.

[7] Le, Q.M. and Lee, H.J. (2023). Mindful Architecture from Text-to-Image AI Perspectives: A Case Study of DALL-E, Midjourney, and Stable Diffusion. *Buildings*, 15(6), 972. https://www.mdpi.com/2075-5309/15/6/972.

[8] S. Sai, A. Gaur and R. Sai (2024). Generative AI for Transformative Healthcare: A Comprehensive Study of Emerging Models, Applications, Case Studies, and Limitations. *IEEE Access*, vol. 12, pp. 31078-31106, 2024, https://ieeexplore.ieee.org/document/10440330.

[9] Ouanes, K. (2024). Generative artificial intelligence in healthcare: current status and future directions. *Italian Journal of Medicine*, 18(3). https://doi.org/10.4081/itjm.2024.1782.

[10] Pinto-Coelho L. (2023). How Artificial Intelligence is Shaping Medical Imaging Technology: A Survey of Innovations and Applications. *Bioengineering (Basel)*. 2023 Dec 18;10(12):1435. doi: 10.3390/bioengineering10121435. PMID: 38136026; PMCID: PMC10740686. https://pmc.ncbi.nlm.nih.gov/articles/PMC10740686/.

[11] Shokrollahi Y., Yarmohammadtoosky S. and Nikahd, M.M. (2023). *A comprehensive review of generative AI in healthcare*. arXiv:2310.00795 Available from: https://arxiv.org/abs/2310.00795.

[12] Rao, V.M., Hla, M. and Moor, M. (2025). Multimodal generative AI for medical image interpretation. *Nature*, 639, 888–896. https://doi.org/10.1038/s41586-025-08675-y.

[13] Röhrich, S., Schlegl, T., Bardach, C. and Prosch, H. (2020). Deep learning detection and quantification of pneumothorax in heterogeneous routine chest computed tomography. *European Radiology Experimental*, 4(1), 26. https://doi.org/10.1186/s41747-020-00152-7.

[14] Hong E.K., Roh B. and Park B. (2025). Value of Using a Generative AI Model in Chest Radiography Reporting: A Reader Study. *Radiology*. 314(3):e241646. doi: 10.1148/radiol.241646. PMID: 40067108. https://pubmed.ncbi.nlm.nih.gov/40067108/.

[15] Jung, H., Kim, Y. and Choi, H. (2024). *Enhancing Clinical Efficiency through LLM: Discharge Note Generation for Cardiac Patients*. Available at: https://arxiv.org/abs/2404.05144.

[16] Hong E.K., Ham J. and Roh B. (2025). Diagnostic Accuracy and Clinical Value of a Domain-specific Multimodal Generative AI Model for Chest Radiograph Report Generation. *Radiology*. 314(3):e241476. doi: 10.1148/radiol.241476. PMID: 40131111. https://pubmed.ncbi.nlm.nih.gov/40131111/.

[17] Choi, Y. (2025). Diagnostic accuracy and clinical value of a domain-specific multimodal generative AI model for chest radiograph report generation. *Radiology*. Vol. 314, No. 3, Mar 25, 2025, https://pubs.rsna.org/doi/10.1148/radiol.241476.

[18] Rashidi, H., Pantanowitz, Chamanzar, A., et al. (2025). *Generative Artificial Intelligence in Pathology and Medicine: A Deeper Dive, Modern Pathology*, Volume 38, Issue 4, 2025, 100687, ISSN 0893-3952, https://doi.org/10.1016/j.modpat.2024.100687. https://www.sciencedirect.com/science/article/pii/S0893395224002679.

[19] McCaffrey, P., Jackups, R. and Seheult, J. (2025). Evaluating Use of Generative Artificial Intelligence in Clinical Pathology Practice: Opportunities and the Way Forward. *Arch Pathol Lab Med*. 2025 Feb 1;149(2):130-141. doi: 10.5858/arpa.2024-0208-RA. PMID: 39384182. https://pubmed.ncbi.nlm.nih.gov/39384182/.

[20] Brodsky, V., Ullah, E. and Bychkov, A. (2025). Generative artificial intelligence in anatomic pathology. *Archives of Pathology & Laboratory Medicine*, 149(4), 298–318. https://doi.org/10.5858/arpa.2024-0215-RA.

[21] Shen, IZ. and Zhang, L. (2025). Digital and Artificial Intelligence-based Pathology: Not for Every Laboratory – A Mini-review on the Benefits and Pitfalls of Its Implementation. *Journal of Clinical and Translational Pathology*. Published online: Apr 3, 2025. doi: 10.14218/JCTP.2025.00007. https://www.researchgate.net/journal/Journal-of-Clinical-and-Translational-Pathology-2771-165X.

[22] Heinke, A., Radgoudarzi, N. and Huang, B.B. (2024). A review of ophthalmology education in the era of generative artificial intelligence. *Asia Pac J Ophthalmol (Phila)*. 13(4):100089. doi: https://doi.org/10.1016/j.apjo.2024.100089 . Epub 2024 Aug 10. PMID: 39134176; PMCID: PMC11934932.

[23] ShuYuan, C. and Wen, B. (2025). Artificial intelligence technology in ophthalmology public health: current applications and future directions. *Frontiers in Cell and Developmental Biology*. Volume

13, https://www.frontiersin.org/journals/cell-and-developmental-biology/articles/10.3389/fcell.2025.1576465, DOI=10.3389/fcell.2025.1576465.

[24] Giovanni. A., (2025). Dynamic Modeling of Ocular Disease Progression with Generative AI – The Ophthalmologist, issue 2025, January, accessed April 18, 2025, https://theophthalmologist.com/issues/2025/articles/jan/dynamic-modeling-of-ocular-disease-progression-with-generative-ai.

[25] Gulshan, V. (2016). Development and validation of a deep learning algorithm for detection of diabetic retinopathy. *JAMA*, 316(22), 2402-2410. https://doi.org/10.1001/jama.2016.17216.

[26] Lam, C. (2018). Automated detection of diabetic retinopathy using deep learning. *Ophthalmology*, 125(7), 962-969. https://doi.org/10.1016/j.ophtha.2018.01.034.

[27] Pekala, M., Joshi, N. and Liu TYA (2019). Deep learning based retinal OCT segmentation. *Comput Biol Med.* 2019 Nov;114:103445. doi: 10.1016/j.compbiomed.2019.103445. Epub 2019 Sep 17. PMID: 31561100. https://pubmed.ncbi.nlm.nih.gov/31561100/.

[28] Veena, H., Muruganandham, A. and Kumaran, T. (2022). A novel optic disc and optic cup segmentation technique to diagnose glaucoma using deep learning convolutional neural network over retinal fundus images, *Journal of King Saud University - Computer and Information Sciences*, Volume 34, Issue 8, Part B, Pages 6187-6198, ISSN 1319-1578, https://doi.org/10.1016/j.jksuci.2021.02.003.

[29] Ting, D.S.W. (2017). Development and validation of a deep learning system for diabetic retinopathy and related eye diseases. *JAMA*, 318(22), 2211–2223. https://doi.org/10.1001/jama.2017.18152.

[30] Jia, Y., Chen, G. and Chi, H. (2024). Retinal fundus image super-resolution based on generative adversarial network guided with vascular structure prior. *Sci Rep.* 14, 22786, https://doi.org/10.1038/s41598-024-74186-x.

[31] Huang L., Chieu D. and Mehta M. (2024). *Self-Supervised Learning Featuring Small-Scale Image Dataset for Treatable Retinal Diseases Classification.* https://ar5iv.labs.arxiv.org/html/2404.10166.

[32] Chelaramani, S., Gupta, M. and Agarwal, V. (2021). Multi-Task Knowledge Distillation for Eye Disease Prediction. 2021 IEEE Winter Conference on Applications of Computer Vision (WACV), Waikoloa, HI, USA, pp. 3982–3992, doi: 10.1109/WACV48630.2021.00403. https://openaccess.thecvf.com/content/WACV2021/papers/Chelaramani_Multi-Task_Knowledge_Distillation_for_Eye_Disease_Prediction_WACV_2021_paper.pdf.

[33] Burlina, P., Paul, W. and Liu TYA (2022). Detecting Anomalies in Retinal Diseases Using Generative, Discriminative, and Self-supervised Deep Learning. *JAMA Ophthalmol.* 1;140(2):185-189. doi: 10.1001/jamaophthalmol.2021.5557. PMID: 34967890; PMCID: PMC8719271. https://pubmed.ncbi.nlm.nih.gov/34967890/.

[34] Shalini, R. and Gopi, V.P., (2024). Multiresolution cascaded attention U-Net for localization and segmentation of optic disc and fovea in fundus images. *Sci Rep.* 14, 23107 (2024). https://doi.org/10.1038/s41598-024-73493-7.

[35] Shi, D., Zhang, W. and Chen, X. (2024). *EyeFound: A Multimodal Generalist Foundation Model for Ophthalmic Imaging*. arXiv preprint arXiv:2405.11338. https://www.semanticscholar.org/paper/EyeFound%3A-A-Multimodal-Generalist-Foundation-Model-Shi-Zhang/adfe039bfb169016617b0d1dcf25ee693e860b38.

[36] Qiu, J., Wu, J. and Wei, H. (2023). *VisionFM: a Multi-Modal Multi-Task Vision Foundation Model for Generalist Ophthalmic Artificial Intelligence*. DOI: 10.48550/ARXIV.2310.04992, https://dblp.org/rec/journals/corr/abs-2310-04992.html.

[37] Atik, M.E., Kocak, İ. and Sayin, N. (2025). Integration of Optical Coherence Tomography Images and Real-Life Clinical Data for Deep Learning Modeling: A Unified Approach in Prognostication of Diabetic Macular Edema. *Journal of Biophotonics*, 18(3), e202400315. https://doi.org/10.1002/jbio.202400315.

[38] Shahgir, H.A.Z.S., Sayeed, K.S. and Zaman, T.A. (2023). *Ophthalmic Biomarker Detection Using Ensembled Vision Transformers and Knowledge Distillation.* arXiv preprint arXiv:2310.14005. https://arxiv.org/abs/2310.14005.

[39] Corradetti, G. (2025). Prediction of structural OCT biomarkers in intermediate AMD using deep learning. *Envision Summit 2025.* https://www.ophthalmologytimes.com/view/envision-summit-2025-prediction-of-structural-oct-biomarkers-in-intermediate-amd-using-deep-learning.

[40] Maldonado-Garcia, C., Zakeri, A., Frangi, A.F. and Ravikumar, N. (2025). Integrating Deep Learning with Fundus and Optical Coherence Tomography for Cardiovascular Disease Prediction. In Predictive Intelligence in Medicine. PRIME 2024. *Lecture Notes in Computer Science*, vol 15155. Springer, Cham. https://doi.org/10.1007/978-3-031-74561-4_14.

[41] Ashtari-Majlan, M., Dehshibi, M.M. and Masip, D. (2023). *Deep Learning and Computer Vision for Glaucoma Detection: A Review.* arXiv:2307.16528.

[42] Zhang, P., Shi, J. and Kamel Boulos, M.N. (2024). Generative AI in Medicine and Healthcare: Moving Beyond the 'Peak of Inflated Expectations'. *Future Internet*, 16(12), 462. https://doi.org/10.3390/fi16120462.

[43] Meng, X., Yan, X. and Zhang, K. (2024). *The application of large language models in medicine: A scoping review. iScience.* Volume 27, Issue 5, 2024, 109713, ISSN 2589-0042, https://doi.org/10.1016/j.isci.2024.109713. https://www.sciencedirect.com/science/article/pii/S2589004224009350.

[44] Gao, Y., Li, R., Croxford, E. and Caskey, J. (2025). Leveraging Medical Knowledge Graphs Into Large Language Models for Diagnosis Prediction: Design and Application Study. *JMIR AI.* 4:e58670. doi: 10.2196/58670. PMID: 39993309; PMCID: PMC11894347.

[45] Ma, M.D., Wang, X. and Xiao, Y. (2025). Memorize and Rank: Elevating Large Language Models for Clinical Diagnosis Prediction. *Proceedings of the AAAI Conference on Artificial Intelligence*, 39(23), 24786-24794. https://doi.org/10.1609/aaai.v39i23.34660.

[46] Takita, H., Kabata, D. and Walston, S.L. (2025). A systematic review and meta-analysis of diagnostic performance comparison between generative AI and physicians. *NPJ Digit Med.* 2025 Mar 22;8(1):175. doi: 10.1038/s41746-025-01543-z. PMID: 40121370; PMCID: PMC11929846.

[47] Incoronato, M., Aiello, M. and Infante, T. (2020). Integrating imaging and omics data: a review. *Frontiers in Oncology*, 10, 1065. https://doi.org/10.3389/fonc.2020.01065.

[48] Agbareia, R., Omar, M. and Soffer, S. (2025). Visual-textual integration in LLMs for medical diagnosis: A preliminary quantitative analysis. *Computational and Structural Biotechnology Journal.* Volume 27, Pages 184-189. ISSN 2001-0370. https://doi.org/10.1016/j.csbj.2024.12.019.

[49] Wang, J., Wang, K. and Yu, Y. (2025). Self-improving generative foundation model for synthetic medical image generation and clinical applications. *Nat Med.* 31(2):609-617. doi: 10.1038/s41591-024-03359-y. Epub 2024 Dec 11. PMID: 39663467. https://www.nature.com/articles/s41591-024-03359-y.

[50] Yi, X., Walia, E. and Babyn, P. (2023). Generative artificial intelligence for synthetic data augmentation in medical imaging: A review of techniques, applications, and challenges. *Artificial Intelligence in Medicine*, 145, 102618. https://doi.org/10.1016/j.artmed.2023.102618.

[51] Munia, N. and Imran, A. (2025). Prompting Medical Vision-Language Models to Mitigate Diagnosis Bias by Generating Realistic Dermoscopic Images - arXiv, accessed April 18, 2025, https://arxiv.org/html/2504.01838v1.

[52] Lewis, P., Perez, E. and Piktus, A. (2023). Retrieval-augmented generation for knowledge-intensive NLP tasks. *Communications of the ACM*, 66(7), 94-103. https://doi.org/10.1145/3536223.

[53] Shin, H.C. (2018). Medical Image Synthesis for Data Augmentation and Anonymization Using Generative Adversarial Networks. In: Gooya, A., Goksel, O., Oguz, I., Burgos, N. (eds) Simulation and Synthesis in Medical Imaging. *SASHIMI 2018.* Lecture Notes in Computer Science, vol 11037. Springer, Cham. https://doi.org/10.1007/978-3-030-00536-8_1.

[54] Pezoulas, V., Zaridis, D. and Mylona, E. (2024). *Synthetic data generation methods in healthcare: A review on open-source tools and methods, Computational and Structural Biotechnology Journal*, Volume 23, 2024, Pages 2892-2910, ISSN 2001-0370, https://doi.org/10.1016/j.csbj.2024.07.005.

[55] Luo, R., Sun, L. and Xia, Y. (2022). *BioGPT: generative pre-trained transformer for biomedical text generation and mining, Briefings in Bioinformatics*, Volume 23, Issue 6, bbac409, https://doi.org/10.1093/bib/bbac409.

[56] Sunil Mallya, S., Overhage, J. and Srivastava, N. (2019). *Effectiveness of LSTMs in Predicting Congestive Heart Failure Onset*, abs/1902.02443, http://arxiv.org/abs/1902.02443, https://dblp.org/rec/journals/corr/abs-1902-02443.bib.

[57] Khader, F., Müller-Franzes, G. and Tayebi Arasteh, S. (2023). Denoising diffusion probabilistic models for 3D medical image generation. *Sci Rep* 13, 7303. https://doi.org/10.1038/s41598-023-34341-2.

[58] Jayaraman, P., Desman, J. and Sabounchi M. (2024). A Primer on Reinforcement Learning in Medicine for Clinicians. *NPJ Digit Med.* 7(1):337. doi: 10.1038/s41746-024-01316-0. PMID: 39592855; PMCID: PMC11599275.

[59] Kalpélbé, B., Adaambiik, A.G. and Peng, W. (2025). *Vision Language Models in Medicine.* Available at: https://arxiv.org/html/2503.01863v1.

[60] Mashood Mohammad Mohsan, Muhammad Usman Akram, Ghulam Rasool, Norah Saleh Alghamdi, Muhammad Abdullah Aamer Baqai et al. Vision Transformer and Language Model Based Radiology Report Generation. IEEE Access. 6 January 2023. DOI: 10.1109/ACCESS.2022.3232719. https://ieeexplore.ieee.org/stamp/stamp.jsp?arnumber=9999689.

[61] Liu, Q., Tian, Y. and Zhou, T. (2024). *A few-shot disease diagnosis decision making model based on meta-learning for general practice, Artificial Intelligence in Medicine*, Volume 147, 102718, ISSN 933-3657, https://doi.org/10.1016/j.artmed.2023.102718.

[62] Huang, S.C., Pareek, A. and Jensen, M. (2023). Self-supervised learning for medical image classification: a systematic review and implementation guidelines. *NPJ Digit. Med.* 6, 74. https://doi.org/10.1038/s41746-023-00811-0.

[63] Zhang, K., Khosravi, B. and Vahdati, S. (2024). *FDA Review of Radiologic AI Algorithms: Process and Challenges. Radiology*. 2024 Jan;310(1):e230242. doi: 10.1148/radiol.230242. PMID: 38165243. https://pubmed.ncbi.nlm.nih.gov/38165243/.

7 Empirical Evaluation using Generative AI models for the Multiclass Classification of Retinal Diseases Images

Pavneet Singh[1], Shranya Suri[2], Shweta Taneja[3*], Palak Girdhar[4] and Bhawna Suri[5]

This study applies Super Resolution Generative Adversarial Networks (SRGAN) to enhance retinal disease diagnosis. Synthetic images for CNV, DRUSEN, DME, and NORMAL classes were generated using SRGAN and added to the Mendley dataset. A custom CNN trained on this augmented data achieved macro and weighted average scores of 99%, outperforming existing methods.

7.1 Introduction

Generative AI (Gen AI) leverages advanced deep learning and modeling techniques to create new content—including images, text, audio, and video—as illustrated in Figure 7.1.

GenAI has broad real-world applications across marketing, media, entertainment, and healthcare. In healthcare, it supports research, diagnostics, and treatment with high accuracy—enabled by advances from machine learning to deep learning [1]. Tools like chatbots and virtual assistants automate routine clinical tasks, improving patient engagement and operational efficiency. GenAI also drives innovation in education, retail, and customer service through personalization and intelligent interaction [2].

Generative AI presents several challenges and ethical considerations,including:

- **Misinformation:** GenAI can produce deepfakes or misleading content, requiring ethical safeguards to prevent misuse.
- **Bias:** AI trained on biased data may generate discriminatory outputs, impacting fairness in critical domains.

[1,3-5] Department of Computer Science and Engineering, Bhagwan Parshuram Institute of Technology, GGSIPU, Delhi, India.

[2] Government Doon Medical College, Dehradun, India.
E-mail: pavneetsingh.5013@gmail.com[1]; shranyasuri@gmail.com[2]; palakgirdhar@bpitindia.com[4]; bhawnasuri@bpitindia.com[5]

* Corresponding author: shwetataneja@bpitindia.com

DOI: 10.1201/9781003670582-7

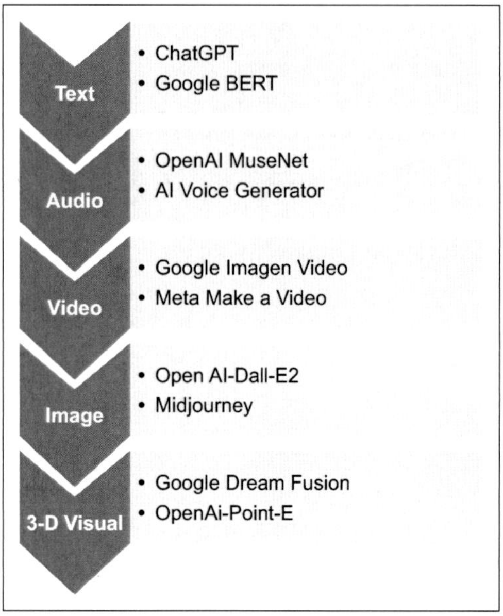

Fig. 7.1 Different GenAI Models.

- **Intellectual Property:** Ownership of AI-generated content remains an unresolved legal concern for businesses and policymakers.

GenAI is poised to reshape how we live and interact with technology, with deeper integration across daily life. Future virtual assistants may anticipate needs and personalize interactions, while entertainment could see dynamic storytelling and custom media experiences powered by generative models. Beyond personal use, GenAI is revolutionizing sectors like education, marketing, design, journalism, and notably healthcare—enhancing decision-making, research, and patient engagement. As GenAI becomes more integrated into society, ethical concerns—data privacy, bias, misinformation, IP rights, and equitable access—must be addressed to ensure fair benefits. Transparent design, inclusive innovation, and responsible governance are vital to building trust and preventing misuse.

In summary, GenAI holds immense potential, but realizing its benefits depends on responsible development and ethical deployment—ensuring it serves the greater good.

7.1.1 Generative AI in Healthcare

GenAI holds transformative promise in healthcare—accelerating drug discovery, enabling personalized treatments, and advancing predictive models. By simulating complex patterns, synthetic data reduces diagnostic and development costs. However, verifying data accuracy and integrating GenAI with legacy systems remain key challenges requiring investment and training [3]. In personalized medicine, GenAI's synthetic data helps address data scarcity, while LLMs enhance diagnostic decision-making [4].

This review highlights the role of GANs and LLMs in healthcare and radiology, emphasizing GenAI's ability to generate secure, high-quality synthetic medical data. Models like ChatGPT and BERT have significantly advanced radiology applications, while emerging initiatives such as LLaVa-Med integrate LLMs with vision models for enhanced diagnostic capabilities [5]. Reference [6] explores GenAI applications across the healthcare AI lifecycle—spanning data collection, model development, and implementation—highlighting privacy and security risks. It presents opportunities, challenges, and mitigation strategies, offering practical guidance for stakeholders. The study underscores the importance of responsible GenAI integration to ensure ethical, secure, and effective adoption in healthcare, reinforcing its emerging potential.

7.1.2 Overview of SRGAN

Super-Resolution GAN (SRGAN) enhances low-resolution images using deep residual and recursive networks. By optimizing SSIM, MSE, and perceptual loss, it preserves structural fidelity and achieves high performance—99.04% accuracy, 3.19 loss, SSIM of 0.97, PSNR of 34.6, and MSE of 0.012. The architecture includes a generator for upscaling and a discriminator for validation. The architecture includes a generator for upscaling and a discriminator for validation.

Chapter sections detail the state-of-art (Section 2), proposed methodology (Section 3), implementation and results (Section 4), and conclusion (Section 5).

7.2 Related Work

Rapid technological shifts have moved healthcare from traditional data mining and machine learning toward advanced GenAI tools. Early ML methods enabled adaptive, rule-free learning [7], widely applied in diagnostics, patient care, and operational efficiency. Business Intelligence (BI) has supported strategic decision-making and departmental performance, with successful case studies in cancer, diabetes, and liver disorders [8]. Recent research explores GenAI's impact on healthcare through digital media analysis, highlighting its potential in clinical automation and patient communication [9]. LLMs like GPT-4 and Bard offer transformative support in documentation and insurance workflows but raise ethical and regulatory concerns due to privacy risks [10]. SRGAN-based models improve image quality via residual and perceptual loss integration [11]. Applications in EHR summarization, medical term translation, and wearable-driven personalized care leverage NLP and speech recognition techniques [12]. Comprehensive reviews emphasize RLHF, few-shot learning, and the need for inclusive governance frameworks to guide responsible deployment of GenAI and LLMs [13].

Numerous studies have applied GenAI models for disease detection. In [14], GANs were used to generate synthetic OCT images for glaucoma diagnosis, with performance evaluated using 100 real and 100 synthetic samples reviewed by clinical experts.

Several studies have applied GAN-based models for disease detection and medical image synthesis [17]. In [16], Pix2Pix GAN, CycleGAN and Deep Pix2Pix GAN were used to generate brain images. Reference [15] introduced Paired Unpaired CycleGANs (PUPC GANs) for MRI and CT scans, and combined CycleGAN with a Dual Path Network (DPN) for breast cancer diagnosis. GANs helped address class imbalance in Alzheimer's datasets by generating minority class images [18], while [19] used GANs to support early Tuberculosis detection and clinical decision-making. In conclusion, integrating ML, BI, and GenAI is reshaping healthcare by enabling predictive analytics, strategic planning, and personalized diagnostics. Tools like ChatGPT and GPT-4 enhance clinical workflows, while GANs support disease detection across imaging domains. Realizing their full potential requires ethical oversight, regulatory alignment, and collaborative innovation. Together, these technologies promise to elevate patient care and healthcare efficiency system-wide.

7.3 Proposed Work

Optical coherence tomography (OCT) is widely used for retinal imaging, producing high-resolution scans. While traditional OCT remains the gold standard, this study explores enhancing subsampled OCT images using SRGAN-based super-resolution techniques. The approach aims to improve image quality for diagnostic and research applications, as illustrated in Figure 7.2.

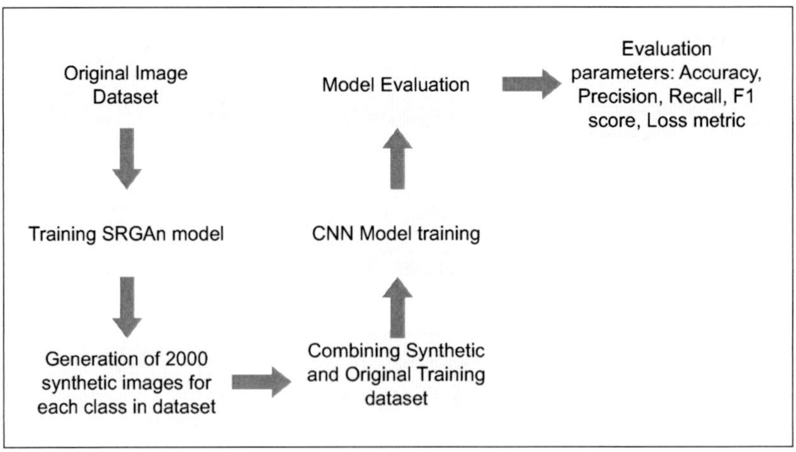

Fig. 7.2 Proposed Approach.

7.3.1 Generator Architecture

Figure 7.3 illustrates the generator module of the SRGAN model, which converts low-resolution (64×64×3) images into high-resolution (256×256×3) outputs. The architecture—based on convolutional layers, residual blocks, and upsampling—draws inspiration from ResNets to ensure high-quality generation and stable training for super-resolution tasks.

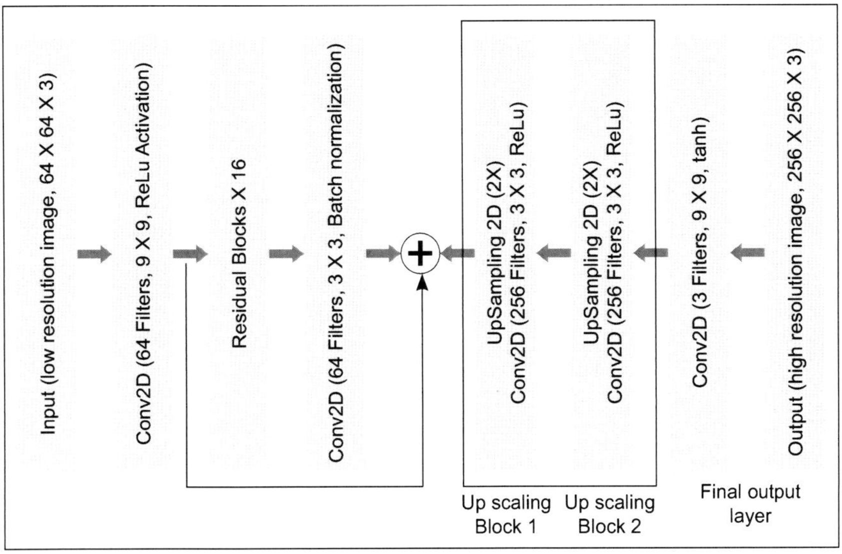

Fig. 7.3 Generator module of SRGAN.

7.3.1.1 Input and Initial Convolution

The generator begins with a 9×9 convolutional layer using 64 filters and ReLU activation, designed to extract low-level features like edges and textures from the input image. This wide kernel establishes a rich feature foundation for deeper processing in subsequent layers.

Residual Blocks
As shown in Figure 7.4, the residual block is a crucial element of the SRGAN generator, enabling efficient feature learning for high-resolution image synthesis.

7.3.1.2 Output Layer

The generator's final layer uses a 9×9 convolution with 3 filters and a tanh activation, integrating features from a wide receptive field for smoother textures. The tanh function scales the output between -1 and 1, aligning with the normalized training data.

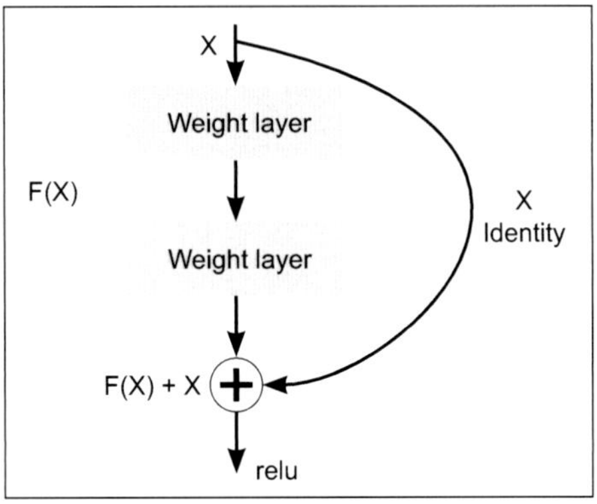

Fig. 7.4 Residual Block.

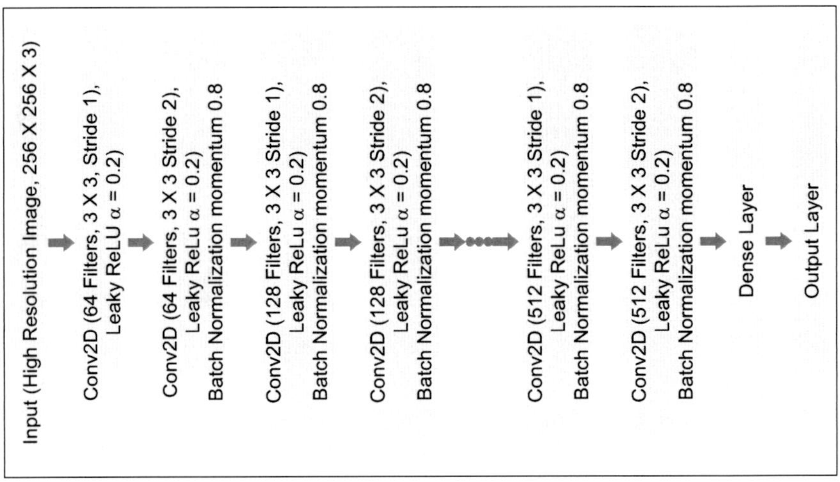

Fig. 7.5 Discriminator Module.

7.3.2 Discriminator Network

As illustrated in Figure 7.5, the SRGAN discriminator is a binary classifier built on a deep CNN architecture. It distinguishes real high-resolution images from those generated by the SRGAN, following a multi-phase processing pipeline.

7.3.2.1 Input Layer

- **Input:** The discriminator takes a 256×256×3 high-resolution image—real or synthetic—as input for feature extraction and classification.
- **Purpose:** The process begins with feature extraction, preserving spatial and color details essential for accurate image discrimination in later layers.

7.3.2.2 Convolutional Feature Extraction

The network uses eight convolutional layers with increasing filter counts and downsampling operations, progressively learning abstract and complex features at each stage. **The first two convolutional layers use 64 filters with a 3×3 kernel and LeakyReLU** (α=0.2) to prevent neuron inactivity. The first layer extracts edges and textures without altering spatial resolution, while the second applies stride 2 for **downsampling, enabling deeper abstraction with reduced computational load. The third and fourth convolutional layers use 128 filters with strides of 1 and 2, respectively, followed by LeakyReLU and Batch Normalization. The increased filter count enhances feature complexity, while downsampling in the fourth layer reduces spatial dimensions for focused discrimination.** The later layers increase filter counts to 256 and 512, retaining existing parameters to compress feature maps into compact representations optimal for classification.

7.3.2.3 Dense Layers for Final Classification

After abstracting spatial features through convolutional layers, the network transitions to fully connected (dense) layers for final classification:

- **First Dense Layer:**
  - **Operation:** The flattened feature maps are fed into a Dense layer with 1024 neurons for high-level feature integration.
  - **Activation:** A LeakyReLU activation introduces non-linearity, allowing small gradients even when units are inactive to improve learning.
  - **Purpose:** This layer consolidates learned features and connects convolutional outputs to the final binary classification stage.
- **Output Dense Layer:**
  - **Operation:** The final Dense layer comprises a single neuron with a Sigmoid activation to output a binary classification score.
  - **Purpose:** The Sigmoid function maps the output between 0 and 1, enabling binary classification during adversarial training to determine whether an input image is real (1) or synthetic (0). Loss Function and Training
- **Loss Function:** The discriminator is trained using mean squared error (MSE) loss function loss and accuracy metrics, with MSE helping stabilize training in GAN-based architectures.
  - **Purpose:** Minimizing MSE loss trains the discriminator to accurately classify real versus generated images, delivering strong feedback to guide generator improvement.

7.3.2.4 VGG 19 Feature Extractor

In the SRGAN framework, VGG19 serves as a pre-trained feature extractor to compute perceptual loss. Instead of relying on pixel-wise comparisons, it evaluates deeper-layer semantic features from both real and generated images. This encourages the generator to produce sharper, more realistic textures, improving image quality and stabilizing training.

7.3.3 Adversarial Training

The generator aims to produce high-resolution images indistinguishable from real ones, while the discriminator is trained to accurately classify inputs as real or fake. This sets up a dynamic adversarial framework: –

- The discriminator learns from both genuine HR images (labelled as real) and super-resolved outputs from the generator (labelled as fake).
- The generator updates its parameters using feedback from the discriminator, with the objective of fooling it into recognizing generated images as real.

7.3.4 Loss Functions

The overall loss function for the generator is a weighted sum of:

- **Adversarial Loss:** Typically using binary cross-entropy, this loss guides the generator to create images that the discriminator recognizes as real.
- **Perceptual Loss (Feature Loss):** Perceptual loss is computed as the mean squared error (MSE) between feature maps of real images extracted via VGG19 . It directs the generator to preserve high-level features like texture and content. Some implementations also include pixel-wise MSE to further enhance output fidelity.

The discriminator is trained to maximize classification accuracy between real and generated images, using a loss function that penalizes misclassifications and supplies strong gradients to improve generator performance.

7.3.5 Generation of Synthetic Images

Post adversarial training, the generator is deployed to produce synthetic high-resolution images—2,000 per class (CNV, DME, DRUSEN, NORMAL)—to augment the dataset.

7.3.6 Convolutional Neural Network Model

The CNN model is applied to the augmented dataset, using layered feature extraction and dimensionality reduction to classify images into CNV, DRUSEN, NORMAL, or DME. To address class imbalance during preprocessing, majority classes were under-sampled, resulting in a balanced dataset with equal class representation and unbiased CNN performance.

Model Architecture

The CNN architecture progressively extracts hierarchical features through stacked layers:

- Convolutional Layers (Conv2D): Initial layers detect low-level features using 60 filters (5×5), followed by smaller kernels (4×4, 3×3) with ReLU activation for non-linearity. Max-Pooling Layers (MaxPooling2D): Applied after each convolutional set to reduce spatial dimensions via 2×2 pooling, retaining key features and minimizing overfitting. Dropout Layers: Added post-convolution and dense layers to prevent overfitting. Flatten Layer: Converts 3D feature maps to a 1D vector for dense layer input. Fully Connected Layers (Dense): A 5000-neuron dense layer with ReLU activation enables high-level learning, followed by an output layer with four neurons for classification (CNV, DME, DRUSEN, NORMAL).
- The output layer uses Softmax to generate class probabilities, selecting the highest as the model's prediction.

7.3.6.1 Model Training

The model uses the Adam optimizer (learning rate: 0.001) for adaptive gradient updates, with categorical cross-entropy loss to handle multi-class classification. Together, they minimize error and enhance accuracy during training. Batch Size: The model uses a batch size of 256, updating weights every 256 images to stabilize learning and enhance generalization.

- Epochs: The model trains for 50 epochs, each representing a full pass through the dataset to iteratively refine its parameters.
- Validation: The model's performance is assessed on a separate validation set comprising unseen images.

7.3.6.2 Custom Callback and Learning Rate Adjustment

A custom callback monitors accuracy per epoch and dynamically reduces the learning rate by 0.9 to ensure smooth convergence and training efficiency.

7.4 Implementation and Results

This section discusses the dataset and implementation details.

7.4.1 Dataset

The Mendeley dataset comprises ~84,000 OCT retinal images (JPEG), collected between July 2013 and March 2017 from institutions including UC San Diego's Shiley Eye Institute, Beijing Tongren Eye Center, Medical Center Ophthalmology Associates, and Shanghai First People's Hospital [20][21]. Images are labeled across four classes: NORMAL, CNV, DRUSEN, and DME.

SRGAN is trained for 5001 epochs, with sample outputs shown at epochs 0, 2500, and 5000 (Figs. 7.6 to 7.8).

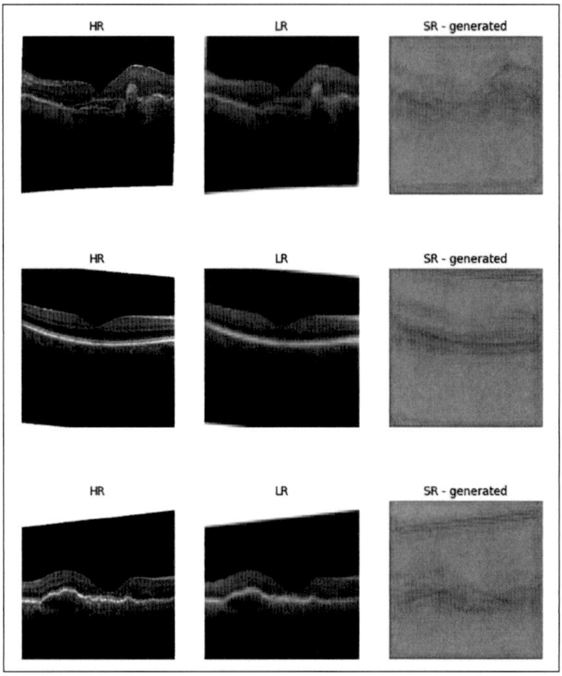

Fig. 7.6 SRGAN Images at end of Epoch 0.

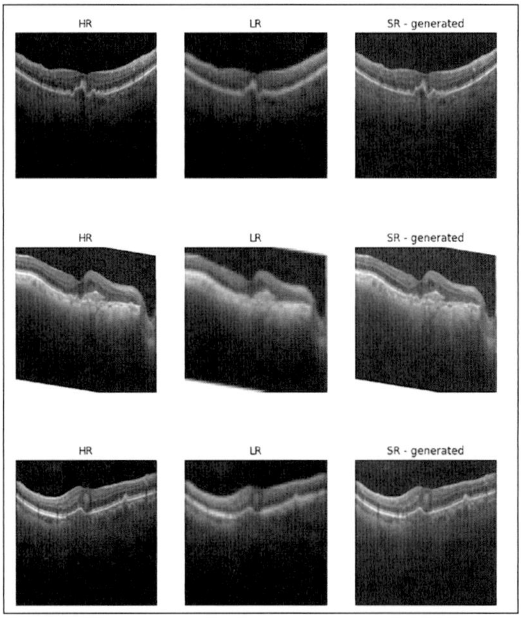

Fig. 7.7 SRGAN images at end of 2500 epochs.

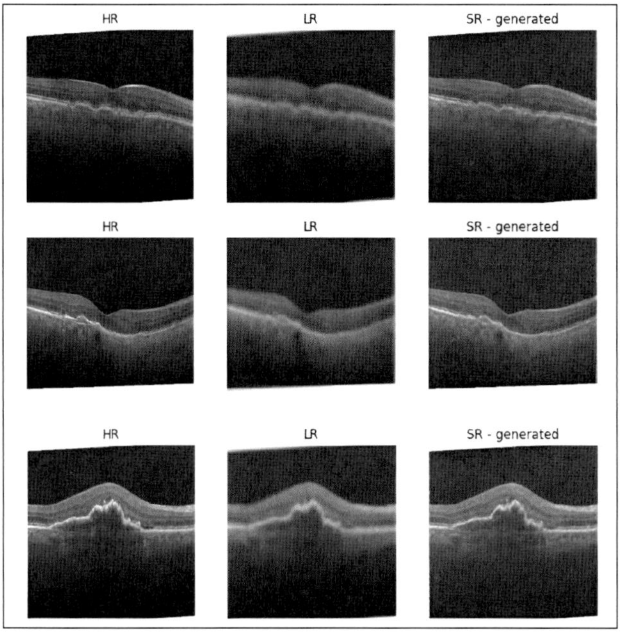

Fig. 7.8 SRGAN Images at end of epoch 5000.

The figures illustrate comparative visual outcomes of image super-resolution (SR) applied to retinal OCT (Optical Coherence Tomography) scans using the SRGAN model. Each figure presents three columns:

- **High-Resolution (HR):** Original, sharp OCT image.
- **Low-Resolution (LR):** Downsampled/blurry image simulating degraded input.

SR-Generated: Super-resolved image produced by SRGAN, aimed at reconstructing fine details from the LR input. During the training phase of SRGAN, different plots are obtained like loss function (Fig. 7.9), PSNR (Fig. 7.10), SSIM (Fig. 7.11) are obtained for the Generator and Discriminator modules.

Figures 7.9 to 7.11 plot SRGAN evaluation metrics across training epochs. In Figure 7.9, Discriminator (blue) and Generator (orange) losses are shown—Discriminator loss fluctuates initially and stabilizes around 0.39; Generator loss remains smoother and lower. Both losses steadily decline, indicating improved image generation and discrimination, with stable GAN training free from mode collapse.

Figure 7.10 shows PSNR trends for Discriminator and Generator across epochs—rising quickly in the first 1000 epochs and stabilizing between 6–10 dB, indicating improved image fidelity with reduced distortion. Figure 7.11 illustrates SSIM progression, increasing until epoch 1000 and saturating near 0.2–0.3. This reflects consistent preservation of structural features essential in medical imaging.

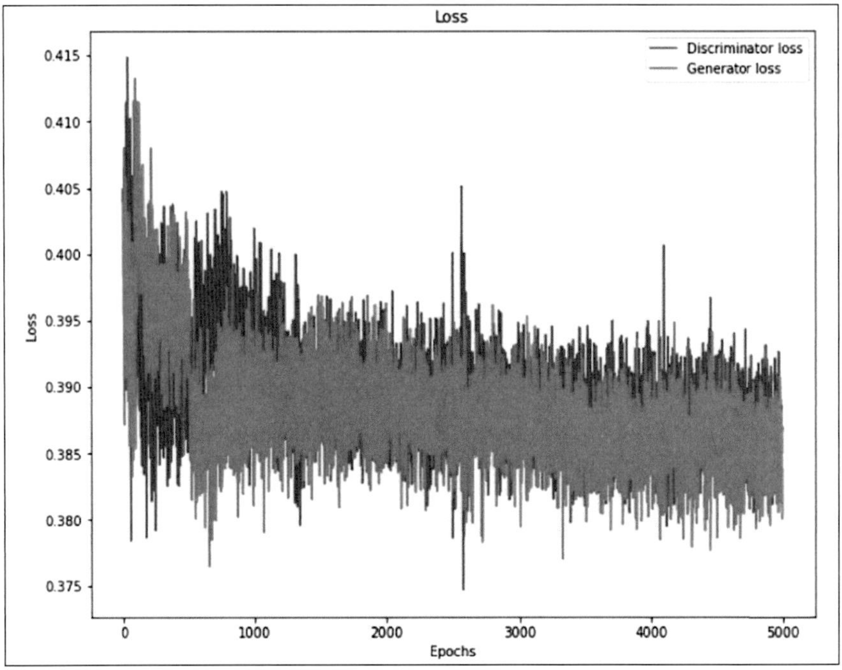

Fig. 7.9 Generator & Discriminator Loss vs Epoch.

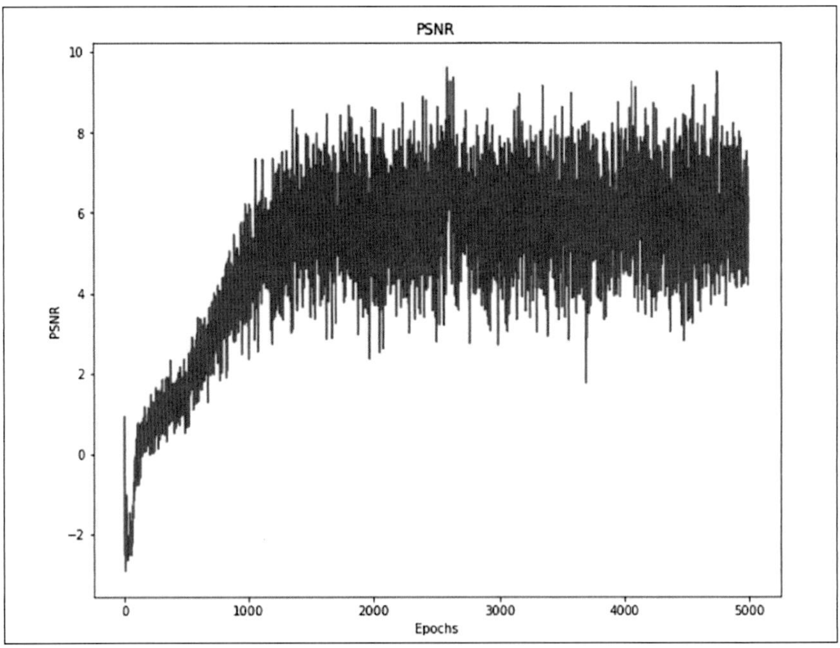

Fig. 7.10 PSNR vs Epoch plot for SRGAN for SRGAN.

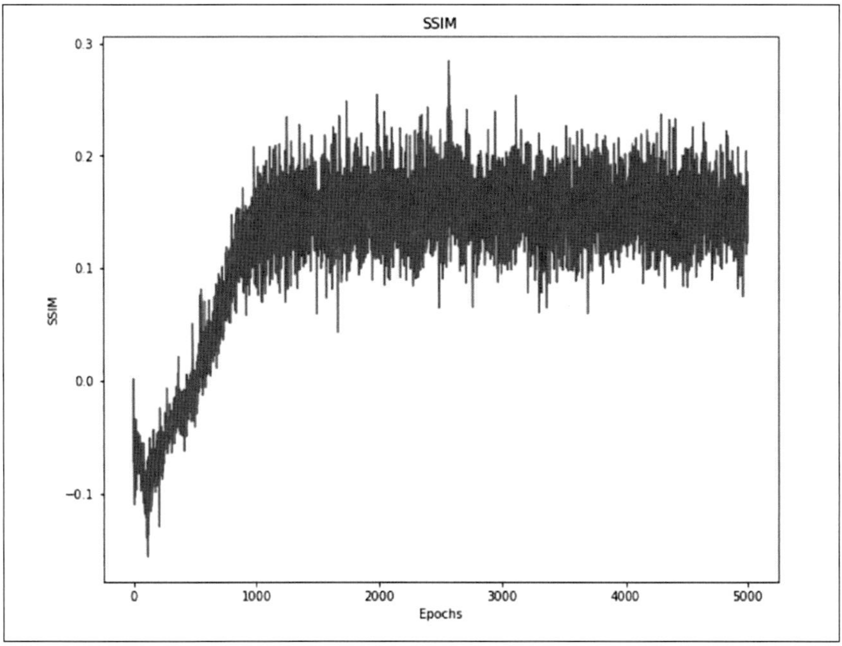

Fig. 7.11 SSIM vs Epoch plot for SRGAN.

The model exhibits stable training with converging losses, rising PSNR, and improving SSIM—confirming that the GAN consistently enhances image resolution and effectively reconstructs high-quality OCT scans from low-resolution inputs. CNN performance was tracked using accuracy, comparing training and validation results per epoch (Figs. 7.12 and 7.13) to check for overfitting. Figure 7.14 confirms that Random Under-Sampling effectively balanced class labels in the dataset. Trained on an augmented and balanced dataset, the CNN model was evaluated using accuracy and loss metrics (Tables 7.1 and 7.2). By combining Random Under-Sampling, data augmentation, and dropout, it achieved strong generalization across unseen retinal images—establishing a robust baseline for automated medical image classification in healthcare.

Figure 7.12 displays CNN loss curves over 50 epochs, with training loss (blue) and validation loss (orange). Both drop sharply early on and stabilize, indicating effective learning. Validation loss remains consistently lower, suggesting noisier training data and good generalization without signs of overfitting.

Figure 7.13 presents training and validation accuracy curves over 50 epochs. Accuracy improves rapidly in the first 10 epochs, with training accuracy rising from ~0.55 to ~0.98 and validation accuracy reaching ~1.0 early and remaining stable. The model shows effective learning and strong generalization. This CNN model:

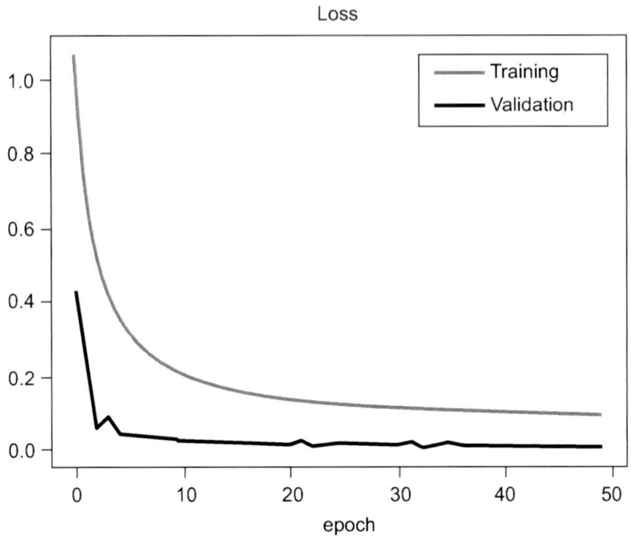

Fig. 7.12 Training and Validation Loss vs Epoch vs for CNN Model

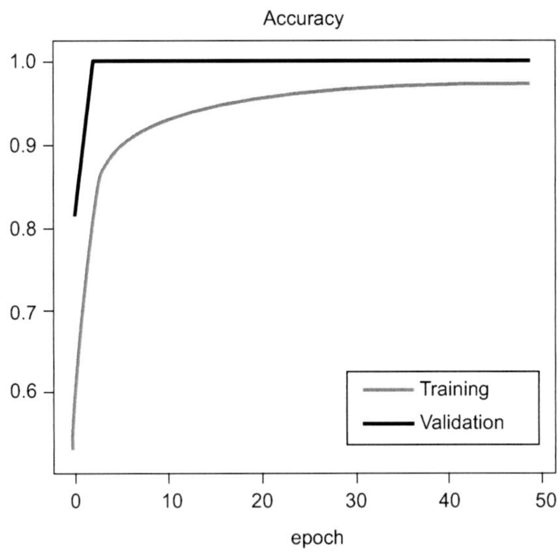

Fig. 7.13 Training and Validation Accuracy Epoch for CNN Model.

- Achieves very high accuracy on both training and validation datasets.
- Is well-trained and generalizes well to unseen data.
- Does not appear to overfit.
- Likely benefits from good data preprocessing, balanced datasets, and/or regularization techniques.

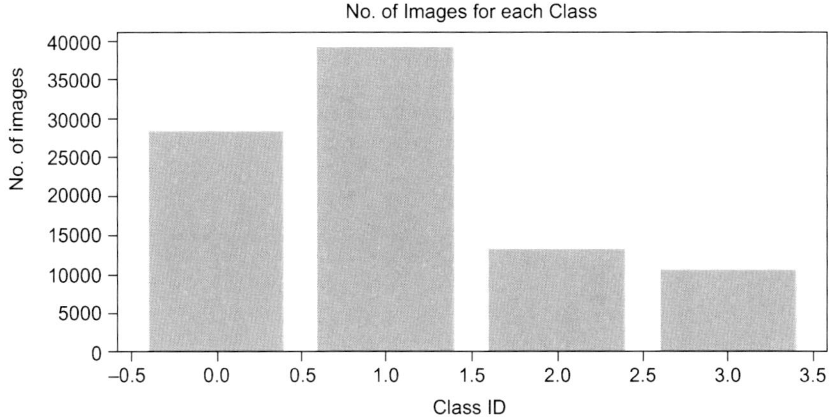

Fig. 7.14 Number of Images in each class of Training dataset before under sampling.

Table 7.1 Performance metrics for each class.

Class ID	*Precision*	*Recall*	*F1 Score*	*Support*
NORMAL	1.00	1.00	1.00	242
CNV	1.00	0.99	0.99	242
DME	0.99	0.99	0.99	242
DRUSEN	1.00	1.00	1.00	242

Table 7.2 Multiclass Performance metrics.

Class	*Precision*	*Recall*	*F1 Score*	*Support*
Macro average	0.99	0.99	0.99	968
Weighted average	0.99	0.99	0.99	968

Figure 7.14 shows class-wise image distribution, revealing imbalance—Class NORMAL has nearly 3× more samples than PME. This disparity may bias the model toward majority classes, reducing accuracy for underrepresented ones.

Table 7.1 shows strong performance across all classes, with only slight drops (0.01) in CNV and DME—indicating near-perfect, balanced classification and excellent generalization.

Table 7.2 presents aggregated multiclass metrics for the CNN model, with Macro Averages of Precision, Recall, and F1 Score all at 0.99—demonstrating consistently high performance across all four classes (NORMAL, CNV, DME, DRUSEN).

Similarly in Table 7.2 shows identical macro and weighted averages (0.99), reflecting equal class support (242 samples) and confirming that the CNN model achieves unbiased, high-accuracy performance across all classes—even in scenarios where weighted metrics typically highlight imbalance.

The CNN model achieved a Cohen's kappa score of 0.9931, with its confusion matrix illustrated in Figure 7.15.

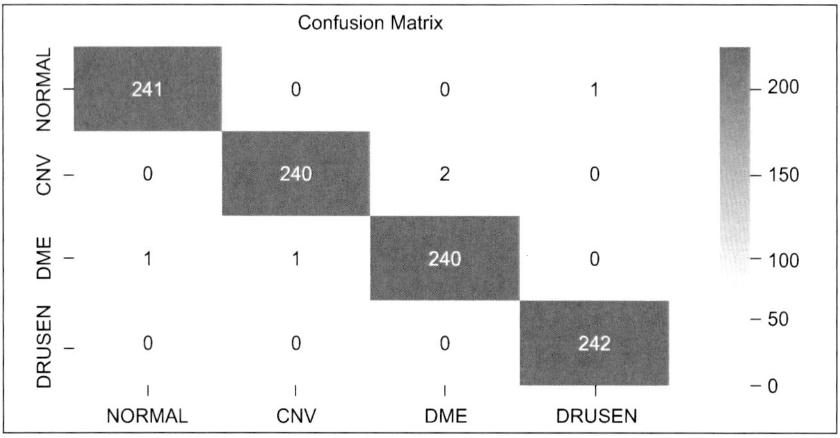

Fig. 7.15 Confusion Matrix

This image shows a confusion matrix for a multi-class classification model with four classes: NORMAL, CNV, DME, and DRUSEN. The model demonstrates excellent classification accuracy and very few errors. Misclassifications are minimal and distributed, suggesting no major confusion between any two particular classes. This confusion matrix validates the high F1-scores shown in performance metrics Tables 7.1 and 7.2.

Conclusion

This study employed SRGAN—a Generative AI model—to enhance retinal OCT datasets with 2000 synthetic images per class (CNV, DRUSEN, DME, NORMAL) for multiclass classification. A CNN trained on this augmented dataset achieved near-perfect results, with macro and weighted averages for precision, recall, and F1-score at 99%. The balanced performance across all classes highlights the model's robustness and generalization. The proposed GenAI-powered pipeline offers a scalable and accurate solution for early detection and diagnosis of retinal diseases.

References

[1] Sai, S., Gaur, A., Sai, R., Chamola, V., Guizani, M. et al. (2024). Generative ai for transformative healthcare: A comprehensive study of emerging models, applications, case studies and limitations. *IEEE Access*.

[2] Chatterjee, S., Fruhling, A., Kotiadis, K. and Gartner, D. (2024). Towards new frontiers of healthcare systems research using artificial intelligence and generative AI. *Health Systems*, 13(4), 263–273.

[3] MULUKUNTLA, S. (2022). Generative ai-benefits, limitations, potential risks and challenges in healthcare industry. *EPH-International Journal of Medical and Health Science*, 8(4), 1–9.

[4] Ghebrehiwet, I., Zaki, N., Damseh, R. and Mohamad, M.S. (2024). Revolutionizing personalized medicine with generative AI: a systematic review. *Artificial Intelligence Review*, 57(5), 128.

[5] Kim, K., Cho, K., Jang, R., Kyung, S., Lee, S. et al. (2024). Updated primer on generative artificial intelligence and large language models in medical imaging for medical professionals. *Korean Journal of Radiology*, 25(3), 224.

[6] Chen, Y. and Esmaeilzadeh, P. (2024). Generative AI in medical practice: in-depth exploration of privacy and security challenges. *Journal of Medical Internet Research*, 26, e53008.

[7] Sathya, D., Sudha, V. and Jagadeesan, D. (2020). Application of machine learning techniques in healthcare. In *Handbook of Research on Applications and Implementations of Machine Learning Techniques* (pp. 289–304). IGI global.

[8] Suri, B., Taneja, S. and Kalsi, H.S. (2020). Decision Making with BI in Healthcare Domain. In *Big Data Analytics and Intelligence: A Perspective for Health Care* (pp. 153–172). Emerald Publishing Limited.

[9] Xu, R. and Wang, Z. (2024). ChatGPT in Healthcare from the Perspective of Digital Media: Applications, Opportunities and Challenges. *Heliyon*.

[10] Meskó, B. and Topol, E.J. (2023). The imperative for regulatory oversight of large language models (or generative AI) in healthcare. *NPJ digital medicine*, 6(1), 120.

[11] Abbas, R. and Gu, N. (2023). Improving deep learning-based image super-resolution with residual learning and perceptual loss using SRGAN model. *Soft Computing*, 27(21), 16041–16057.

[12] Nova, K. (2023). Generative AI in healthcare: advancements in electronic health records, facilitating medical languages, and personalized patient care. *Journal of Advanced Analytics in Healthcare Management*, 7(1), 115–131.

[13] Yu, P., Xu, H., Hu, X. and Deng, C. (2023, October). Leveraging generative AI and large Language models: a Comprehensive Roadmap for Healthcare Integration. In *Healthcare* (Vol. 11, No. 20, p. 2776). MDPI.

[14] Kumar, A.J.S., Chong, R.S., Crowston, J.G., Chua, J., Bujor, I. et al. (2022). Evaluation of generative adversarial networks for high-resolution synthetic image generation of circumpapillary optical coherence tomography images for glaucoma. *JAMA ophthalmology*, 140(10), 974–981.

[15] Taneja, S., Suri, B., Kumar, A., Chowdhry, A., Kumar, H. et al (2023). PUPC-GANs: A Novel Image Conversion Model using Modified CycleGANs in Healthcare. *Recent Advances in Computer Science and Communications (Formerly: Recent Patents on Computer Science)*, 16(7), 66–73.

[16] Aljohani, A. and Alharbe, N. (2022). Generating synthetic images for healthcare with novel deep pix2pix gan. *Electronics*, 11(21), 3470.

[17] Chopra, P., Junath, N., Singh, S.K., Khan, S., Sugumar, R. et al (2022). [Retracted] Cyclic GAN Model to Classify Breast Cancer Data for Pathological Healthcare Task. *BioMed Research International*, 2022(1), 6336700.

[18] Tufail, H., Ahad, A., Puspitasari, I., Shayea, I., Coelho, P.J. et al (2024). Deep Learning in Smart Healthcare: A GAN-based Approach for Imbalanced Alzheimer's Disease Classification. *Procedia Computer Science*, 241, 146–153.

[19] Fatima, N. and Kapoor, S. (2024, November). GAN-Powered Predictive Analytics for the Detection and Diagnosis of Tuberculosis. In *2024 3rd Edition of IEEE Delhi Section Flagship Conference (DELCON)* (pp. 1–7). IEEE.

[20] Kermany, D., Zhang, K. and Goldbaum, M. Large Dataset of Labeled Optical Coherence Tomography (OCT) and Chest X-ray Images. *Mendeley Data.* 2018, 3, pp. 10–17632.

[21] Yang, J., Fong, S., Wang, H., Hu, Q., Lin, C. et al. Artificial intelligence in ophthalmopathy and ultra-wide field image: A survey. *Expert Syst. Appl.* 2021, 182, 115068.

8 Implementing Robotics and Generative AI in Healthcare: Challenges and Opportunities

Raman Dhand[1*], Disha Tuteja[2*], Hemang Vats[3] and Stephin George[4]

Robotics and generative AI are transforming healthcare by enhancing clinical efficiency, improving patient outcomes, and optimizing workflows. Their growing adoption in surgery, diagnostics, recovery, and administration supports faster decisions and better patient care. However, challenges persist—particularly around ethics, privacy, interoperability, and staff training. Addressing these will unlock their full potential, enabling safer, more effective, and patient-centric healthcare systems.

8.1 Introduction

Rising treatment costs and a shortage of medical professionals are driving a shift toward smarter, tech-enabled healthcare solutions [1]. Generative AI and robotics are emerging as transformative tools poised to reshape service delivery and future healthcare practices. Robotics is advancing swiftly in rehabilitation and minimally invasive surgery, offering precision and automation that reduce risks and accelerate recovery. Robotic arms deliver enhanced reach and flexibility, especially in complex procedures beyond human capability. Generative AI supports personalized treatment planning, risk assessment, scenario simulation, and emergency readiness by analyzing large datasets [2,3]. Its growing impact spans precision-driven fields such as drug development, medical imaging, personalized care, and predictive analytics—collectively advancing a proactive and efficient healthcare ecosystem.

According to Grand View Research, the global AI healthcare market is projected to grow from USD 26.57 billion in 2024 to USD 187.69 billion by 2030, with a CAGR of 38.62% [4]. Figure 8.1 visualizes this market trajectory.

The healthcare sector has heavily invested in AI-powered solutions, with 75% of major organizations adopting or expanding generative AI use in operations [5]. GenAI's rapid progress is evident from studies showing ChatGPT outperforming physicians on performance and patient-specific metrics [6]. This chapter reviews the expanding role of robotics and generative AI in healthcare, highlighting their

[1-4] ECE, Guru Tegh Bahadur Institute of Technology, New Delhi, India.
E-mail: hemangvats05@gmail.com[3]; georgestephin16@gmail.com[4]
* Corresponding author(s): raman19.gtbit@gmail.com[1]; dishatuteja20@gmail.com[2]

DOI: 10.1201/9781003670582-8

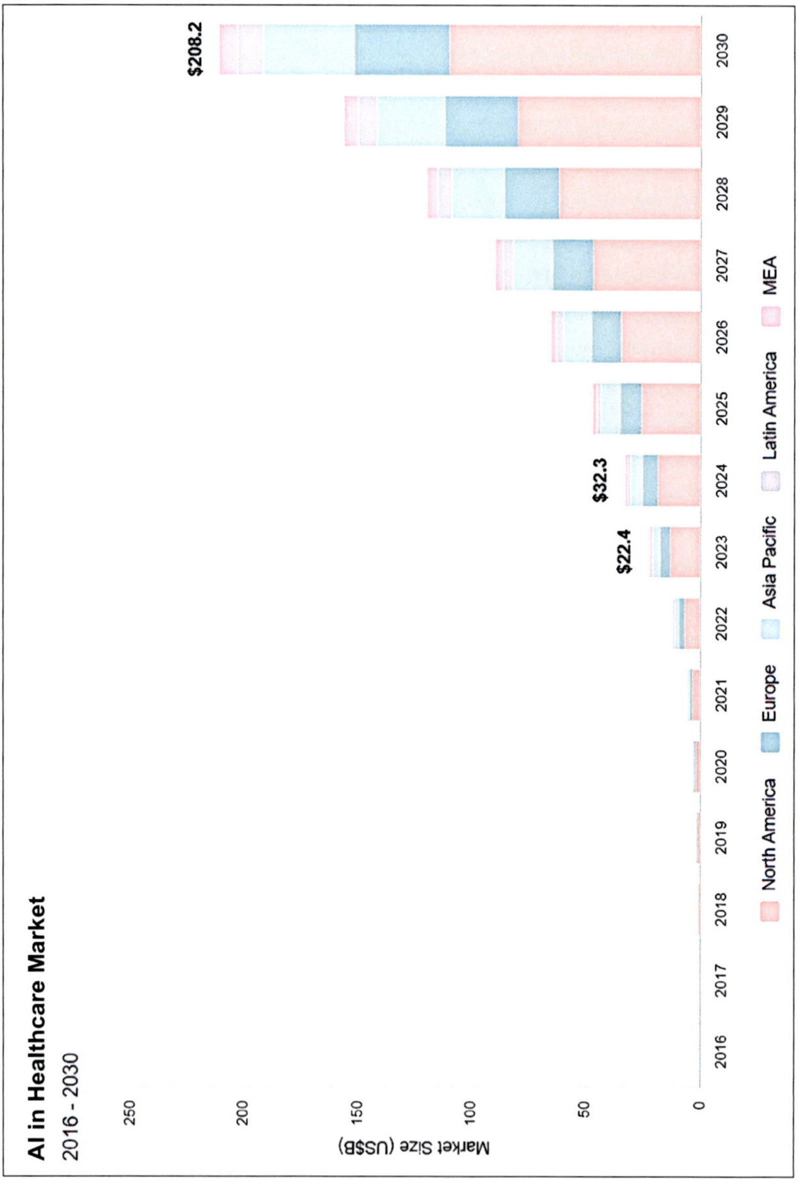

Fig. 8.1 Global AI in healthcare market.

potential to improve patient outcomes, streamline operations, and reduce costs [7]. Technologies like robotic surgery and AI-driven diagnostics are reshaping care delivery. However, challenges—including diagnostic errors, data privacy risks, algorithmic bias, and decision-making ambiguity—raise concerns about trust, safety, and equity. The chapter reviews current deployments of robotics and generative AI in healthcare, identifies key research and implementation gaps, and outlines future directions. It highlights ethical, practical, and policy considerations for developers, clinicians, and decision-makers to responsibly advance these technologies.

8.2 Literature Review

Healthcare professionals rely on diverse data and clinical expertise to devise effective treatment plans. Robotics and generative AI are reshaping healthcare by cutting costs, boosting operational efficiency, and improving care delivery [7]. Robotics streamlines routine tasks and enhances surgical precision [8], while generative AI supports drug discovery, simulations, and predictive diagnostics using comprehensive medical databases. AI excels in trend detection, disease prediction, and personalized care planning [9]. Additionally, generative AI automates tasks like scheduling and prescriptions, boosting healthcare productivity [10]. These advancements contribute to improved patient outcomes, faster recoveries, and reduced costs [11]. AI enables early disease detection and personalized treatments by processing extensive health data. However, deploying AI and robotics also raises concerns—including algorithmic bias, data privacy, workforce displacement, and ethical decision-making risks [12]. Responsible integration demands transparency, accountability, and safeguards for fairness and human oversight in clinical contexts [13].

Despite their promise, AI and robotics face key implementation hurdles—namely, integration with existing healthcare systems and clinical reliability [14]. Cybersecurity concerns, outdated protocols, and cost-related access disparities further limit adoption, especially in low-resource settings. Addressing ethical, technical, and financial challenges is crucial for equitable integration and sustainable impact.

8.3 Research Gaps in the Implementation of Robotics and Generative AI in Healthcare

Robotics and generative AI are rapidly advancing healthcare through faster decision-making, personalized treatments, and streamlined workflows. However, key research gaps must be addressed to ensure responsible, safe, and inclusive adoption across diverse clinical settings.

Algorithmic bias remains a critical challenge in AI systems, driven by non-representative training data—what goes in is what comes out [14]. Without diversity across socioeconomic, racial, ethnic, and gender lines, outputs risk unfair or inaccurate recommendations. Targeted research is needed to ensure data quality, equity, and reliability in clinical decision support. Algorithmic bias remains a critical challenge in AI systems, driven by non-representative training data—what goes in is what comes out [14]. Without diversity across socioeconomic, racial, ethnic, and gender lines, outputs risk unfair or inaccurate recommendations. Targeted research is needed to ensure data quality, equity, and reliability in clinical decision support.

Integrating AI and robotics into hospital workflows remains challenging due to infrastructure demands and compatibility issues with EHR and clinical systems. Poor integration can disrupt processes, highlighting the need for multidisciplinary research to ensure seamless, efficient deployment in daily healthcare operations. The human–technology interface in healthcare requires attention, as many clinicians lack data science experience. Complex systems may erode trust and hinder adoption. AI and robotics must be intuitive and user-friendly, supported by clear training resources, dashboards, and visual tools suited for time-constrained clinical settings. Legal and ethical challenges—such as data ownership, privacy, and liability for AI-driven decisions—must be addressed before widespread adoption. Questions around informed consent, autonomy, and algorithmic transparency remain unresolved. Additionally, disparities in access pose a risk of widening the digital divide, especially in under-resourced settings. For robotics and generative AI to deliver global impact, they must be adaptable and scalable across diverse healthcare environments. Research must also examine how AI affects healthcare professionals—potentially reducing task burdens but raising concerns about job roles if reskilling is lacking. Understanding its impact on workplace dynamics, job satisfaction, and professional identity is vital for building trust and long-term acceptance. Engaging patients in the research process is vital, yet their perspectives on AI and robotics remain underexplored. Integrating their feedback into design and testing enhances trust, usability, and adoption. Inclusive research and continuous collaboration can drive responsible, patient-centered innovation in healthcare.

8.4 Proposed Methodology

The flowchart in Figure 8.2 shows a clear overview of the approach used for the proposed method.

Now that we have a fundamental understanding of the steps, let us examine each one in detail to understand its function and significance.

8.4.1 Define Research Objectives and Scope

A thorough literature review on robotics and generative artificial intelligence in healthcare begins by defining clear research objectives and scope. Key questions should address their benefits and limitations, integration requirements, and ethical, legal, and regulatory considerations essential for responsible implementation.

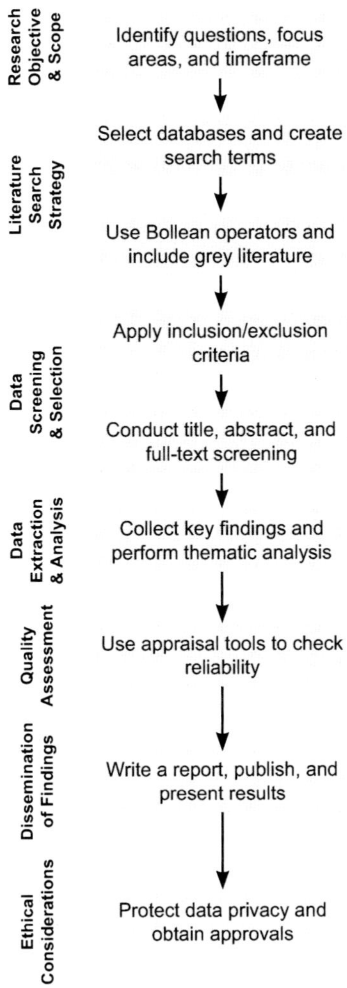

Fig. 8.2 Flowchart depicting proposed methodology.

The evaluation should assess how robotics and generative AI improve patient outcomes, service delivery, and cost efficiency. A defined scope should focus on specific applications—such as telemedicine, AI diagnostics, robotic surgery, or patient monitoring—and targeted healthcare settings, including hospitals, clinics, or home-based care. Setting a 5–10 year timeframe for the literature review helps ensure relevance. Defining the geographic scope—regional or global—enhances contextual understanding. A clear goal and scope keep the review focused, manageable, and aligned with research objectives.

8.4.2 Literature Search Strategy

A systematic literature search is essential for sourcing reliable research. Key databases—Google Scholar, ACM Digital Library, IEEE Xplore, Web of Science, PubMed, and Scopus—provide access to extensive scholarly content on robotics, AI, and healthcare. To capture a broad range of relevant studies, use keywords covering robotics (e.g., surgical robots), AI (e.g., machine learning, generative AI), and healthcare applications (e.g., diagnosis, treatment). Boolean operators (AND, OR, NOT) refine or expand search precision within these parameters. Alongside peer-reviewed journals and conference papers, grey literature—such as government reports, white papers, and policy briefs—offers practical insights into current issues often overlooked in academia. Including these sources ensures comprehensive coverage and enhances analytical depth through systematic, well-structured searches.

8.4.3 Data Screening and Selection

A rigorous two-step screening process ensures inclusion of high-quality, relevant studies. Initial title and abstract review filters out non-essential material; full-text analysis follows to confirm alignment with inclusion criteria. Preference is given to empirical research, systematic reviews, and peer-reviewed publications, while opinion pieces and uncited articles are excluded to maintain academic integrity.

8.4.4 Data Extraction and Analysis

After selecting relevant studies, data should be meticulously extracted using standardized forms to capture objectives, methods, key findings, limitations, and ethical considerations—ensuring consistency and organization. Thematic analysis helps identify recurring patterns and insights aligned with research questions. By grouping findings under major themes and highlighting research gaps, it enables clear interpretation and supports a foundation for future discussions and recommendations.

8.4.5 Quality Assessment

Assessing article quality strengthens the reliability of a literature review. Tools like the Joanna Briggs Institute Critical Appraisal Tool support standardized evaluation. Key indicators—study design, sample size, data collection, and analysis—help determine validity. Excluding subpar studies ensures the review is based on robust, credible evidence.

8.4.6 Dissemination of Findings

The final step involves sharing key insights, challenges, and opportunities uncovered in the review. Findings should inform future research, influence policy, and guide clinical practice. Dissemination through conferences, peer-reviewed publications, and stakeholder engagement ensures broad impact and supports safe, effective adoption of robotics and generative AI in healthcare.

8.4.7 Ethical Concerns

Ethical concerns must remain central throughout the research process. Ensuring patient confidentiality and data safety is critical, especially when handling sensitive medical information. Researchers must document each step—from data selection to analysis—to uphold accountability and enable reproducibility [15]. Researchers must obtain ethical approval from their institution's review board or ethics committee before initiating the study to ensure compliance with established ethical standards. Prioritizing ethical considerations enables researchers to better understand the strengths and limitations of generative AI and robotics in medicine. This foundation supports the development of safe, efficient, and reliable systems. Responsible research ensures future AI applications benefit both patients and healthcare professionals.

Fig. 8.3 Challenges of AI & Robotics in healthcare.

8.5 Key Findings & Analysis: Implementing Robotics & Generative AI in Healthcare

8.5.1 Challenges

- **Privacy and Ethics Matter:** Robotics and generative AI present ethical challenges, particularly around patient confidentiality and data security as they become routine in medical practice. Trust hinges on how safely and accountably these systems operate. While they support clinical decisions, they must complement—not replace—human judgment and compassion. Future efforts should focus on balancing technological advancement with ethical, patient-centered care [16].
- **Establishing Trust Through Comprehension:** One of the problems is that many people do not understand the workings. Many patients remain skeptical of AI in healthcare due to limited understanding and a preference for face-to-face care. Studies show greater trust in human consultants, viewing AI as a supportive tool—not a replacement [17]. Building trust requires transparency about AI's role in augmenting, not replacing, clinical expertise. Patient comfort is essential for successful integration.
- **Technical Issues:** Transitioning to AI-based systems faces significant technical hurdles, including costly hardware (GPUs, FPGAs) and limited user training among healthcare staff. AI's "black-box" nature and reliance on unstructured data reduce trust and transparency. Poor interoperability with EHRs and insufficient high-quality training data further hinder reliable deployment. Addressing these challenges is essential for safe, effective integration of AI and robotics in clinical practice [16].
- **AI Adoption in Clinical Care:** As AI takes on greater decision-making roles in healthcare, concerns grow around diminished clinical judgment, privacy risks, and lack of accountability in AI systems. Patients fear reduced human oversight, while professionals worry about decreased autonomy. Hesitation to challenge AI recommendations may impact outcomes, highlighting the need for careful integration into daily practice [17]. Limited familiarity with AI tools and varying digital literacy across healthcare professionals can hinder adoption. Effective integration requires comprehensive training, support, and guidance to ensure clinicians are confident and comfortable with these technologies [18].
- **Challenges of Regulatory, Cost, and Acceptance in Surgery:** Successful AI-assisted surgeries rely on well-trained, confident surgeons. Without proper training, errors and uncertainty may arise. Regulatory approval remains a challenge due to the lack of safety standards for AI tools. High costs—equipment, maintenance, and training—can deter adoption, though they may benefit high-volume institutions. Patient and clinician acceptance is vital, requiring transparency, education, and trust-building to ease discomfort and highlight real-world benefits [19].

8.5.2 Opportunities

- **Technology advancements:** Technological innovations are reshaping healthcare, especially with an expected doubling of the elderly population by 2050. Socially assistive robots and AI-powered tools are addressing growing care demands by enhancing elder support and promoting self-management. Sensor-based devices allow heart failure patients to monitor their health from home. In medical training, AI improves image analysis and decision-making, while VR simulators offer safe environments for surgical practice. Beyond clinical settings, modern apps empower individuals to actively manage health and fitness.
- **AI-Powered Diagnosis and Monitoring:** AI is revolutionizing patient monitoring and diagnosis through predictive analytics and personalized care. Misdiagnosis contributes to around 80,000 deaths annually, often due to system overload and incomplete data—AI helps minimize such errors with faster, more accurate detection [20]. Its role in early cancer diagnosis and disease tracking improves outcomes and lowers costs. Emerging tools like smart textiles, nanorobots, and digital pills support comprehensive health monitoring, from wound care to emotional well-being. Predictive models further identify high-risk cases and anticipate deterioration, enabling timely intervention and efficient treatment [18].
- **Accuracy and precision:** Surgical robots enhance precision beyond human capability, enabling stable, controlled movements that reduce errors and improve outcomes—even in prolonged or intricate procedures. Advanced features like 3D visualization and superior dexterity also aid quicker recovery. AI software accelerates tasks like mitosis rate analysis in cancer diagnostics, improving accuracy and freeing clinicians for more critical care. As AI systems continually learn from vast datasets, their diagnostic performance now rivals or surpasses human specialists. Ongoing research suggests AI will increasingly support clinicians by identifying overlooked areas and reducing treatment errors [21].
- **Minimally Invasive Surgery Revolutions in Surgery:** Robotic surgery enhances complex procedures by enabling minimally invasive techniques using precise, sensor-equipped robotic arms. These systems allow for smaller incisions, reduced blood loss, less physical trauma, and faster recovery. Their advanced dexterity improves control in tight surgical spaces and lowers complication risks. Widely adopted, robotic systems not only elevate surgical outcomes but also reduce physical strain on surgeons.
- **Robotic Reach and Dexterity for More Sustainable Surgery:** Robotic surgical arms now allow access to previously unreachable areas, enabling precise movements even in confined or complex regions. Their flexibility reduces surgeon fatigue and improves procedural outcomes, particularly in high-precision surgeries [22]. Complementing this, AI software enhances surgical planning and decision-making with accuracy that rivals or exceeds

human experts. By learning from vast medical data, these systems help reduce errors and identify critical issues early, making surgery safer and more efficient [21].

- **Reducing Surgeon Fatigue by Robotic Support:** Robotic systems significantly reduce surgeon fatigue during long or complex procedures by providing spinal support and stable positioning. Operating from a console eliminates the need for prolonged standing, easing physical strain and minimizing wear and tear, which enhances comfort and focus throughout surgery. Robotic support helps surgeons maintain prolonged focus and precision by reducing fatigue, which in turn boosts stamina and consistency in care. Fewer errors and improved surgical quality lead to better patient outcomes overall.
- **Phases of drug development:** Generative AI is increasingly vital to drug development, supporting tasks like molecule generation, property prediction, virtual screening, synthesis planning, and drug repurposing. Virtual screening, in particular, accelerates candidate identification while cutting costs. Researchers are exploring how AI can create novel chemical structures for early-stage innovation. As development advances, digital twins—virtual models of biological systems—are gaining momentum, with generative AI expected to drive their integration [23, 24]. These technologies streamline the path from discovery to market by optimizing candidate evaluation and repurposing. Experts widely agree on AI's future role, despite ongoing challenges in automation and system integration [25].
- **Virtual Health Assistant:** AI-powered virtual health assistants (VHAs) are reshaping healthcare by offering round-the-clock access—especially benefiting rural and underserved populations. VHAs interpret symptoms, provide tailored care guidance, and assist with referrals when needed. They also promote treatment adherence by managing medications, flagging side effects, and issuing reminders. Remote monitoring through AI further boosts accessibility, enabling early diagnosis and timely intervention without frequent hospital visits. These advancements make care more proactive, personalized, and convenient [26]. Robotics and generative AI are driving a transformative shift in healthcare, enhancing patient care, productivity, and clinical outcomes. Their benefits span AI-assisted diagnosis, robotic surgeries, personalized treatments, and streamlined administration. Yet, challenges persist—ethical concerns like algorithmic bias, data privacy, and job displacement require robust safeguards and equitable decision-making. Technically, these systems demand reliable data, infrastructure integration, and ongoing maintenance. Successful adoption hinges on collaboration among clinicians, engineers, data experts, ethicists, and policymakers. With responsible implementation, these technologies can catalyze lasting advancements in pharmacy and medicine [27].

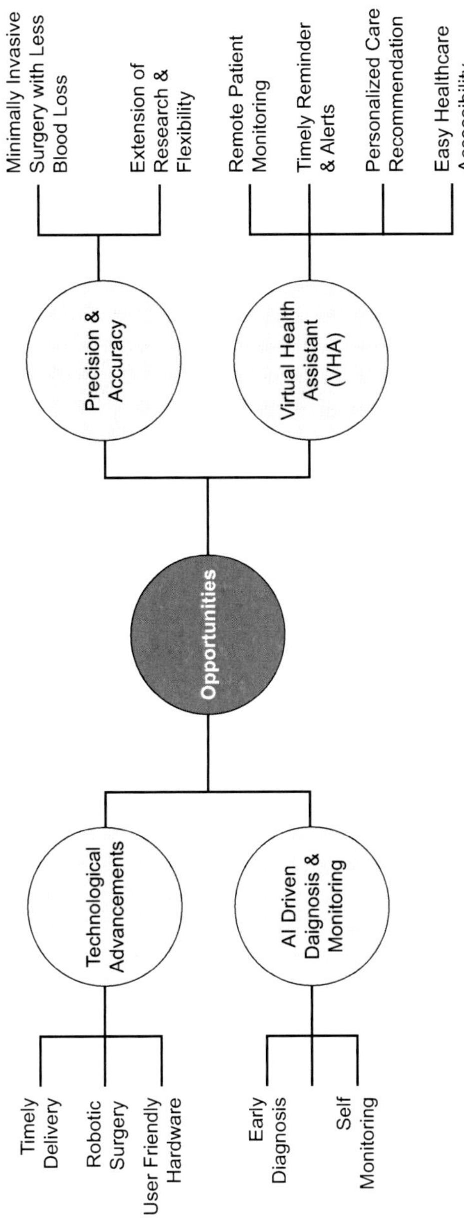

Fig. 8.4 Opportunities for AI and Robotics in healthcare.

8.6 Future Scope of Implementing Robotics and Generative AI in Healthcare

The integration of robotics and generative AI into healthcare is set to revolutionize diagnostics, treatment personalization, and overall care delivery—enhancing precision, efficiency, and patient outcomes. AI-driven precision medicine is reshaping healthcare by tailoring treatments to individual environmental, lifestyle, and genetic factors. This personalized approach boosts therapeutic effectiveness and reduces the risk of adverse side effects—marking a major leap in medical innovation. Generative AI is poised to transform drug discovery by rapidly designing novel molecules, predicting therapeutic effects, and identifying viable targets—far beyond traditional methods. More broadly, AI is driving global healthcare innovation through enhanced diagnostics, smarter decision-making, accelerated research, and support for public health initiatives. Supercomputing underpins AI advancements by tackling complex scientific challenges and processing large healthcare datasets, especially in drug design and discovery. Robotic process automation (RPA) further streamlines pharmacy and clinical workflows by automating repetitive tasks like prescription filling and claims processing—boosting operational efficiency and enabling greater focus on patient-centred care [27]. Robotics technologies are enhancing minimally invasive surgeries with improved precision, fewer complications, and shorter recovery times—demonstrated by systems like the da Vinci Surgical System [28]. They also support rehabilitation by aiding physical therapy and post-surgical recovery. The "da Vinci Surgical System" by Intuitive Surgical is a state-of-the-art robotic platform enabling highly precise, minimally invasive procedures across specialties such as urology, gynecology, cardiothoracic, and general surgery. It facilitates delicate operations that exceed the capabilities of traditional open or laparoscopic techniques [28]. The da Vinci system comprises three components: the surgeon's console, patient-side cart, and vision system. From the console, surgeons control robotic arms via hand and foot inputs, with motions scaled for precision. The patient-side cart holds the robotic instruments and a high-definition 3D endoscopic camera, enabling detailed visualization and precise surgical actions. The da Vinci system's vision component offers a magnified 3D view of the surgical field, allowing surgeons to clearly see fine anatomical structures and operate with enhanced spatial awareness during complex procedures.

The table below represents the benefits of robotic-assisted therapies:

AI-powered disease management and diagnostics support early detection and timely care, with generative AI improving scan accuracy for conditions like cancer and cardiovascular disease [28]. Remote monitoring systems enable continuous assessments, allowing healthcare providers to respond quickly and proactively. AI improves healthcare efficiency and access by streamlining operations and enabling care in underserved areas through telemedicine [14]. Its adoption depends largely on supportive financial reimbursement models. AI also automates routine tasks like billing, claims, and scheduling, allowing healthcare staff to prioritize patient care

Benefits	*Description*
Intensifying rehabilitation programs	Robotic systems may allow for more frequent and longer therapy sessions.
Assistance based on needs	Robots can provide varying levels of support depending on the patient's abilities.
Feedback delivery on the efficacy of the rehabilitation program	Robots can track progress and provide data-driven feedback on treatment effectiveness.
Quantification of the patient's movement performance	Robotic systems can precisely measure and record various aspects of a patient's movements.

Fig. 8.5 Benefits of Robotic Therapies.

[29]. Breakthroughs in robotics and AI signal an exciting future for healthcare. Elderly and chronically ill patients will benefit from smart robotic and virtual assistants, while AI-powered analytics are driving collaborative, data-informed clinical decisions. Widespread adoption of digital health solutions hinges on their scalability, financial sustainability, and public acceptance [27]. Addressing algorithmic bias, data privacy, and ethical use is essential, supported by robust regulatory frameworks. Ultimately, responsible AI integration requires public trust and equitable access across all regions and communities.

Conclusion

Robotics and AI are transforming healthcare across diagnostics, treatment, surgery, and drug discovery—driving greater precision, personalization, and efficiency. Systems like the da Vinci Surgical System enable minimally invasive procedures with better recovery, reduced trauma, and enhanced surgeon comfort. Generative AI improves imaging analysis for early disease detection, while remote monitoring expands access in low-resource settings. Robotic process automation streamlines pharmacy operations, and supercomputing supports large-scale drug development by accelerating molecular analysis.However, ethical concerns such as data privacy, informed consent, and algorithmic bias must be addressed. Ensuring equitable access, clear regulations, and public trust is essential. Successful integration also requires continuous training, collaboration, and strong governance. Ultimately, AI and robotics should complement—not replace—human judgment to advance safe, patient-centered care [28].

Human values like empathy, ethics, and compassion must remain central as AI and robotics reshape healthcare. This technological revolution should be carefully guided to support—not replace—clinical judgment. Thoughtfully designed, these tools can enhance care delivery and healing while preserving the vital human connection at the heart of medicine.

Declarations

- The authors received no specific funding for this study.
- The authors declare that they have no conflicts of interest to report regarding the present study.
- No human subject or animals are involved in the research.
- All authors have mutually consented to participate.
- All the authors have given their consent for publishing this paper.

Authors declare that all the data sources used in the design and production of this work have been mentioned

References

[1] Mohammed Yousef Shaheen. Applications of Artificial Intelligence (AI) in healthcare: A review. ScienceOpen Preprints. 2021. DOI: 10.14293/S2199-1006.1.SOR-.PPVRY8K.v1.

[2] Generative AI use cases | Google Cloud. Available from: https://cloud.google.com/use-cases/generative-ai?hl=en. Accessed May 31, 2024.

[3] AI future of healthcare. Available from: https://www.asianhhm.com/information-technology/ai-future-of-healthcare. Accessed May 31, 2024.

[4] AI In Healthcare Market Size, Share, And Trends Analysis Report By Component (Hardware, Services), By Application, By End Use, By Technology, By Region (North America, Europe, APAC, Latin America, MEA), And Segment Forecasts, 2025–2030,Report ID: GVR-3-68038-951-7.

[5] Generative AI in Healthcare. Deloitte. Available from: https://www2.deloitte.com/us/en/pages/life-sciences-and-health-care/articles/generative-ai-in-healthcare.html. Accessed May 31, 2024.

[6] Study Finds ChatGPT Outperforms Physicians in High-Quality, Empathetic Answers to Patient Questions. UC San Diego Today. Available from: https://today.ucsd.edu/story/study-finds-chatgpt-outperforms-physicians-in-high-quality-empathetic-answers-to-patient-questions. Accessed May 31, 2024.

[7] Next-Gen Surgery: AI Robots Leading the Way in Healthcare, October 2024, Archives of Community Medicine and Public Health 10(4):013-017,DOI:10.17352/2455-5479.000210.

[8] Morgan AA, Abdi J, Syed MAQ, Kohen GE, Barlow P, Vizcaychipi MP. Robots in Healthcare: a Scoping Review. *Curr Robot Rep*. 2022;3(4):271–280. doi: 10.1007/s43154-022-00095-4. Epub 2022 Oct 22. PMID: 36311256; PMCID: PMC9589563.

[9] Chatterjee, S. and Das S. "Advancements in robotic surgery: innovations, challenges and future prospects," January 2024, *Journal of Robotic Surgery* 18(1), DOI:10.1007/s11701-023-01801-w.

[10] Mohamed Khalifa, Mona Albadawy, Artificial Intelligence for Clinical Prediction: Exploring Key Domains and Essential Functions, Computer Methods and Programs in Biomedicine Update, Volume 5, 2024, 100148, ISSN 2666-9900, https://doi.org/10.1016/j.cmpbup.2024.100148.

[11] Devi, Kharibam & Alghamdi, Wajdi & N, Divya & Alkhayyat, Ahmed & Sayyora, Artikbaeva & Sathish, T.. (2023). Artificial Intelligence in Healthcare: Diagnosis, Treatment, and Prediction. E3S Web of Conferences. 399. 10.1051/e3sconf/202339904043.

[12] Elendu C, Amaechi DC, Elendu TC, Jingwa KA, Okoye OK, John Okah M, Ladele JA, Farah AH, Alimi HA. Ethical implications of AI and robotics in healthcare: A review. Medicine (Baltimore). 2023 Dec 15;102(50):e36671. doi: 10.1097/MD.0000000000036671. PMID: 38115340; PMCID: PMC10727550.

[13] Harishbhai Tilala M, Kumar Chenchala P, Choppadandi A, Kaur J, Naguri S, Saoji R, Devaguptapu B. Ethical Considerations in the Use of Artificial Intelligence and Machine Learning in Health Care: A Comprehensive Review. Cureus. 2024 Jun 15;16(6):e62443. doi: 10.7759/cureus.62443. PMID: 39011215; PMCID: PMC11249277.

[14] Singh RP, Hom GL, Abramoff MD, Campbell JP, Chiang MF; AAO Task Force on Artificial Intelligence. Current Challenges and Barriers to Real-World Artificial Intelligence Adoption for the Healthcare System, Provider, and the Patient. Transl Vis Sci Technol. 2020 Aug 11;9(2):45. doi: 10.1167/tvst.9.2.45. PMID: 32879755; PMCID: PMC7443115.

[15] Prager EM, Chambers KE, Plotkin JL, McArthur DL, Bandrowski AE, Bansal N, Martone ME, Bergstrom HC, Bespalov A, Graf C. Improving transparency and scientific rigor in academic publishing. Cancer Rep (Hoboken). 2019 Feb;2(1):e1150. doi: 10.1002/cnr2.1150. Epub 2018 Dec 2. PMID: 32721132; PMCID: PMC7941525.

[16] Wubineh BZ, Deriba FG, Woldeyohannis MM. Exploring the opportunities and challenges of implementing artificial intelligence in healthcare: A systematic literature review. Urol Oncol. 2024 Mar;42(3):48-56. doi: 10.1016/j.urolonc.2023.11.019. Epub 2023 Dec 14. PMID: 38101991.

[17] Scott IA, Carter SM, Coiera E. Exploring stakeholder attitudes towards AI in clinical practice. BMJ Health Care Inform. 2021 Dec;28(1):e100450. doi: 10.1136/bmjhci-2021-100450. PMID: 34887331; PMCID: PMC8663096.

[18] Hazarika I. Artificial intelligence: opportunities and implications for the health workforce *International Health*, Volume 12, Issue 4, July 2020, Pages 241–245, https://doi.org/10.1093/inthealth/ihaa007.

[19] Deo N. and Anjankar A. Artificial Intelligence With Robotics in Healthcare: A Narrative Review of Its Viability in India. *Cureus*. 2023 May 23;15(5):e39416. doi: 10.7759/cureus.39416. PMID: 37362504; PMCID: PMC10287569.

[20] Bera, K., Schalper, K.A. and Rimm, D.L. Artificial intelligence in digital pathology—new tools for diagnosis and precision oncology. *Nat Rev Clin Oncol* 16, 703–715 (2019). https://doi.org/10.1038/s41571-019-0252-y.

[21] Lee, D. and Yoon, S.N. (2021). Application of Artificial Intelligence-Based Technologies in the Healthcare Industry: Opportunities and Challenges. *International Journal of Environmental Research and Public Health*, *18*(1), 271. https://doi.org/10.3390/ijerph18010271.

[22] Padhan S, Mohapatra A, Ramasamy S, et al. (August 03, 2023) Artificial Intelligence (AI) and Robotics in Elderly Healthcare: Enabling Independence and Quality of Life. Cureus 15(8): e42905. doi:10.7759/cureus.42905.

[23] Bordukova, M., Makarov, N., Rodriguez-Esteban, R., Schmich, F., and Menden, M.P. et al. (2024). Generative artificial intelligence empowers digital twins in drug discovery and clinical trials. *Expert opinion on drug discovery*, 19(1), 33–42.

[24] Gangwal A., Ansari A., Ahmad I., Azad A.K., Kumarasamy, V. et al. Generative artificial intelligence in drug discovery: basic framework, recent advances, challenges, and opportunities. Front Pharmacol. 2024 Feb 7;15:1331062. doi: 10.3389/fphar.2024.1331062. PMID: 38384298; PMCID: PMC10879372.

[25] Chan, H.C.S., Shan, H., Dahoun, T., Vogel, H., and Yuan, S. (2019). Advancing Drug Discovery via Artificial Intelligence. *Trends in pharmacological sciences*, *40*(8), 592–604. https://doi.org/10.1016/j.tips.2019.06.004.

[26] Kavyanjali Reddy (2023) Advancements in Robotic Surgery: A Comprehensive Overview of Current Utilizations and Upcoming Frontiers, PMCID: PMC10784205 PMID: 38222213 2023 Dec 12;15(12):e50415. doi: 10.7759/cureus.50415

[27] Stasevych, M. and Zvarych, V. (2023). Innovative Robotic Technologies and Artificial Intelligence in Pharmacy and Medicine: Paving the Way for the Future of Health Care—A Review. *Big Data and Cognitive Computing*, 7(3), 147. https://doi.org/10.3390/bdcc7030147.

[28] Collins, F.S. and Varmus, H. (2015). A New Initiative on Precision Medicine. *The New England Journal of Medicine*, 372, 793-795. https://doi.org/10.1056/NEJMp1500523.

[29] Esteva (2019). Dermatologist-level classification of skin cancer with deep neural networks. *Nature*, 542, 115–118. https://doi.org/10.1038/nature21056.

9 Generative AI in Healthcare: Transforming Delivery and Redefining Patient–Provider Dynamics

Amritanshu Raj[1], Shilpa Gupta[2*], Renuka Sharma[3], Ayush Kaushik[4] and Ronit Mathur[5]

Generative AI is reshaping medicine through major gains in diagnostics, personalized treatments, drug discovery, and clinical workflows. Using models like Transformers, GANs, and Diffusion Models, AI rapidly analyzes complex medical data to detect anomalies in scans, tailor therapies using genetic history, and generate novel drug compounds with greater efficiency and lower costs. However, its deployment raises ethical, legal, and social concerns—including bias, lack of transparency, data privacy under HIPAA and GDPR, and risk of widening healthcare disparities. Responsible use and robust safeguards are essential to maximize benefits and minimize risks. This article explores both transformative applications and the need for ethical frameworks to guide AI's integration into modern medicine.

9.1 Introduction

Generative AI is revolutionizing healthcare by enhancing diagnostics, treatment, and research through advanced models and natural language processing (NLP) [1]. It enables rapid pattern recognition in large medical datasets, automates clinical workflows, and supports robot-assisted care. AI applications have improved medical imaging, oncogenomics, patient monitoring, and drug development—leading to fewer diagnostic errors and more personalized interventions [2]. With AI-powered tools, healthcare providers can analyze complex data swiftly, enabling earlier diagnoses and better clinical outcomes [3]. Generative AI has rapidly entered medical practice, powered by breakthroughs in deep learning and NLP. GANs enable realistic medical image synthesis and enhancement of limited datasets [4–6], while Transformer-based LLMs are revolutionizing clinical documentation and decision support. These tools offer potential for more accurate diagnosis, personalized treatment, and streamlined workflows—but also raise concerns

[1-5] Department of Computer Science and Engineering, JIMS Engineering Management Technical Campus, Greater Noida, Uttar Pradesh, India.
E-mail: rajamritanshu69@gmail.com[1]; renukas090@gmail.com[3]; kaushikayushh@gmail.com[4]; ronit.oct11@gmail.com[5]
* Corresponding author: shilpagupta21@gmail.com

DOI: 10.1201/9781003670582-9

around bias [7], interpretability [8], and the erosion of humanism in healthcare [9]. Generative AI deployment in medicine faces key challenges: data privacy, ethical concerns, and bias—demanding careful oversight to protect patient confidentiality and ensure responsible use. Against this backdrop, this work contributes by:

- Examining key pathways through which AI has impacted healthcare delivery and outcomes.
- Exploring **AI's influence** on patient–provider relationships,including communication, trust, and decision-making dynamics.
- Establishing a **rigorous mathematical foundation** underpinning AI models and algorithms used in clinical applications.
- Present ethical and practical **challenges,** supported by empirical evidence, highlighting concerns around bias, transparency, and data governance.

This chapter presents a comprehensive overview of Generative AI in healthcare. Section 2 outlines its background and relevance. Section 3 introduces key models—Transformers, GANs, and Diffusion Models—highlighting their mechanisms and medical applications. Section 4 explores real-world use cases alongside ethical, regulatory, and technical challenges. Section 5 addresses broader ethical, legal, and societal implications, concluding with an assessment of Generative AI's transformative potential in modern medicine.

9.2 Literature Review

AI has gained widespread adoption across sectors, especially in healthcare, driving intelligent product design, service innovation, and new business models—despite concerns around privacy, security, and individual rights [10]. In medicine, generative AI models like Transformers and Diffusion Models play a pivotal role in analyzing medical data, supporting imaging tasks (e.g., reconstruction, synthesis, classification), predicting protein structures, interpreting clinical notes, aiding diagnostics, and accelerating drug design. These applications have enhanced disease detection, data processing, and treatment development.This review provides a comprehensive overview of generative AI in medicine, focusing on current applications, existing limitations, and future directions to guide researchers and practitioners [11].

Natural Language Processing (NLP) is a core AI field aimed at enabling computers to understand and generate human language in natural context [12]. In healthcare, it helps extract insights from large datasets like EHRs, clinical literature, and patient-generated content [13]. NLP techniques such as named entity recognition support identification of medications, conditions, and test names [14,15], while also detecting adverse drug events from unstructured text [16]. Additionally, NLP models aid in disease prediction, enabling early intervention and better health outcomes [17].

Large language models like GPT-4 are transforming clinical documentation and patient communication. Singhal et al. (2023) showed that LLMs can generate reliable clinical notes from interviews, reducing administrative load [45]. Advances like AlphaFold 3 (2024) have improved drug-target modeling at atomic resolution, boosting drug discovery efficiency [47]. Yet, ethical challenges remain—WHO [37] called for inclusive regulatory frameworks to prevent widening healthcare inequities.

9.3 Generative AI Models in Healthcare

Generative AI has significantly advanced medical imaging, diagnostics, clinical decision-making, and drug discovery. Models such as Transformers, Diffusion Models, and GANs enable enhanced medical data analysis—supporting tasks like image synthesis, anomaly detection, and molecular generation. GPT-4 and other LLMs are increasingly used in clinical documentation for summarizing patient histories and translating medical terminology [45].

9.3.1 Transformers in Healthcare

Transformers have advanced NLP across healthcare by leveraging attention mechanisms to handle sequential data—enabling applications in EHR management, disease classification, and medical chatbots [18]. BioBERT improves biomedical text mining for drug and disease identification [19], while ClinicalAlbert enhances patient prognosis from EHR data. Vision Transformers (ViT) excel in analyzing MRI and X-ray scans, boosting diagnostic accuracy and anomaly detection [20].

9.3.2 Diffusion models in Healthcare

Diffusion models have been used to improve medical imaging by enhancing CT and MRI scans while minimizing patient radiation exposure [21]. DDPMs, in particular, have shown improved detail in low-dose CT reconstructions, boosting diagnostic accuracy [21]. They also support histopathology by generating synthetic tissue images to enrich AI datasets [22], and are being explored for tumor segmentation in MRI scans to aid early cancer detection [27].

9.3.3 Generative Adversarial Networks (GANs) in Healthcare

Generative Adversarial Networks (GANs) offer powerful capabilities in healthcare by generating synthetic data, supporting disease prediction, and identifying anomalies. Using a generator-discriminator framework, GANs produce high-resolution CT, MRI, and X-ray images—helping train deep learning models when labeled data is limited [23]. In drug discovery, models like MolGAN accelerate molecular generation for faster testing and synthesis [24]. GANs also aid in anonymizing patient data for research without compromising privacy [25]. Despite challenges like mode collapse and unstable training, ongoing work addresses these limitations to enable real-world medical applications [26].

Figure 1 illustrates how Generative AI models—Transformers, Diffusion Models, and GANs—enable key healthcare applications. Transformers enhance EHR analysis, clinical documentation, and radiology interpretation; Diffusion Models support image reconstruction and tumor detection; GANs generate synthetic medical images, assist drug discovery, and anonymize patient data. The diagram underscores their role in improving diagnostics, streamlining workflows, and advancing medical research.

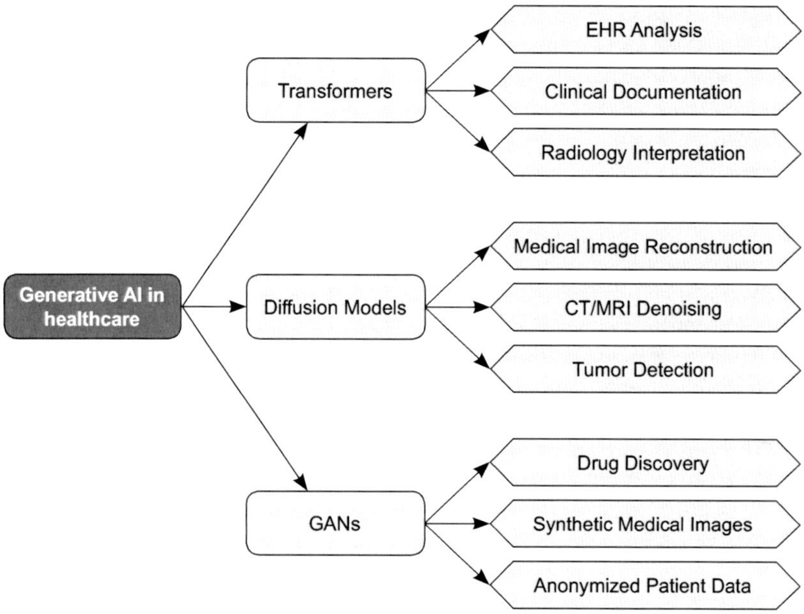

Fig. 9.1 Flow Diagram: Generative AI in Healthcare.

9.4 Applications of Generative AI in Healthcare

Generative AI is reshaping healthcare by advancing clinical decisions, diagnostics, drug development, administration, and medical imaging. This chapter highlights the impactful applications of key generative AI models across these domains.

9.4.1 Medical Imaging and Diagnostics

Generative AI significantly advances medical imaging through reconstruction, enhancement, segmentation, and synthesis. GANs and diffusion models refine low-resolution CT/MRI scans by reducing noise and preserving detail [28]. AI-driven segmentation boosts early cancer detection accuracy using MRI data [29], while GANs generate synthetic medical images to support training of deep learning disease models [30]. A study using denoising diffusion probabilistic models (DDPMs) significantly improved low-dose CT image resolution while minimizing patient radiation exposure [31]. StyleGAN3 GAN generated high-resolution brain MRI scans, enabling LIAM AI models to effectively train for brain disease recognition.

9.4.2 Personalized Medicine and Drug Discovery

AI empowers personalized medicine by simulating patient-specific conditions and tailoring therapies. Generative models analyze complex clinical and genomic data to recommend individualized treatments [1]. In drug discovery, these models enable virtual screening and molecule generation, accelerating early-stage research. Similarity measurements — such as the Tanimoto coefficient,

$$T(A, B) = \frac{|A \cap B|}{|A \cup B|} \quad ...(1)$$

are commonly applied to compare molecular structures and predict biological activity. Miotto et al. [33] further highlight how deep learning approaches can transform personalized care by integrating multi-omics data.

- AlphaFold transformed protein structure prediction by achieving atomic-level accuracy in modeling protein shapes [33].
- AI-driven molecular optimization models identified anticancer drug leads in nearly half the time of conventional methods [32].

9.4.3 Clinical Workflow Optimization

AI systems are are transforming clinical practice by automating routine tasks and optimizing workflows. Deep learning enhances EHR documentation, patient scheduling, and data handling [34], while Transformer-based conversational agents provide 24/7 support, boosting engagement [35]. Integrating these tools reduces administrative burdens and focuses clinician attention on complex care needs. Recent surveys affirm AI's role in streamlining clinical operations [36].

9.4.4 Decision Support and Multi-Modal Integration

Generative AI enables the integration of multi-modal data—genomic sequences, imaging, and clinical notes—into robust decision support systems [34,36]. This fusion enhances diagnostic precision and treatment planning for complex clinical cases [37]. Ching et al. [38] emphasize multi-modal fusion as key to personalized risk stratification and predictive analytics. Figure 9.2 segments healthcare applications of Generative AI: medical imaging holds the largest share (30%) for improving diagnostics via advanced image analysis [41]; decision support systems (25%) aid in clinical reasoning and treatment planning [39]; drug discovery (20%) accelerates molecule generation and protein prediction [40]; administration (15%) benefits from automation of coding and billing tasks [42]; and predictive analytics (10%) uses EHRs to identify at-risk patients [2]. Collectively, these highlight AI's expanding role across healthcare [3].

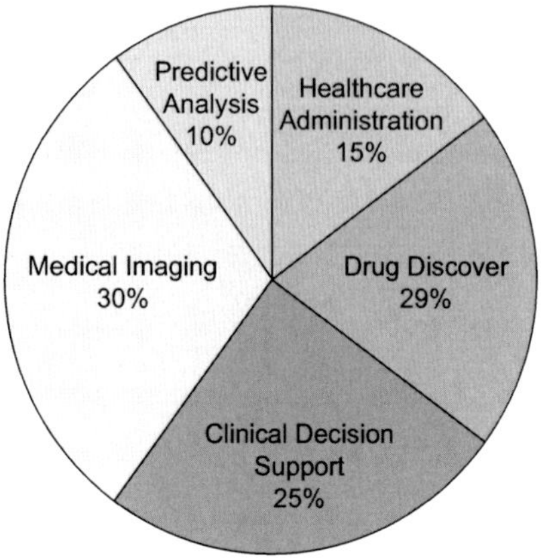

Fig. 9.2 Distribution of Generative AI Applications in Healthcare.

9.5 Ethical, Legal, and Social Implications

9.5.1 *Bias and Fairness*

AI systems rely heavily on the quality and representativeness of training data. As shown by [7], biased datasets can lead to unequal treatment outcomes. Addressing this requires robust data governance, audits, and bias-mitigation strategies [8]. Transparency and validation are essential for fair clinical use. It was further revealed by [7] that AI-based pulse oximeters misread oxygen levels in patients with darker skin, delaying care [48]—underscoring the urgency of auditing training data for fairness.

9.5.2 *Transparency and Accountability*

Transparency underpins ethical AI in healthcare. Clinicians and patients must understand how AI-derived recommendations are generated, especially when guiding critical decisions [6,9]. Legal frameworks need to evolve to clarify accountability for adverse outcomes [9]. Trust requires clear guidelines and rigorous validation of AI systems.

9.5.3 *Data Privacy and Security*

Extensive patient data collection raises major privacy risks. Adherence to HIPAA and GDPR is critical [43], alongside secure encryption, access control, and protected data storage. Regular audits and monitoring help maintain data integrity and safeguard patient trust.

Socioeconomic and Ethical Considerations

AI deployment in healthcare carries notable socio-economic impacts, with risks of uneven benefit distribution that may worsen access disparities [1, 44]. To ensure equitable outcomes, ethical frameworks must guide AI adoption, prioritizing inclusivity for all patient groups—especially underserved populations [1, 9].

9.6 Challenges and Barriers to Adoption

Generative AI is transforming medicine by enhancing diagnosis, treatment planning, and patient engagement. However, its clinical adoption faces challenges—from technical limitations and workflow misalignment to ethical concerns, data privacy issues, and clinician resistance. Overcoming these requires coordinated, evidence-driven solutions across technology, regulation, and healthcare practice.

9.6.1 Technical Limitations & Integration Hurdles

Generative AI's vast medical potential faces technical barriers in real-world deployment. A key challenge is its poor interoperability with existing EHR systems—most tools remain siloed, creating fragmented workflows that frustrate clinicians. Nair and associates identified data integration, workflow misalignment, and system inertia as top hurdles [49]. The opaque nature of LLMs ("black box" logic) undermines physician trust, as explainable AI (XAI) tools lack sufficient clarity for clinical use. Inconsistent data quality and format variability across institutions further jeopardize reliability. Without standard protocols like FHIR, AI adoption remains limited. Addressing these gaps requires seamless integration, robust governance, and AI tools designed as embedded decision-support systems within clinical workflows.

9.6.2 Clinical Validation and Reliability of Generative AI Instruments

Ensuring reliability and clinical validation is a major hurdle in deploying generative AI in medicine. While models like ChatGPT and Med-PaLM perform well in controlled tests, they often falter in real-world clinical settings—due to human-AI interaction flaws and misleading outputs. Hallucinations, such as fabricated HPO codes and fictional patient data in genetic and radiology reports, pose serious risks [50]. These issues highlight the gap between promising algorithms and safe clinical application.

A key barrier to deploying generative AI in healthcare is the lack of robust regulatory and certified use guidelines. Despite initiatives like FDA action plans and frameworks such as SPIRIT-AI and CONSORT-AI, clinical trials assessing safety and efficacy remain limited. Post-deployment monitoring is also underdeveloped. These models continuously evolve, unlike static software, creating challenges in maintaining performance and accountability. To ensure safe patient care, generative AI must bridge the bench-to-bedside gap, minimize hallucinations, undergo rigorous clinical validation, and adopt strong governance protocols.

9.6.3 Organizational & Human Factors

Organizational and human factors play a critical role in generative AI adoption in healthcare. Many clinicians resist new AI tools due to concerns over job displacement, loss of control, and liability for AI-related errors. Low AI literacy further limits confidence and critical engagement. [51] reported that allied health professionals often felt excluded from AI design, amplifying resistance. Poor integration with existing workflows and lack of actionable outputs also reduce utility. Legal ambiguity around responsibility for AI decisions compounds hesitation. Effective adoption requires change management—through user training, clinician involvement in design, and fostering trust and shared ownership of AI systems.

9.6.4 Mitigation Strategies

Overcoming generative AI adoption barriers in healthcare demands a comprehensive strategy spanning governance, design, education, and regulation. Establishing multidisciplinary AI governance committees ensures ethical oversight, transparency, and accountability. Early involvement of clinicians—highlighted by [49]—enhances usability through user-centered design aligned with clinical workflows. Building AI literacy into medical curricula via workshops and simulations equips providers to interpret AI outputs accurately. Pilot programs and "AI champions" help foster trust and encourage adoption. Finally, collaboration with regulators to establish flexible compliance frameworks supports safe, sustainable integration of evolving AI tools.

9.7 Future Prospects of Generative AI in Healthcare

Generative AI—spanning GANs, VAEs, and Transformer models—is reshaping healthcare by generating unique data, personalizing therapies, and refining clinical workflows. This chapter outlines its evolving impact, practical applications, and the ethical and legal considerations essential for responsible adoption.

9.7.1 Personalized Medicine

Generative AI is reshaping personalized healthcare by tailoring treatments to individual genomic, lifestyle, and physiological profiles. By integrating diverse data sources, it enables precise therapy planning, reduces trial-and-error prescribing, and models disease progression for timely interventions. Real-time EHR-based response tracking allows dynamic adjustments, boosting treatment accuracy, minimizing side effects, and enhancing resource use. This shift marks a move from reactive care to adaptive, patient-centric medicine.

9.7.2 *Medical Imaging and Diagnostics*

Generative AI is pivotal in advancing medical imaging and diagnostics. It enhances low-quality scans for faster, more accurate diagnoses—particularly where traditional imaging falls short [52]. GAN-generated synthetic images address data scarcity and class imbalance, improving model training and supporting rare disease detection. These techniques are especially valuable in resource-limited settings lacking advanced tools or labeled datasets [53], boosting diagnostic equity and clinical outcomes.

9.7.3 *Ethical, Regulatory, and Societal Considerations*

Generative AI could reshape healthcare, but it brings ethical, regulatory, and societal concerns. Skewed training data risks deepening health disparities [54], and opaque "black box" models undermine trust and informed consent. Regulatory bodies like the FDA and EMA are embracing AI, but strict compliance with HIPAA, GDPR, and national laws remains vital for data protection [55]. To ensure responsible use, AI systems must be fair, transparent, and human-centered—supported by equitable algorithms, peer oversight, and public accountability.

9.7.4 *Mental Health and Emotional Intelligence*

Generative AI is rapidly advancing mental health care, particularly through language-based support. Enhanced models enable empathetic interactions, simulate therapy sessions, and monitor mood shifts over time. Virtual tools guide users in identifying harmful thought patterns, while AI-powered chatbots offer 24/7 support—critical for those in remote areas or facing stigma. These innovations are making mental health services more accessible, personalized, and discreet, blending emotional intelligence with technology [56, 57].

9.7.5 *Virtual Health Assistants and Patient Interaction*

Generative AI is driving the rise of virtual medical assistants, improving patient engagement and care delivery. Conversational AI supports scheduling, symptom assessment, and medication guidance—making healthcare info more accessible and boosting treatment adherence. In chronic disease management, these systems analyze health patterns to deliver tailored support and real-time interventions for conditions like diabetes and hypertension. Virtual health assistants boost patient engagement, expand access to care, and ease administrative workloads. As technology evolves, these tools foster a proactive, informed, and connected healthcare experience across diverse settings [58][59].

Conclusion

Generative AI is reshaping healthcare by improving diagnostics, personalizing treatments, and streamlining clinical workflows. Its ability to process complex health data, enhance imaging, and accelerate drug discovery enables early, accurate disease detection and tailored therapies with fewer side effects. In drug development, it predicts molecular interactions and designs new compounds, cutting time and cost. However, concerns over data privacy, security, and ethical use remain. Transparent, fair, and accountable AI systems—supported by strong governance and ethical standards—are essential. Future collaboration among researchers, clinicians, and policymakers will be key to realizing a more equitable and patient-centered healthcare landscape.

References

[1] Topol, E.J. (2019). High-performance medicine: the convergence of human and artificial intelligence. *Nature medicine*, 25(1), 44–56.

[2] Yu, K.H., Beam, A.L. and Kohane, I.S. (2018). Artificial intelligence in healthcare. *Nature biomedical engineering*, 2(10), 719–731.

[3] Esteva, A., Robicquet, A., Ramsundar, B., Kuleshov, V., DePristo, M. et al. (2019). A guide to deep learning in healthcare. *Nature medicine*, 25(1), 24–29.

[4] Goodfellow, I., Pouget-Abadie, J., Mirza, M., Xu, B., Warde-Farley, D. et al. (2014). Generative adversarial nets. In *Advances in Neural Information Processing Systems*, 27.

[5] Frid-Adar, M., Klang, E., Amitai, M., Goldberger, J. and Greenspan, H. et al. (2018). Synthetic data augmentation using GAN for improved liver lesion classification. *IEEE Transactions on Medical Imaging*, 38(3), 589–597.

[6] Yi, X., Walia, E. and Babyn, P. (2019). Generative adversarial network in medical imaging: A review. *Medical Image Analysis*, 58, 101552.

[7] Obermeyer, Z., Powers, B., Vogeli, C. and Mullainathan, S. (2019). Dissecting racial bias in an algorithm used to manage the health of populations. *Science*, 366(6464), 447–453.

[8] Bender, E.M., Gebru, T., McMillan-Major, A. and Shmitchell, S. (2021). On the dangers of stochastic parrots: Can language models be too big? In *Proceedings of the 2021 ACM Conference on Fairness, Accountability, and Transparency*.

[9] Verghese, A., Shah, N.H. and Harrington, R.A. (2018). What this computer needs is a physician: Humanism and artificial intelligence. *JAMA*, 319(1), 19–20.

[10] Matheny, M. "Artificial intelligence in health care: The hope, the hype, the promise, the peril." *Washington, DC: National Academy of Medicine* 10 (2019).

[11] Shokrollahi, Yasin. "A comprehensive review of generative AI in healthcare." *arXiv preprint arXiv:2310.00795* (2023).

[12] Patel, A.A. and Ajay U.A. *Applied natural language processing in the enterprise*. "O'Reilly Media, Inc.", 2021.

[13] Kilicoglu, Halil. "SemMedDB: a PubMed-scale repository of biomedical semantic predications." *Bioinformatics* 28.23 (2012): 3158–3160.

[14] Wu, Yonghui, "A study of neural word embeddings for named entity recognition in clinical text." *AMIA annual symposium proceedings*. Vol. 2015. 2015.

[15] Śniegula, Anna, Aneta Poniszewska-Marańda, and Łukasz Chomątek. "Towards the named entity recognition methods in biomedical field." *SOFSEM 2020: Theory and Practice of Computer Science: 46th International Conference on Current Trends in Theory and Practice of Informatics, SOFSEM 2020, Limassol, Cyprus, January 20–24, 2020, Proceedings 46*. Springer International Publishing, 2020.

[16] Chen, L. "Extracting medications and associated adverse drug events using a natural language processing system combining knowledge base and deep learning." *Journal of the American Medical Informatics Association* 27.1 (2020): 56–64.

[17] Wu, S.T. "Automated chart review for asthma cohort identification using natural language processing: an exploratory study." *Annals of Allergy, Asthma & Immunology* 111.5 (2013): 364–369.

[18] Vaswani, A. "Attention is all you need." *Advances in Neural Information Processing Systems (NeurIPS)*, vol. 30, 2017, pp. 4137–4149.

[19] Lee, J. "BioBERT: a pre-trained biomedical language representation model for biomedical text mining." *Bioinformatics*, vol. 36, no. 4, 2020, pp. 1234–1240.

[20] Dosovitskiy, A. "An Image is Worth 16x16 Words: Transformers for Image Recognition at Scale." *IEEE Transactions on Pattern Analysis and Machine Intelligence*, vol. 43, no. 7, 2021, pp. 6000–6014.

[21] Song, Y. "Denoising Diffusion Probabilistic Models for Image Reconstruction." *IEEE Transactions on Medical Imaging*, vol. 40, no. 2, 2021, pp. 456–467.

[22] Rombach, R. "Generative models for histopathology image synthesis." *Nature Biomedical Engineering*, vol. 6, no. 5, 2022, pp. 302–316.

[23] Goodfellow, I. "Generative adversarial nets." *Advances in Neural Information Processing Systems (NeurIPS)*, vol. 27, 2014, pp. 2672–2680.

[24] De Cao, N. and Kipf, T. "MolGAN: An Implicit Generative Model for Small Molecular Graphs." *Journal of Chemical Information and Modeling*, vol. 58, no. 1, 2018, pp. 76–89.

[25] Beaulieu-Jones, BK. "Privacy-preserving generative deep neural networks support clinical data sharing." *Nature Medicine*, vol. 25, no. 7, 2019, pp. 1038–1040.

[26] Arjovsky, M. "Wasserstein GAN." *Proceedings of the International Conference on Machine Learning (ICML)*, 2017, pp. 214–223.

[27] Karras, T. "Training Generative Neural Networks for Medical Image Synthesis." *Medical Image Analysis*, vol. 68, 2021, pp. 77–89.

[28] Chen, C.-H. et al. "Low-dose CT image denoising using generative adversarial networks." *Medical Physics*, vol. 46, no. 1, 2019, pp. 89–98.

[29] Liu, Q. "Deep learning-based tumor detection in MRI scans." *Computerized Medical Imaging and Graphics*, vol. 87, 2020, pp. 1245–1260.

[30] Costa, P. "Medical image synthesis for data augmentation and anonymization using GANs." *Artificial Intelligence in Medicine*, vol. 101, 2019, pp. 567–580.

[31] Wolterink, J.M. "Denoising low-dose CT with deep learning." *Medical Image Analysis*, vol. 55, 2019, pp. 789–800.

[32] Stokes, J.M., Yang, K., Swanson, K., Jin, W., Cubillos-Ruiz, A. et al. (2020). A deep learning approach to antibiotic discovery. *Cell, 180*(4), 688-702.

[33] Senior, A.W., Evans, R., Jumper, J., Kirkpatrick, J., Sifre, L. et al. (2020). Improved protein structure prediction using potentials from deep learning. *Nature*, *577*(7792), 706–710.

[34] Rajkomar, A., Oren, E., Chen, K., Dai, A.M., Hajaj, N. et al. (2018). Scalable and accurate deep learning with electronic health records. *NPJ Digital Medicine*, 1(1), 1–10.

[35] Bickmore, T.W. and Giorgino, T. (2006). Health dialog systems for patients and consumers. *Journal of Biomedical Informatics,* 39(5), 556–571.

[36] Kazeminia, S.M., Razzak, M.I. and Imran, M. (2020). A review on deep learning for medical image segmentation. *Medical Image Analysis*, 68, 101855.

[37] Shen, D., Wu, G. and Suk, H.-I. (2017). Deep learning in medical image analysis. *Annual Review of Biomedical Engineering,* 19, 221–248.

[38] Ching, T., Himmelstein, D.S., Beaulieu-Jones, B.K., Kalinin, A.A., Do, B.T. et al (2018). Opportunities and obstacles for deep learning in biology and medicine. *Journal of The Royal Society Interface*, 15(141), 20170387.

[39] Huang, K., Altosaar, J. and Ranganath, R. (2019). ClinicalBERT: Modeling clinical notes and predicting hospital readmission. *Journal of Biomedical Informatics*, 100, 56–67.

[40] Jumper, J., Evans, R., Pritzel, A., Green, T., Figurnov, M. et al. (2021). Highly accurate protein structure prediction with AlphaFold. *Nature*, 596, 583–589.

[41] Liu, Y., Chen, P. H.C. and Krause, J. (2021). Deep learning for medical image analysis: Advances, challenges, and applications. *Annual Review of Biomedical Engineering*, 23, 341–367.

[42] Xie, P., Jiang, H. and Fu, Y. (2021). AI-powered medical coding for billing optimization. *Journal of the American Medical Informatics Association*, 28(2), 901–912.

[43] Chen, M., Hao, Y., Cai, Y., Wang, Y. and Wei, Z. et al. (2020). Artificial intelligence in health care: Anticipated challenges to ethics, privacy, and bias. *IEEE Access*, 8, 232132–232146.

[44] Ching, T., Himmelstein, D.S., Beaulieu-Jones, B.K., Kalinin, A.A., Do, B.T. et al. (2018). Opportunities and obstacles for deep learning in biology and medicine. *Journal of The Royal Society Interface*, 15(141), 20170387.

[45] Singhal, K. (2023). Large language models encode clinical knowledge. *Nature*, 620(7972), 172–180.

[46] WHO. (2023). Ethics and governance of AI for health. *World Health Organization.*

[47] Jumper, J. (2024). Highly accurate structure prediction of biomolecular interactions with AlphaFold 3. *Nature*, 625(7993), 1–9.

[48] Obermeyer, Z. (2023). Diagnostic racial bias in pulse oximetry: A case study of algorithmic fairness. *NEJM AI*, 1(1), 1–10.

[49] Nair, Monika. "A comprehensive overview of barriers and strategies for AI implementation in healthcare: mixed-method design." Plos one 19.8 (2024): e0305949.

[50] Du, Xinsong, et al. "Generative large language models in electronic health records for patient care since 2023: a systematic review." medRxiv (2024).

[51] Hoffman, Jane. "Overcoming barriers and enabling artificial intelligence adoption in allied health clinical practice: A qualitative study." Digital Health 11 (2025): 20552076241311144.

[52] Yang, Guang. "DAGAN: deep de-aliasing generative adversarial networks for fast compressed sensing MRI reconstruction." *IEEE transactions on medical imaging* 37.6 (2017): 1310–1321.

[53] Yi, X., Walia, E. and Babyn, P. (2019). Generative adversarial network in medical imaging: A review. *Medical image analysis*, 58, 101552.

[54] Mehrabi, N., Morstatter, F., Saxena, N. and Galstyan, A. (2023). *A survey on bias and fairness in AI healthcare systems. Nature Digital Medicine*, 6(1), 78.

[55] Vincent, C., Ramakrishnan, N. and Tiwari, A. (2024). *Privacy-preserving frameworks for AI in healthcare: Regulatory challenges and opportunities. Health Informatics Journal*, 30(1), 1–15.

[56] Gupta, S., Bose, A. and Narayanan, V. (2023). *Generative AI for cognitive behavioral therapy: Opportunities and ethical considerations. Journal of Digital Psychiatry*, 5(2), 76–89.

[57] Lin, K. and Patel, R. (2024). *AI-enabled emotional intelligence: Redefining mental health support systems. Advances in AI and Mental Health*, 8(1), 22–35.

[58] Singh, R., Gupta, M. and Verma, P. (2023). *Conversational AI in Healthcare: Trends, Applications, and Future Directions. Journal of Medical Systems*, 47(1), 12.

[59] Alami, H., Gagnon, M.P., Fortin, J.P. and Lehoux, P. (2024). *Virtual Health Assistants in Primary Care: A Scoping Review of the Evidence and Ethical Considerations.* Digital Health, 10, 20552076241234567.

10 Revolutionizing Healthcare: The Synergy of Blockchain and Robotics for Secure, Transparent, and Efficient Operations

Samyak Jain[1] and Arpit Singh[2*]

This qualitative study highlights Blockchain Technology's (BT) potential to enhance healthcare data security, transparency, and efficiency. Expert interviews reveal key benefits—such as safeguarding electronic records, automating tasks, and ensuring clinical trial integrity—as well as challenges around interoperability, regulation, and cost. The research also explores synergies between BT and robotics in areas like surgeries and logistics. Despite its limited scope, the study offers useful insights and recommends broader, quantitative research. It emphasizes collaborative, patient-focused solutions and suggests BT integration with AI and IoT could drive future healthcare innovation.

10.1 Introduction

Blockchain Technology (BT) is gaining traction across sectors, especially healthcare, where it offers breakthroughs in secure, transparent data management [2]. Its decentralized nature reduces risks tied to centralized control, aligning with growing concerns over data safety among providers, regulators, and researchers [26, 9]. Fragmented data systems, security gaps, inefficiencies, and high costs are key challenges in healthcare [4]. Disjointed records often delay access to vital patient information, hindering timely and accurate care [18]. Blockchain Technology (BT) offers a solution through secure, distributed ledgers for data storage and sharing [24]. Its immutability and traceability foster trust among stakeholders, including patients, providers, and payers [20]. A key advantage of Blockchain Technology (BT) is eliminating intermediaries, allowing peer-to-peer sharing and seamless data verification [16]. This enhances integrity and accountability, reducing risks like hacking and unauthorized access. In clinical trials, BT ensures tamper-proof records of protocols, consents, and outcomes, improving transparency and regulatory compliance [15]. Blockchain Technology (BT) enhances healthcare by

[1] Actuarial department, EXL, Delhi, India.
[2] Information systems and Analytics, Jindal Global Business School, Sonipat, India.
E-mail: jnsamyak@gmail.com
* Corresponding author: asingh6@jgu.edu.in

DOI: 10.1201/9781003670582-10

improving data security, reducing errors, and speeding up treatment processes [22]. Its secure, transparent data sharing helps eliminate redundancies, cutting major cost drivers like medical mistakes [3]. Smart contracts further streamline administrative tasks—such as insurance claims and supply chain operations—through automated execution, minimizing human delays [5]. Blockchain Technology (BT) adoption in healthcare faces major hurdles: regulatory ambiguity, technical complexity, and resistance to change [11]. Key barriers include poor interoperability with legacy systems and high energy demands of BT protocols—especially concerning sensitive patient data. Clear regulatory guidelines are essential to govern BT use. When combined with robotics, BT can automate surgeries, medication dispensing, and patient monitoring. Robotics enhances data security by executing precise, repetitive tasks like inventory management or surgical operations within BT-linked systems. To accelerate Blockchain Technology (BT) adoption, developers must prioritize user-centric scalability over purely technical upgrades. Solutions should be intuitive, affordable, and compatible with existing workflows. Equally important is stakeholder engagement—including clinicians, tech developers, policymakers, and patients—to foster a supportive adoption environment [11]. This study builds on existing concepts by examining how Blockchain Technology (BT) can be applied and scaled in healthcare. It explores whether BT is an emerging reality or a conceptual promise. The chapter is structured as follows: Section 2 reviews key literature, Section 3 outlines the methodology, Sections 4 and 5 present findings and discussion, and Section 6 concludes with future directions and practical implications for BT's impact on healthcare systems.

10.2 Literature Review

There has been a notable Recent years have seen a surge in research exploring Blockchain Technology (BT) in healthcare—highlighting its potential and challenges. This section reviews key contributions, focusing on BT's role in addressing critical healthcare issues and deployment barriers.

BT: Evolution and Core Capabilities

Blockchain Technology (BT), pioneered by Satoshi Nakamoto in Bitcoin's design [13], laid the foundation for decentralized data systems. Today, BT extends beyond finance into healthcare, offering solutions to inefficiencies, data breaches, and administrative overheads [23]. By removing intermediaries and ensuring encrypted, immutable records, it strengthens trust and privacy [25]. Its impact spans secure EHR sharing, clinical trial integrity, and drug traceability [1]. With healthcare embracing rapid IT advancements, BT is gaining momentum as a transformative force for future innovation.

Enhancing Data Security and Privacy

Protecting sensitive patient data is vital in healthcare, and Blockchain Technology (BT) offers strong security through encryption and decentralization—avoiding single-point failures [12]. Robotics can enhance this by securing data centers and ensuring authorized access via biometric authentication. BT's transparent ledger also supports robust audit trails that help meet regulatory standards like HIPAA [7].

Streamlining Healthcare Operations

Blockchain Technology (BT) streamlines healthcare operations by automating administrative tasks like claims and appointment scheduling through smart contracts—reducing costs and errors [10, 14]. Robotic systems, when integrated with BT, enable precise inventory management and transparent supply chain tracking. They verify medication origin and quality using immutable ledgers, strengthening traceability and counterfeit prevention efforts [8].

10.2.1 Enhancing Interoperability and Data Sharing

Interoperability remains a major hurdle in healthcare data sharing and collaboration. As highlighted by [19], Blockchain Technology (BT) can serve as a unified platform for distributed systems, enabling secure, efficient communication across stakeholders. Its standardized formats and real-time accessibility promote smoother collaboration among clinicians, researchers, and patients.

Adoption of BT and Value Drivers

BT's development can be divided into four generations:

- BT 1.0: It was concerned with secure data transfer, especially in health records and patient data sharing.
- BT 2.0: It brought in smart contracts that automate healthcare services, including insurance claims and clinical trial management.
- BT 3.0: It enabled the development of decentralized healthcare applications, improving service delivery and the patient experience.
- BT 4.0: It empowered integration with artificial intelligence to carry out predictive analytics and personalized care.

Every phase has contributed unique value drivers, from lowering administrative costs to enhancing transparency and trust in healthcare operations. These advancements have paved the way for BT's transformative role in healthcare, but significant barriers still exist to its widespread adoption.

10.2.2 Addressing Challenges in Implementation

Blockchain Technology (BT) faces key hurdles in healthcare implementation, including complex technical integration, scalability limitations, high energy demands, and consensus challenges [6]. Regulatory uncertainty adds further friction due to unclear guidelines [17]. Experts advocate for coordinated efforts among policymakers, technologists, and healthcare professionals to build a supportive environment for BT adoption. *Exploring Patient-Centric Applications*

Blockchain Technology (BT) empowers patients by giving them control over personal health data via BT-based personal health records (PHRs), enabling selective sharing and enhancing privacy and trust. Studies highlight its role in supporting patient autonomy while ensuring data integrity. Robotics complements this by delivering tailored therapy, teleconsultations, mobility support, and secure post-op care—logging progress through BT platforms for traceability and data protection [19, 25]. The literature underscores Blockchain Technology's (BT) transformative potential in healthcare, while highlighting key adoption barriers. Building on these insights, this study explores BT's applicability, scalability, and its practical and future implications for the sector.

10.3 Research Methodology

This study employed a qualitative approach using in-depth interviews with four experts actively engaged in Blockchain Technology (BT) applications in healthcare. Their domain experience provided valuable insights into BT's practical implementation. Respondent profiles are outlined in Table 10.1, and the methodological framework is illustrated in Figure 10.1.

Table 10.1 Details of respondents participating in the study.

Respondent	*Designation*	*Experience (yrs.)*	*Gender*
1	Healthcare IT Specialist	4	Female
2	BT Entrepreneur	3.5	Male
3	Research Scholar	8	Male
4	Assistant Professor	2.5	Male

To meet the research objective, we formulated four questions to guide expert interviews and assess the current state and future potential of Blockchain Technology (BT) in healthcare. The questions are:

- RQ1. What benefits does BT bring to the healthcare industry?
- RQ2. How aware are people in your organization about BT in healthcare?
- RQ3. What significant challenges do you foresee?
- RQ4. How much BT is needed in the healthcare industry?

The interviews began by identifying suitable professionals on LinkedIn using keywords like "BT specialist healthcare" and "healthcare IT consultant." Out of 50 contacted, four agreed to participate. All respondents were assured anonymity and access to the final research findings. Interviews, conducted via phone or Zoom and averaging 15 minutes, faced challenges in steering discussions toward healthcare-specific applications of Blockchain Technology (BT). While respondents offered valuable insights based on their expertise, much of the input remained theoretical due to BT's emerging role in the sector.

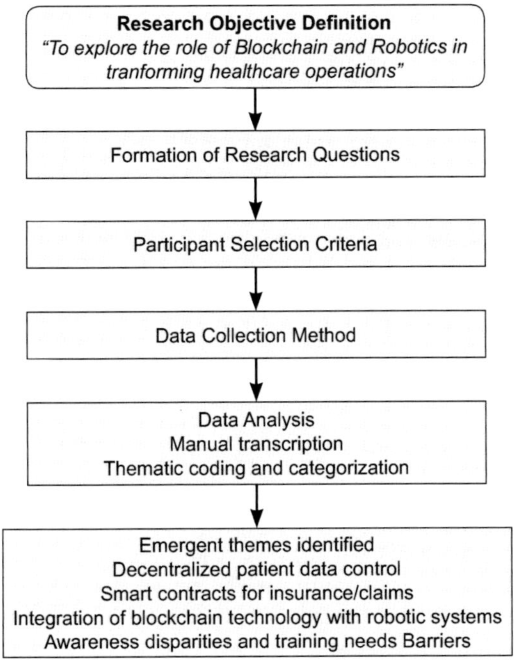

Fig. 10.1 Research methodology.

10.4 Findings

This section summarizes the responses from the interviews, with slight grammatical modifications for clarity.

Respondent 1

For the first research question, the respondent emphasized Blockchain Technology's (BT) potential to disrupt healthcare by decentralizing patient data—enabling secure, transparent, and interoperable systems. BT empowers patients with control over their medical records, ensuring easy yet integrity-preserving data sharing. Smart contracts streamline insurance and consent processes, cutting delays and boosting administrative efficiency. BT also improves drug safety through immutable records that verify origin, manufacture, and distribution. Robotics enhances this impact by automating tasks like diagnostics and surgeries, securely logging data via BT for real-time tracking and improved operational efficiency.

The respondent noted uneven awareness of Blockchain Technology (BT) across the organization—IT teams are more informed, while clinicians and admin staff require further training. This highlights the need for ongoing education and cross-disciplinary collaboration to ensure a unified understanding of BT's healthcare applications. Robotics can support this transition by streamlining workflows and minimizing manual errors, helping build trust in BT systems. The respondent identified key barriers to Blockchain Technology (BT) adoption in healthcare: strict regulations like HIPAA and GDPR pose compliance challenges due to BT's immutable nature; high implementation costs and limited scalability hinder broader deployment; and outdated systems complicate data interoperability. Addressing these issues requires additional funding and integration support. Robotics can assist by automating tasks such as sample handling and supply chain audits, promoting smoother implementation. The respondent emphasized that strategic, phased adoption of Blockchain Technology (BT) is essential. Initial focus should target high-impact areas like clinical trials, insurance claims, and drug traceability. With broader acceptance and technical refinement, BT could extend to advanced uses such as real-time patient monitoring and AI-driven personalized treatment planning—supporting a more integrated care ecosystem.

Respondent 2

Blockchain Technology (BT) enhances data security and accessibility in healthcare, especially in clinical trials where tamper-proof records boost credibility. It also improves system interoperability, reducing delays and improving provider communication. BT's immutable ledger helps prevent insurance fraud by ensuring claims are traceable and accurate. Robotics complements this by automating data collection and transfer in trials, and streamlining scheduling and medication processes to accelerate care delivery. Blockchain Technology (BT) awareness is rising, particularly among healthcare IT teams, but adoption remains slow due to administrative skepticism and concerns over workflow disruption. Bridging this gap requires highlighting clear stakeholder benefits. Showcasing robotics—through patient care enhancements or automated hospital logistics—may help drive broader acceptance of both technologies.

Balancing patient data ownership with provider access remains a key challenge, alongside a lack of professionals skilled in both Blockchain Technology (BT) and healthcare systems. Scalability is also a concern, especially for data-intensive fields like genomics and medical imaging. Integrating robotics with BT could help manage large datasets and eventually support advanced applications such as AI-powered diagnostics and real-time patient monitoring. The respondent proposed Blockchain Technology (BT) as a foundational element for future healthcare systems. Initial adoption should target key areas like fraud prevention, data security, and drug traceability. As BT matures, its use can expand to predictive analytics and secure medical research data sharing—enhancing privacy and trust.

Respondent 3

The respondent viewed Blockchain Technology (BT) as a driver of patient-centered systems, offering individuals control over their medical data to boost transparency and trust. Smart contracts automate insurance claims, reducing delays and errors. BT's decentralized design enhances data security against cyber threats. Robotics can complement this by enabling personalized therapy, securely logging progress, and supporting BT-integrated surgical procedures. Highlighting their combined impact may encourage training and broader adoption of both technologies.

Employee reactions to Blockchain Technology (BT) varied—some departments showed interest, but limited training resources have restricted broader understanding, especially among nontechnical staff. BT's complexity further reduces its perceived relevance, highlighting the need for tailored education efforts. Robotics could help bridge these gaps by streamlining data handling and enabling solutions like robotic telepresence and automated logistics. Participants highlighted technical and ethical challenges in integrating wearable data into Blockchain Technology (BT) systems—particularly concerns around data anonymity and misuse. Cultural resistance also persists among healthcare leaders who remain skeptical of BT's return on investment, further impeding its adoption. The respondent recommended a targeted rollout of Blockchain Technology (BT) to address critical issues like EHR security, billing fraud, and drug safety. If proven effective, BT could expand to support patient record management, AI-based decision-making, and collaborative care networks.

Respondent 4

Blockchain Technology (BT) enables decentralized systems hat maintain data security and accessibility—even during network disruptions. It enhances medical research traceability by securely documenting each stage of clinical trials. BT also supports global collaboration by allowing data exchange across regions while complying with privacy regulations. The respondent saw BT as a foundational tool, with robotics amplifying its impact through automated sample handling and secure data transfers for clinical research. The interviewee noted that Blockchain Technology (BT) awareness is mostly confined to IT teams. For broader healthcare adoption, leadership buy-in and clear demonstrations of BT's value are essential. Robotics can help showcase tangible benefits through applications like automated inventory and secure data collection, enhancing privacy and enabling full traceability—potentially accelerating adoption of both technologies. Blockchain Technology (BT) adoption in healthcare faces major hurdles, including the lack of global standards and persistent privacy concerns—especially around re-identification of anonymized data. Jurisdictional legal differences further complicate cross-border implementations, posing challenges for global health initiatives. In response to the fourth research question, the respondent recommended starting Blockchain Technology (BT) adoption in critical areas like counterfeit drug prevention and emergency data sharing. With greater acceptance, BT could expand into patient data management, AI-assisted diagnostics, and predictive analytics for health planning.

Summary

This thematic analysis draws on qualitative insights from four expert interviews, identifying five core categories: (1) Benefits of Blockchain Technology (BT), (2) Adoption Awareness and Readiness, (3) Implementation Barriers, (4) Strategic BT Application Areas, and (5) Complementary Role of Robotics.

Perceived Benefits of Blockchain in Healthcare

All interviewees emphasized Blockchain Technology's (BT) potential to safeguard patient data, enhance traceability, and increase transparency. Decentralized electronic health records put patients in control while preserving data integrity. Smart contracts were highlighted as tools to automate consent, clinical trials, and insurance processes—reducing errors and streamlining administration.

"BT provides a tamper-proof layer that enhances data trust—from clinical trials to drug traceability." (Respondent 1)

Participants agreed that blockchain streamlines operations by removing intermediaries and minimizing data breach risks. This supports existing research on its role in enabling transparent, trustless interactions ([1]; [23]).

Awareness and Adoption Readiness

Awareness of Blockchain Technology (BT) is uneven across stakeholder groups —IT teams are more informed, while clinicians and administrators show limited understanding. Interviewees stressed the need for targeted training and collaborative learning hubs to bridge this gap. "Clinicians are eager but pretty unaware of how BT can be infused into current work processes." (Respondent 3)

This disparity in awareness highlights the requirement for institutional readiness models bridging technical and clinical spaces.

10.4.1 Implementation Challenges

Key barriers include complex regulations (e.g., GDPR, HIPAA), legacy system incompatibility, high deployment costs, and limited technical expertise. Notably, the immutability of blockchain enhances data integrity but conflicts with legal requirements for data alteration or deletion. "The immutable nature of BT conflicts with the legal obligation to delete patient information in some jurisdictions." (Respondent 4)

A shortage of professionals with expertise in both Blockchain Technology (BT) and healthcare systems emerged as a key capacity gap, echoing concerns noted in [6] and [25].

Strategic Application Areas

Respondents consistently identified three initial high-impact application zones:

- Clinical Trials (for traceable consent and protocols)

- Insurance Claims (via smart contracts)
- Pharmaceutical Supply Chains (for counterfeiting prevention)

"BT should start in areas where existing processes are highly manual and vulnerable to fraud." (Respondent 2)

These insights support a phased implementation approach, where BT is piloted in limited, high-stakes environments before wider adoption.

10.4.2 Synergy with Robotics

All interviewees saw robotics as a possible facilitator of BT adoption, particularly in the spheres of:

- Automated drug dispensing and diagnostic procedures
- Robotics-assisted procedures with BT-supported compliance
- Safe transfer of laboratory and clinical data

"When robotics automates the task and BT provides the audit trail—trust and efficiency are maximized." (Respondent 1)

This co-evolution of robotics and BT is regarded as a driver of operational excellence and patient-centered care. It also sets this study apart by developing the dual-technology lens.

The findings from this research suggest that although BT is generally seen as promising, its adoption into healthcare systems is limited by institutional, regulatory, and technical barriers. However, focused applications—especially when supplemented by robotics—have significant potential for early achievement. A strategic, training-facilitated, and stakeholder-engaged approach is needed for wider adoption.

10.5 Managerial implications

The findings of this research have significant managerial implications for the adoption and implementation of BT technology in the healthcare sector. Managers and decision-makers can leverage these insights to devise strategic approaches that maximize the benefits of BT while addressing its challenges effectively.

- Under the supervision of healthcare managers, BT solutions can be initiated in certain critical-pain areas including drug traceability, fraud prevention, and EHR (electronic health record) security. These areas are classified as crucial pain points where BT technology can provide immediate benefits and, in addition, present a platform for the technology to be broadly adopted in the future.
- To support Blockchain Technology (BT) integration, managers should launch inclusive training programs tailored to diverse employee groups. This will close knowledge gaps and foster collaboration—essential for embedding BT into core healthcare operations. Managers must navigate stringent regulatory frameworks, such as HIPAA and GDPR, which often conflict with BT's immutable nature. Collaborative efforts with regulatory authorities and the

development of hybrid BT models that can manage and control data changes, can mitigate these challenges.

- To overcome Blockchain Technology (BT) cost and scalability challenges, managers should prioritize smart financial planning and phased implementation. Raising funds and collaborating with tech partners is key—initial trials in controlled settings can help validate effectiveness before broader rollout. Successful Blockchain Technology (BT) adoption in healthcare hinges on collaboration among IT experts, clinicians, administrators, and researchers. Managers should establish interdisciplinary teams to pinpoint use cases, streamline processes, and align efforts with strategic goals. Blockchain Technology (BT) empowers managers to shift health data control to patients, fostering transparency and trust. Success depends on building patient-centric solutions that strengthen collaboration and deepen the doctor–patient relationship.

10.6 Conclusion and Future Research Opportunities

This research explores Blockchain Technology's (BT) potential to transform healthcare by boosting data security, transparency, and administrative efficiency. However, it also identifies major hurdles—namely complex regulations, high implementation costs, and skill shortages. This study's main limitations include a small sample size—just four respondents—limiting the diversity of perspectives and stakeholder representation. The findings are largely theoretical and speculative, reflecting future potential rather than real-world BT implementation. Regional biases also constrain generalizability, as participants' views may not account for global healthcare disparities, regulatory differences, or varied BT adoption levels.

Future research on Blockchain Technology (BT) in healthcare should expand sample size and participant diversity—including patients, lawmakers, administrators, and tech vendors—to build a fuller understanding of its impact. Quantitative studies assessing cost savings, reduced malpractice, and improved patient satisfaction are needed. Longitudinal research could track adoption challenges and long-term performance [21]. Additional focus areas include privacy, interoperability, and the use of BT with EHRs, AI, and smart devices. Integrating BT with AI, IoT, and big data may unlock breakthroughs in personalized care, predictive analytics, and real-time monitoring.

Declarations

- The authors received no specific funding for this study.
- The authors declare that they have no conflicts of interest to report regarding the present study.
- No human subject or animals are involved in the research.
- All authors have mutually consented to participate.

- All the authors have given consent for publishing this work.
- Authors declare that all the data sources used in this project have been mentioned.

References

[1] Abbate, S., Centobelli, P., Cerchione, R., Oropallo, E. and Riccio, E. et al. (2022). Blockchain technology for embracing healthcare 4.0. *IEEE Transactions on Engineering Management*, 70(8), 2998–3009.

[2] Agarwal, U., Rishiwal, V., Yadav, M., Aslhammari, M., Yadav, P. et al. (2024). Exploring Blockchain and Supply Chain Integration: State-of-the-Art, Security Issues and Emerging Directions. *IEEE Access*.

[3] Ali, A., Al-Rimy, B.A.S., Alsubaei, F.S., Almazroi, A.A. and Almazroi, A.A. et al. (2023). HealthLock: Blockchain-Based Privacy Preservation Using Homomorphic Encryption in Internet of Things Healthcare Applications. *Sensors*, 23(15), 6762.

[4] Alkhalifa, A.K., Alanazi, M.H., Mahmood, K., Almukadi, W.S. and Qurashi, M. (2024). Harnessing Privacy-Preserving Federated Learning With Blockchain for Secure IoT Applications in Smart Healthcare Systems. *Fractals*, 2540020.

[5] Almaiah, M.A., Ali, A., Alkhdour, T. and Lutfi, A. (2024). Security Risk and Breach Detection Approach Based Blockchain for Medical Applications. *IEEE Access*.

[6] Arbabi, M.S., Lal, C., Veeraragavan, N.R., Marijan, D., Nygård, J.F. et al. (2022). A survey on blockchain for healthcare: Challenges, benefits, and future directions. *IEEE communications surveys & tutorials*, 25(1), 386–424.

[7] Balia, S., Brau, R. and Marrocu, E. (2018). Interregional patient mobility in a decentralized healthcare system. *Regional Studies*, 52(3), 388–402.

[8] Berneis, M. and Winkler, H. (2024). Matching supply chain management challenges with blockchain applications. *Supply Chain Management: An International Journal*, 29(6), 1063–1077.

[9] Chan, H.L., Choi, T.M. and De la Torre, D.M. (2023). The "SMARTER" framework and real application cases of blockchain. *Technological Forecasting and Social Change*, 196, 122798.

[10] Chen, C.L., Deng, Y.Y., Tsaur, W.J., Li, C.T., Lee, C.C. et al. (2021). A traceable online insurance claims system based on blockchain and smart contract technology. *Sustainability*, 13(16), 9386.

[11] Garg, H., Jhunthra, S., Kindra, M., Dixit, V. and Gupta, V. et al. (2025). A deep learning-based integrated voice assistance system for partially disabled people. In *Uncertainty in Computational Intelligence-Based Decision Making* (pp. 293–310). Academic Press.

[12] Halder, R., Das Roy, D. and Shin, D. (2024). A Blockchain-Based Decentralized Public Key Infrastructure Using the Web of Trust. *Journal of Cybersecurity and Privacy*, 4(2), 196–222.

[13] Hussein, Z., Salama, M.A. and El-Rahman, S.A. (2023). Evolution of blockchain consensus algorithms: a review on the latest milestones of blockchain consensus algorithms. *Cybersecurity*, 6(1), 30.

[14] Jain, N., Gupta, V. and Dass, P. (2022). Blockchain: A novel paradigm for secured data transmission in telemedicine. In *Wearable telemedicine technology for the healthcare industry* (pp. 33–52). Academic Press.

[15] Jiang, Y., Xu, X. and Xiao, F. (2022). Attribute-based encryption with blockchain protection scheme for electronic health records. *IEEE Transactions on Network and Service Management*, 19(4), 3884–3895.

[16] Lakshmanan, M., Mala, G.A. and Anandkumar, K.M. (2024). Highly secured EHR management system based on blockchain technology with digitally signed authentication using data sanitization and polynomial interpolation. *Biomedical Signal Processing and Control*, 87, 105412.

[17] Masehela, T.S. and Barros, E. (2023). The African continent should consider a harmonized consultative and collaborative effort towards coordinated policy and regulatory guidelines across the fields of biotechnology. *Frontiers in Bioengineering and Biotechnology*, 11, 1211789.

[18] Mole, J.S. and Shaji, R.S. (2024). Ethereum blockchain for electronic health records: securing and streamlining patient management. *Frontiers in Medicine*, 11, 1434474.

[19] Moreno-Álvarez, S., Paoletti, M.E., Cavallaro, G. and Haut, J. M. (2023). Enhancing Distributed Neural Network Training Through Node-Based Communications. *IEEE transactions on neural networks and learning systems*.

[20] Psarra, E., Apostolou, D., Verginadis, Y., Patiniotakis, I. and Mentzas, G. et al. (2024). Permissioned blockchain network for proactive access control to electronic health records. *BMC Medical Informatics and Decision Making*, 24(1), 303.

[21] Qian, C., Mathur, N., Zakaria, N.H., Arora, R., Gupta, V. and Ali, M. (2022). Understanding public opinions on social media for financial sentiment analysis using AI-based techniques. *Information Processing & Management*, 59(6), 103098.

[22] Quan, G., Yao, Z., Chen, L., Fang, Y., Zhu, W. et al. (2023). A trusted medical data sharing framework for edge computing leveraging blockchain and outsourced computation. *Heliyon*, 9(12).

[23] Raj, A., Sharma, V. and Rani, Z. (2024). Revolutionizing Healthcare Efficiency: Blockchain-Driven Process Enhancement. In *Blockchain for Biomedical Research and Healthcare: Concept, Trends, and Future Implications* (pp. 51–76). Singapore: Springer Nature Singapore.

[24] Shahzad, A., Chen, W., Shaheen, M., Zhang, Y. and Ahmad, F. et al. (2024). A robust algorithm for authenticated health data access via blockchain and cloud computing. *Plos one*, 19(9), e0307039.

[25] Singh, Y., Jabbar, M.A., Kumar Shandilya, S., Vovk, O. and Hnatiuk, Y. et al. (2023). Exploring applications of blockchain in healthcare: road map and future directions. *Frontiers in Public Health*, 11, 1229386.

[26] Vanmathi, C., Farouk, A., Alhammad, S.M., Mangayarkarasi, R., Bhattacharya, S. et al. (2024). The Role of Blockchain in Transforming Industries Beyond Finance. *IEEE Access*.

11 Future Directions and Emerging Trends in Robotics and AI

Shubhra Dixit[1], Surbhi Gupta[2] and Ajay Sharma[3*]

Generative AI is driving a transformative shift in AI and robotics by enhancing machine learning, automation, and human-robot collaboration. Key trends include ethical AI, autonomy, cybersecurity, and sustainability. These models improve robot learning, simulation, and interaction central to next-gen smart systems. As robotics expands across healthcare, manufacturing, and smart cities, challenges like data security, bias, and job loss arise. Ethical frameworks, explainable AI, and tighter regulations are critical for safe deployment. When paired with quantum computing, edge AI, and neuromorphic tech, Generative AI will shape robotics into more efficient, ethical, and human-centric systems.

11.1 Introduction

Generative AI is transforming robotics by enabling machines to simulate tasks, adapt autonomously, and operate effectively in unstructured environments [34],[18]. These models support motion planning, image synthesis, and scenario generation advancing robotics in healthcare, logistics, and manufacturing. Machine learning further enhances robotic perception, pattern recognition, and collaboration in dynamic settings. In factories, autonomous robots use predictive analytics to streamline workflows and prevent downtime. In healthcare, AI robots enable minimally invasive, high-precision surgeries, improving patient outcomes. AI-powered drones are transforming logistics with efficient navigation across urban environments. AI integration in robotics improves decision-making, operational efficiency, and system security [8]. Future advancements will likely involve smarter, more innovative robotic capabilities, fueled by developments in machine learning, computer vision, NLP, reinforcement learning, and generative AI. Figure 11.1 outlines impacted sectors.

[1-3] Amity University, Noida, India.
E-mail: sdixit3@amity.edu; sgupta11@amity.edu
* Corresponding author: asharma3@amity.edu

DOI: 10.1201/9781003670582-11

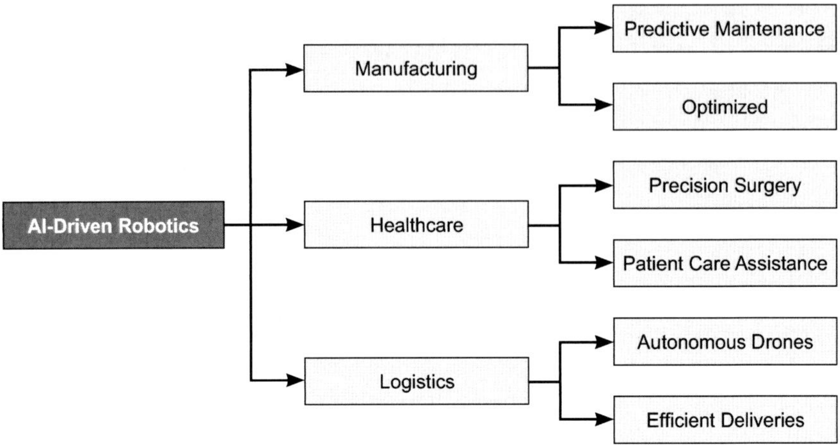

Fig. 11.1 Impact of AI driven robotics.

11.1.1 Reinforcement Learning (RL) and Generative AI

11.1.1.1 Reinforcement Learning (RL) for Autonomous Adaptation

Reinforcement Learning (RL) enables robots to learn optimal actions through trial and error, improving performance without manual programming. Techniques like Proximal Policy Optimization (PPO) and Deep Q-Networks (DQN) [18] support real-time decision-making in robotics and autonomous vehicles. This continuous learning allows systems like self-driving cars to adapt efficiently to dynamic environments, as illustrated in Figure 11.2.

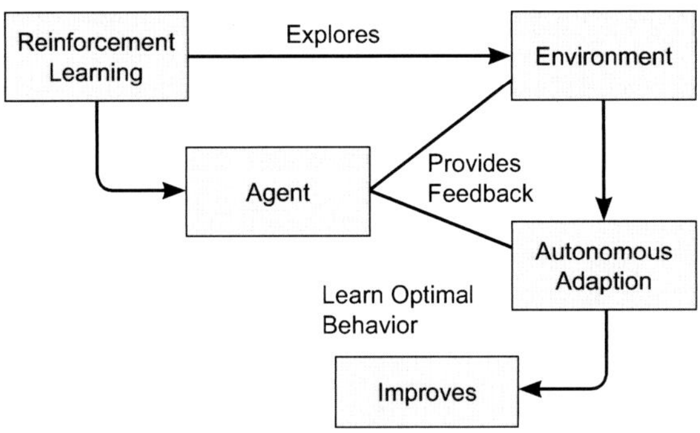

Fig. 11.2 Functioning of Reinforcement Learning.

11.1.1.2 Generative AI for Intelligent Robotics

Generative AI models like GANs enhance robot learning through simulation and data augmentation, enabling robust performance before deployment [34]. They improve motion planning and human-like dexterity for surgical, industrial, and humanoid applications. In human-robot interaction, these models support natural language, gesture, and facial expression recognition, advancing social robotics and customer engagement. Figure 11.3 illustrates these capabilities.

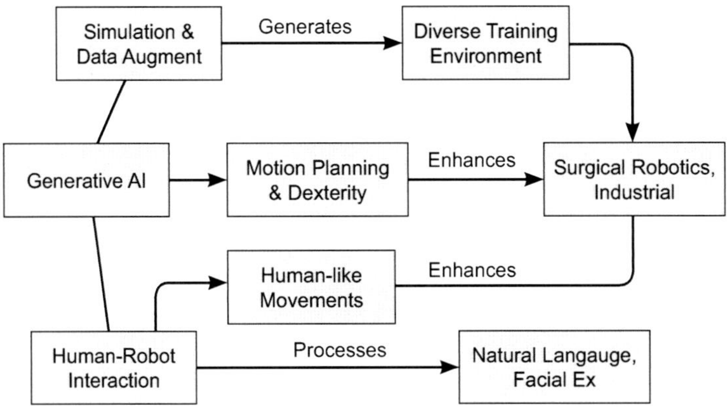

Fig. 11.3 Generative AI contribution.

11.1.2 Explainable AI (XAI) and Trustworthy Robotics

As AI becomes central to robotics, ensuring transparency, reliability, and ethics is vital. Explainable AI (XAI) and Trustworthy Robotics make robotic decisions interpretable and fair for safe human interaction [10]. These approaches build user trust, support regulation, and reduce automation risks (Fig. 11.4).

11.1.2.1 Explainable AI (XAI) for Transparent Decision-Making

AI-driven robots must offer transparent, interpretable decisions, especially in defence, healthcare, and industry. Explainable AI (XAI) techniques—like decision trees and attention models help users understand robotic choices and build trust. In autonomous vehicles, XAI enables regulators to evaluate route selection and braking actions [10].

11.1.2.2 Ensuring Safety, Reliability, and Ethical AI

To ensure fairness, AI in robotics must reduce decision-making bias in critical fields like recruitment, law enforcement, and healthcare. Autonomous robots require fail-safes and error detection to prevent operational failures. Ethical AI development demands compliance with global standards, protecting privacy, security, and human rights. Figure 11.5 illustrates this broad scope.

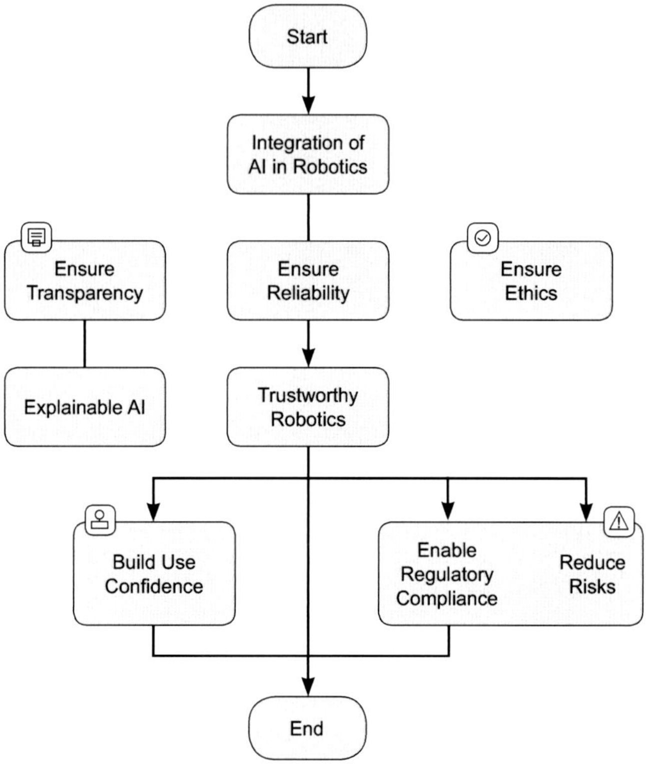

Fig. 11.4 Explainable AI and Trustworthy Robotics.

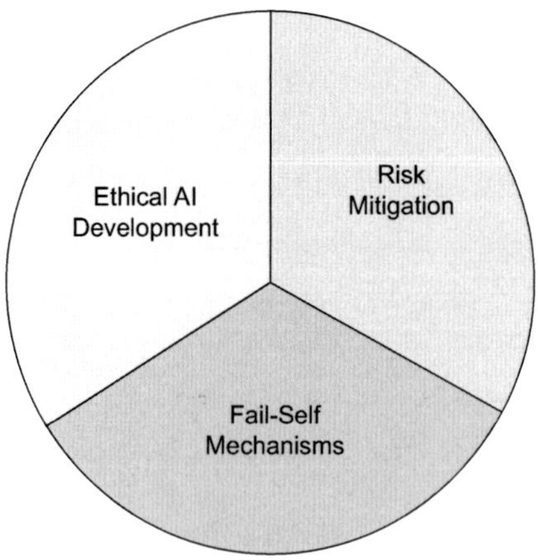

Fig. 11.5 Spread of Ensuring Safety, Reliability, and Ethical AI.

11.1.2.3 Future Impact

AI-driven robotics is enabling autonomous, self-learning systems across healthcare, manufacturing, agriculture, and smart cities. The fusion of AI, IoT, and quantum computing boosts decision-making and adaptability defining the next wave of intelligent automation (Fig. 11.6). **Generative AI**, reinforcement learning, and explainable AI are driving smarter, ethical, and collaborative robotic systems. This chapter examines their evolving role and lasting impact on global industries, highlighting the push toward generative, human-aligned robotics.

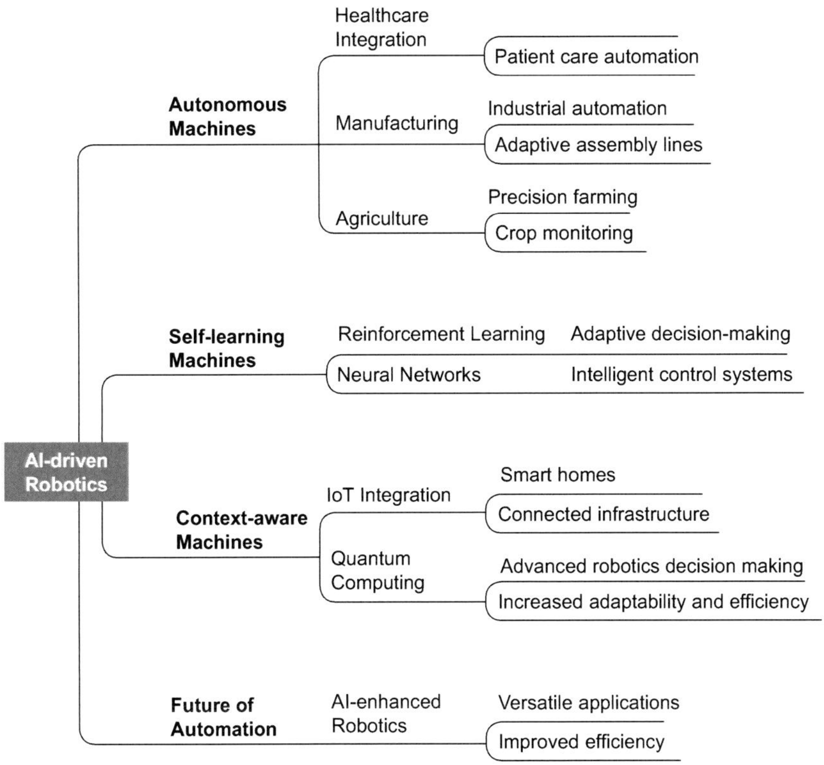

Fig. 11.6 Future impact of AI driven robotics.

11.2 Next-Generation Robotics Technologies

Emerging technologies like soft robotics, swarm intelligence, and quantum computing are reshaping robotics boosting flexibility, efficiency, and adaptability. These innovations enable robots to tackle complex tasks in dynamic settings, expanding their capabilities across diverse applications [17].

11.2.1 Soft Robotics and Bio-Inspired Systems

Soft robotics uses flexible, deformable materials to replicate the movement and adaptability of living organisms. Unlike rigid robots, soft robots safely interact with humans, traverse uneven terrains, and handle delicate objects with precision [15].

Soft robotics uses flexible materials like silicones, polymers, and hydrogels to achieve high adaptability and smooth motion. Powered by fluidic or electroactive actuators, they perform tasks such as grasping, stretching, and navigating tight spaces ideal for delicate operations. Unlike rigid robots, soft robots excel in dynamic environments, making them especially valuable in healthcare, agriculture, and disaster response (Fig. 11.7).

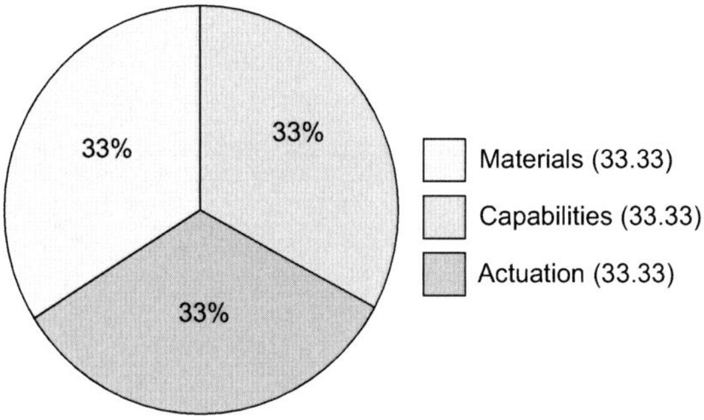

Fig. 11.7 Key Characteristics of Soft Robotics.

Soft robotics, built from flexible and adaptive materials, supports safe automation across diverse fields. In medicine, soft prosthetics and surgical tools improve outcomes with natural motion and precision. Agriculture benefits from gentle robotic grippers that reduce damage during harvesting. In disaster response, soft robots navigate confined spaces, aiding search and rescue where rigid machines fall short. These use cases (Figure 11.8) underscore soft robotics' growing role in real-world problem-solving.

Bio-inspired robotics emulates nature's efficient movement and functionality to solve complex challenges. Gecko-like robots climb walls using adhesive feet; octopus-inspired designs use flexible tentacles for agile underwater exploration; and snake robots navigate tight spaces, ideal for inspections and search operations. These biologically modeled systems offer innovative solutions across exploration, industry, and beyond.

11.2.2 Swarm Robotics and Collective Intelligence

Swarm robotics features groups of simple robots that self-organize, communicate, and make decentralized decisions to achieve shared goals modeled after natural swarms like ants, bees, and fish [25].

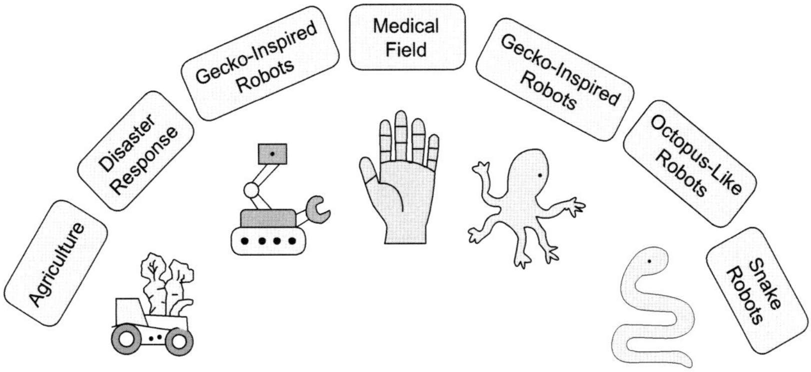

Fig. 11.8 Spectrum of Soft and Bio inspired Robotics.

Advantages of Swarm Robotics includes:
Swarm robotics offers key advantages across diverse applications. Its scalability allows teams to grow or shrink as needed, optimizing resource use and adaptability. These systems are resilient individual failures don't disrupt overall function—and highly efficient, enabling coordinated coverage of large areas. This makes them ideal for search and rescue, environmental monitoring, and exploration.

Applications of Swarm Robotics in various fields are:
Swarm robotics significantly enhances efficiency and adaptability across key applications (Fig. 11.9). In disaster management, drone swarms rapidly survey affected zones and support search and rescue in hard-to-reach areas. In industrial automation, synchronized robots streamline warehouse tasks, boosting inventory accuracy and workflow speed. For environmental monitoring, swarms track pollution, assess ecosystem health, and enable large-scale data collection for informed conservation.

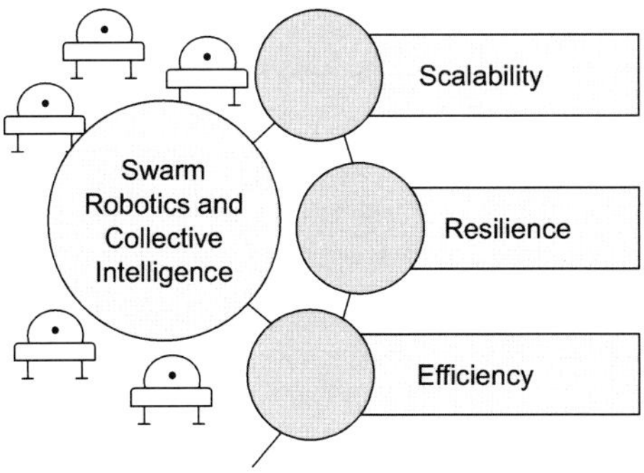

Fig. 11.9 Advantages of SR and CI.

11.2.3 Quantum Computing in Robotics

Quantum computing is set to transform robotics by vastly boosting speed and efficiency. By using qubits capable of parallel calculations it enhances decision-making and optimization processes in autonomous systems [13].

11.2.3.1 Impact of Quantum Computing on Robotics

Advanced algorithms and computational methods boost robotic performance across domains. They enable faster path planning, reduce delays, and enhance real-time efficiency. Improved machine learning accelerates data processing, supporting better pattern recognition and sensor fusion [23], leading to smarter, adaptive behavior. These advancements also optimize resource allocation, improving decision-making in sectors like healthcare, logistics, and transportation (Fig. 11.10).

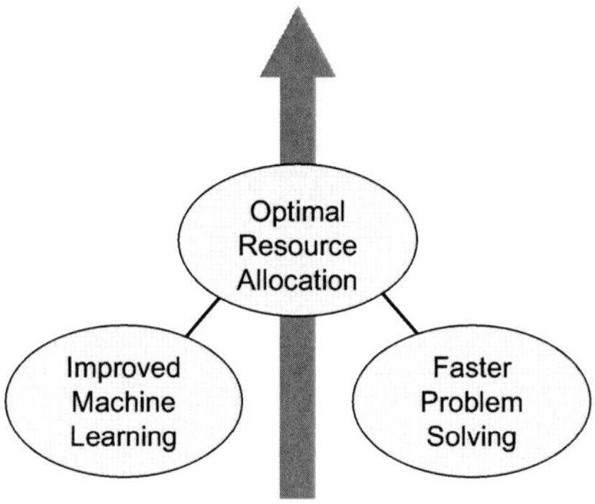

Fig. 11.10 Impact of Quantum Robotics.

11.2.3.2 Potential Applications of Quantum Robotics

High-speed computational technologies are reshaping robotics across key sectors. In autonomous vehicles, faster processing boosts navigation and obstacle detection, enhancing safety and efficiency. In healthcare, AI-powered labs accelerate molecular research and drug development. In smart manufacturing, advanced computing streamlines workflows and robot coordination improving productivity and adaptability. Next-gen robotics will merge soft, swarm, and quantum technologies to build efficient, intelligent, and adaptive systems. These robots will advance healthcare, automation, space exploration, and environmental conservation (Fig. 11.11), fueling progress across industries [12].

11.3 Human-Robot Collaboration and Ethical Considerations

Human-Robot Collaboration (HRC) is reshaping sectors like manufacturing, healthcare and logistics by allowing robots to handle repetitive tasks while humans

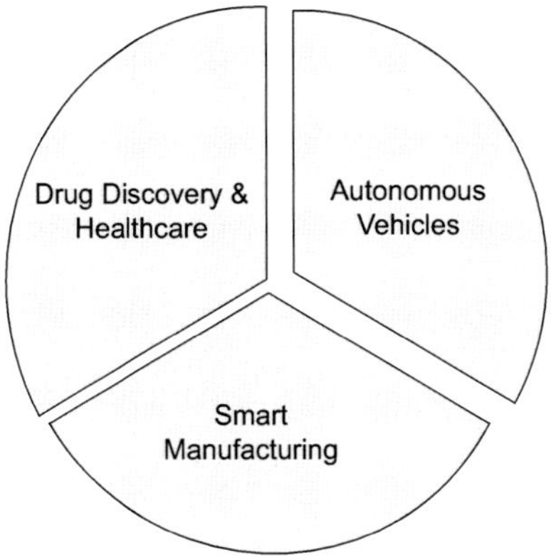

Fig. 11.11 Broader Applications of Quantum Robotics.

focus on creative and strategic roles [3]. As this synergy grows, ethical concerns around safety, privacy, fairness, and job displacement must be addressed to ensure responsible integration.

11.3.1 Collaborative Robots (Cobots) and Their Role

Cobots are built to collaborate safely with humans in shared spaces unlike isolated industrial robots. With AI, adaptive learning, and advanced sensors, they boost productivity while maintaining safe interaction (Fig. 11.12). Cobots are designed for safe, flexible collaboration with human workers across industries. With sensors and force detection, they adjust movements in real time to prevent injuries. Easily reprogrammable, cobots adapt to diverse tasks and boost productivity by automating repetitive work freeing humans to focus on creative and strategic responsibilities. Cobots are gaining traction across sectors for their versatility and safe human collaboration. In manufacturing, they assist with assembly, welding, and quality control enhancing precision and productivity [3], [16]. In healthcare, cobots aid surgeons and support rehabilitation. In retail and service, they automate inventory and interact with customers, driving efficiency and engagement.

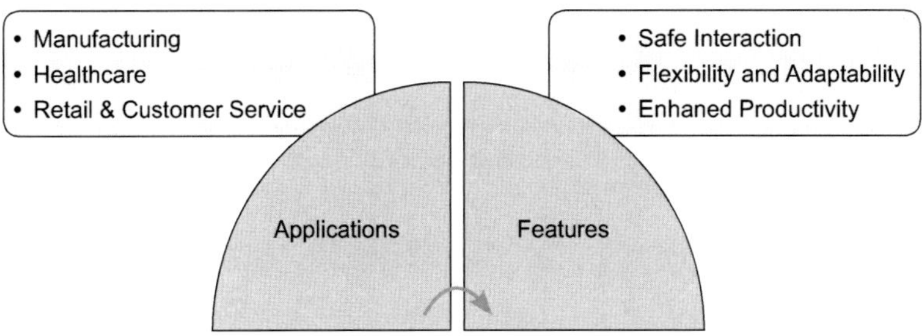

Fig. 11.12 Features and Applications of Cobots.

11.3.2 Brain-Computer Interfaces (BCI) in Robotics

Brain-Computer Interfaces (BCI) enable neural signal-based control of robots, transforming assistive devices, remote operations, and cognitive human–robot interaction [35].

Brain-Computer Interface (BCI) technology enables direct control of robots through neural signals, revolutionizing assistive and human-machine interaction. Electrodes or wearables detect brain activity, which AI algorithms interpret into actionable commands for robotic response. Real-time execution allows seamless interaction, benefiting neurorehabilitation, prosthetics, and assistive robotics with enhanced independence and quality of life. Brain-Computer Interface (BCI) technology enables thought-controlled robotics, transforming human–machine interaction. In assistive tech, it empowers users to operate prosthetics, wheelchairs, and exoskeletons for greater independence. BCI also enables remote control of drones and surgical robots, crucial in high-risk environments. It advances cognitive robotics by helping machines respond to human emotions, fostering more intuitive and empathetic interactions.

11.3.3 Ethical Challenges in Human-Robot Collaboration

Expanding human-robot collaboration raises ethical concerns that demand careful attention to ensure responsible integration and societal acceptance [7].

(a) Safety and Reliability in Robotics

Robots require fail-safe systems to avoid malfunctions and accidents. AI-driven models must ensure transparent decision-making to foster trust (Fig. 11.13). Enforcing rigorous safety standards is essential—especially in defence, healthcare, and autonomous transport sectors [31].

(b) Privacy and Data Security

Robots handle large volumes of personal data, raising risks of unauthorized access and misuse. Robust cybersecurity is vital to prevent breaches, while strict regulations must govern the handling of biometric and behavioral information.

(c) Workforce Impact and Job Displacement

Automation boosts efficiency but risks job displacement especially in manufacturing, logistics, and customer service. To prepare for AI-driven roles, governments and industries must invest in upskilling initiatives. A balanced approach should position robots as collaborators, not replacements, fostering sustainable employment models.

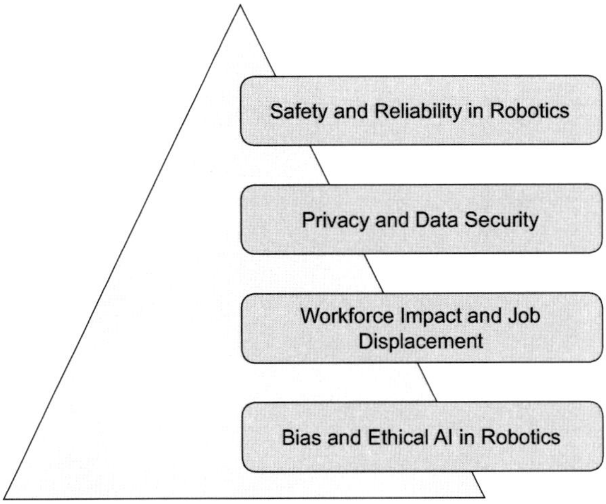

Fig. 11.13 Ethical challenges in Human-Robot Collaboration.

(d) Bias and Ethical AI in Robotics

AI robots must be trained on diverse datasets to avoid biased decisions. Transparency in algorithms ensures fairness and accountability, especially in hiring, law enforcement, and healthcare. Ethical AI frameworks should guide robotic development to uphold human rights and values. Advances in NLP, adaptive learning, and emotional intelligence will shape future robotics-human collaboration making robots more responsive to human needs [21]. Ethical development will be crucial to ensure trust, safety, and fairness in deployment.

11.4 Autonomous Systems and Smart Robotics

Autonomous robotics is reshaping industries by enabling machines to operate independently with minimal human input. Using advanced sensors, AI, and real-time decision-making, these systems perform complex tasks safely and efficiently across applications like self-driving cars, industrial automation, and healthcare support [20].

11.4.1 Key Features of Autonomous Systems

Autonomous systems integrate advanced technologies to operate with minimal human input. Key features include perception through LiDAR, radar, cameras, and ultrasonic sensors; real-time decision-making via AI; and navigation aided by SLAM and GPS [22]. Adaptive learning refines behavior over time, while NLP and gesture recognition enhance intuitive human interaction (Fig. 11.14).

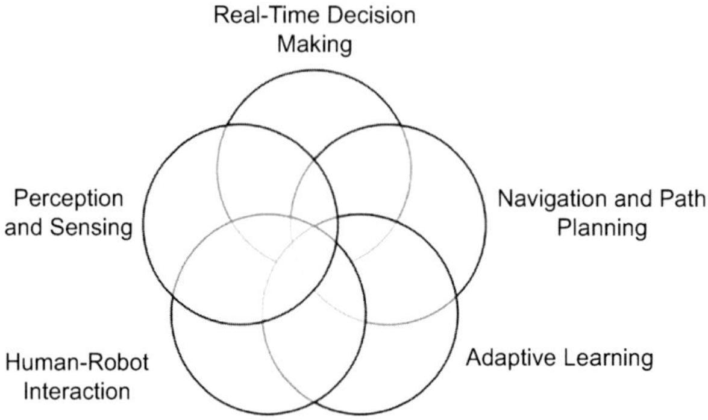

Fig. 11.14 Key Features of Autonomous Systems.

11.4.2 Applications of Autonomous Robotics

Autonomous robotics is revolutionizing industries by enabling machines to function independently with minimal human input. Applications span manufacturing automation, self-driving transport, AI-driven drones, precision agriculture, healthcare robotics, and service roles in retail and hospitality enhancing safety, productivity, and efficiency across sectors (Fig. 11.15).

(a) Self-driving vehicles and smart transportation systems are reshaping mobility by improving safety and reducing traffic congestion. Autonomous cars, drones, and transit systems rely on sensors like LiDAR, cameras, and GPS, while AI algorithms process real-time data for smooth navigation. Integrated with V2X communication, these systems optimize traffic flow and fuel efficiency enhancing overall transport sustainability [24].

(b) Industrial and warehouse robotics are revolutionizing operations through autonomous transport, precision manufacturing, and predictive maintenance. AMRs autonomously manage inventory and materials, while AI-powered robotic arms ensure high-quality assembly. Embedded sensors enable proactive maintenance, boosting reliability and reducing downtime across logistics and factory workflows.

(c) Smart agricultural robotics are enhancing farming by improving resource use and boosting yields. AI-guided drones monitor crop health and soil conditions via high-res imaging, while autonomous tractors and harvesters handle planting and harvesting with minimal human input. Sensor-equipped irrigation systems adjust water use based on soil moisture ensuring growth and reducing waste. These innovations make agriculture more efficient, sustainable, and data-driven.

(d) Healthcare robotics improve precision, efficiency, and accessibility in patient care. Surgical robots support minimally invasive procedures, rehab systems aid recovery, and robotic nurses enhance caregiving. Diagnostic and telemedicine robots advance imaging and enable remote surgeries reshaping healthcare delivery and outcomes [6], [22].

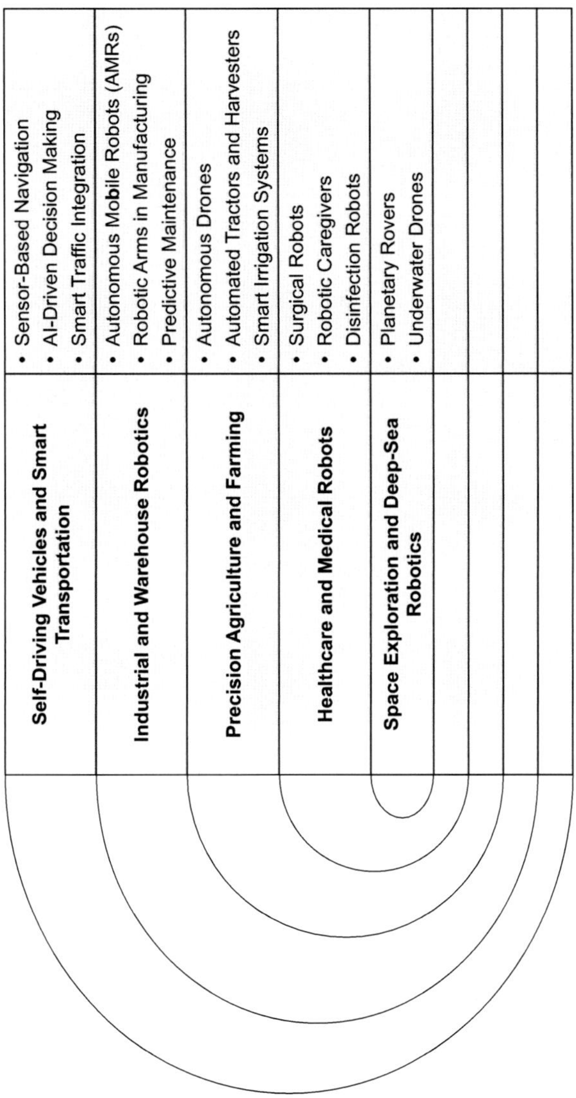

Fig. 11.15 Applications of Autonomous Robotics.

Robotic technologies are advancing healthcare by improving precision, outcomes, and patient support. Surgical robots enable minimally invasive procedures with faster recovery, while robotic caregivers assist the elderly and disabled enhancing independence and quality of life [11]. Disinfection robots maintain hygiene using UV light and automated systems, boosting safety and operational efficiency. Robotics is unlocking access to extreme environments, both in space and underwater. Autonomous rovers and probes explore planets, gather data, and support satellite maintenance, while deep-sea drones map ocean floors and inspect marine ecosystems [33]. These systems endure harsh conditions, delivering vital insights and expanding human knowledge beyond physical limits.

11.4.3 Challenges and Ethical Considerations in Autonomous Robotics

Autonomous robotics faces key challenges in safety, accountability, bias, and privacy. Reliable decision-making is critical in high-stakes fields like healthcare, defence, and autonomous transport. Ethical concerns—such as job loss, biased AI decisions, and data misuse—require urgent attention. Clear regulations, transparency, and human oversight are essential for safe and responsible integration [2], [7] (Fig. 11.16).

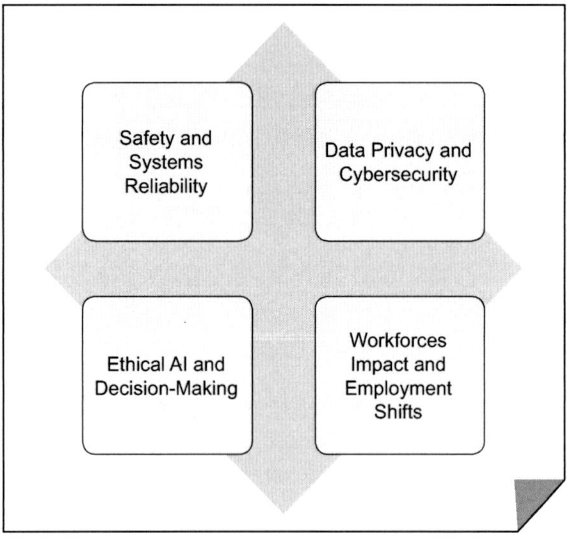

Fig. 11.16 Challenges and Ethical Considerations.

(a) Safety and System Reliability

Autonomous machines must achieve high accuracy to prevent accidents especially in healthcare and transportation. Rigorous testing and validation are essential before real-world deployment.

(b) Data Privacy and Cybersecurity

Autonomous systems gather large volumes of data, prompting privacy concerns and risks of unauthorized access. Strong cybersecurity is essential to prevent breaches and protect system integrity.

(c) Ethical AI and Decision-Making

In high-stakes scenarios like collision avoidance robots must make ethical decisions based on clear frameworks. Transparent AI logic is vital to ensure public trust and prevent bias.

(d) Workforce Impact and Employment Shifts

Automation may displace jobs in manufacturing and logistics. To support workforce transition, governments and industries must invest in reskilling for emerging roles in AI and robotics.

11.4.4 The Future of Robotics

The future of smart robotics will be shaped by rapid progress in AI, machine learning, and edge computing enabling faster, real-time decisions in dynamic settings. Human-centric AI will foster emotionally aware, adaptive robots that collaborate naturally with humans. As autonomous systems grow, regulatory frameworks will be vital to address privacy, safety, and accountability. Integration with IoT and smart city infrastructure will support seamless urban automation, positioning robotics as a catalyst for enhanced productivity and innovation across industries.

11.5 Convergence of Robotics with Emerging Technologies

Robotics is evolving through convergence with AI, IoT, 5G, blockchain, biotechnology, and quantum computing enhancing autonomy, precision, and adaptability [4]. These integrated technologies are revolutionizing healthcare, manufacturing, logistics, and space exploration by boosting efficiency and driving innovation [1], [5] (Fig. 11.17).

11.5.1 Artificial Intelligence (AI) in Robotics

AI boosts robotic intelligence, adaptability, and automation by enabling data-driven decision-making. Machine learning allows robots to refine actions through pattern recognition and experience-based learning. Advances in computer vision and NLP enhance object detection and human interaction. These capabilities power real-time defect detection in factories, precise navigation in autonomous vehicles, and improved diagnostics and care in healthcare transforming industry and daily life.

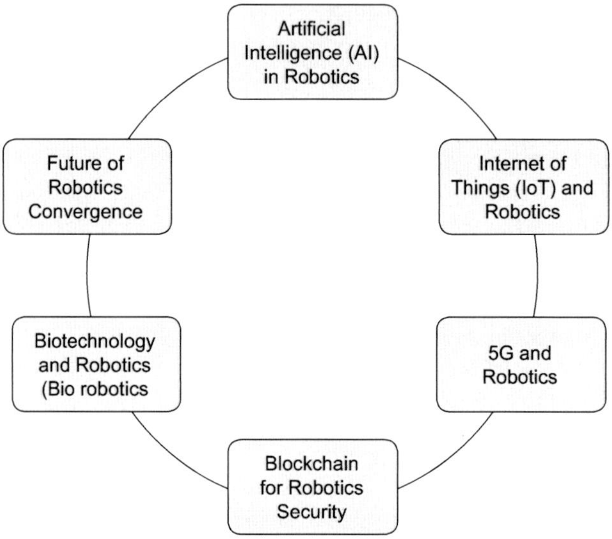

Fig. 11.17 Convergence of Robotics with Emerging Technologies.

11.5.2 Internet of Things (IoT) and Robotics

IoT-connected robotics enhance real-time data exchange and automation by linking machines with cloud platforms, sensors, and smart systems. This integration boosts productivity across industries through remote control, predictive maintenance, and smart manufacturing. Applications range from inventory tracking in logistics to remote patient monitoring in healthcare and data-driven irrigation in agriculture driving greater efficiency, sustainability, and operational resilience.

11.5.3 5G and Robotics

5G technology is revolutionizing robotics by enabling ultra-fast data transfer, low latency, and high connectivity. This supports real-time robot coordination, precise remote operations like telesurgery, and seamless integration in smart city ecosystems. In healthcare, manufacturing, and transport, 5G-powered robots respond instantly, boosting accuracy, safety, and productivity.

11.5.4 Blockchain for Robotics Security

Blockchain enhances robotics security by ensuring data integrity, transparency, and resilience against cyber threats. Decentralized ledgers allow secure, authority-free data sharing, while smart contracts enable tamper-proof automation in supply chains. It also strengthens identity verification and swarm coordination, improves auditability, and protects autonomous systems from unauthorized control—critical across sectors like defence, healthcare and manufacturing [26], [27]. Blockchain integration strengthens robotics through enhanced security, transparency, and efficiency. Tamper-proof records improve trust, while decentralized networks boost resilience against cyber threats. Smart contracts enable secure, automated transactions essential for supply chains. Applications span fraud prevention, verified drone deliveries, and encrypted financial operations, ensuring safe and trustworthy robotic workflows.

11.5.5 Biotechnology and Robotics (Bio robotics)

Bio-robotics blends biological principles with robotic technology to revolutionize healthcare, prosthetics, and bio-inspired automation. AI-powered bionic limbs and exoskeletons restore mobility and aid rehabilitation, while soft and biohybrid robots support precision surgery and medical research. Microbots enable targeted drug delivery, and bio-manufacturing advances regenerative medicine enhancing patient care and personalized treatments. Neural interfaces enable brain-controlled robotic systems, helping patients with severe disabilities regain mobility and control. Robotic bioprinting supports 3D-printed tissues and organs, advancing treatment and transplant options. Innovations include AI-driven smart prosthetics, mobility-assisting exoskeletons, and microbots for targeted drug delivery—transforming healthcare and personalized care.

11.5.6 Future of Robotics Convergence

The future of robotics convergence involves integrating AI, IoT, biotechnology, and quantum computing to create intelligent, autonomous systems. Robotics will seamlessly collaborate with human augmentation, enabling advanced prosthetics and brain-computer interfaces. AI- powered swarm robotics will enhance automation in industries like agriculture, logistics, and space exploration. Edge computing and 5G will enable real-time decision-making in autonomous vehicles and smart cities. Human-robot collaboration (HRC) will expand in workplaces, improving efficiency and safety [30]. Ethical AI frameworks will ensure transparency and fairness. As robotics converges with emerging technologies, it will revolutionize healthcare, industry, and daily life, driving a more connected, intelligent world.

- Fully Automated Smart Factories powered by AI and IoT.
- Human-Robot Collaboration enhanced by 5G and blockchain security.
- Autonomous AI-driven cities where robots manage infrastructure and logistics.
- Self-Adaptive Robots that continuously evolve through AI and quantum computing.

As robotics technology advances, its convergence with other fields will redefine industries and reshape everyday life, driving innovation and efficiency across multiple sectors.

11.6 Challenges, Ethics, and Future Roadmap

The rapid advancement of robotics and artificial intelligence (AI) brings numerous opportunities but also presents significant challenges and ethical concerns. As robots become more autonomous and integrated into society, addressing these challenges is crucial to ensure their responsible development and deployment. This section explores the key obstacles, ethical dilemmas, and the future roadmap for robotics and AI.

11.6.1 Challenges in Robotics and AI

Despite remarkable progress, robotics faces several hurdles that must be addressed to enhance reliability, safety, and efficiency. Figure 18 illustrates the key factors that contribute to the development of a safe and effective robot. Robotic systems rely on high processing power, precise sensors, and advanced algorithms to perform effectively in various tasks. However, several challenges hinder their full potential. One of the main issues is limited perception and adaptability, as robots often struggle to navigate and make decisions in unstructured environments, making real-time decision-making difficult. Additionally, the high energy consumption required by these systems can significantly limit their operational efficiency, particularly for autonomous robots that need to run continuously without frequent recharge. Furthermore, hardware reliability remains a concern, as the mechanical components of robots can wear out over time, leading to increased maintenance needs and downtime, as noted by [29]. These challenges highlight the ongoing need for advancements in robot design and technology to improve their effectiveness and longevity. Human-Robot Interaction focuses on seamless communication and collaboration between humans and robots. Challenges include understanding human intent, emotions, and natural language. Advancements in AI, machine learning, and sensor technologies improve safety, adaptability, and trust, enabling robots to assist in industries like healthcare, manufacturing, and service automation. Ensuring seamless collaboration between humans and robots is essential for maximizing the benefits of automation while maintaining a productive and comfortable work environment. One critical factor is the development of intuitive interfaces that allow robots to understand and respond to natural language and human gestures, making interactions more fluid and user-friendly. Equally important is fostering trust and acceptance among human workers, as there can be significant reluctance to work alongside machines due to concerns about potential malfunctions or fears of job displacement. Building reliable, transparent robotic systems and promoting education about their roles can help bridge this gap, enabling more effective and harmonious human-robot collaboration. Safety and Security Risks in robotics and AI involve system failures, cyber threats, and unintended consequences. Risks include hacking, data breaches, autonomous malfunctions, and physical harm in human-robot interactions. Ensuring robust cybersecurity, fail-safe mechanisms, ethical AI policies, and regulatory oversight is crucial for safe and reliable AI-driven robotics deployment.

Robots operating in industrial, medical, and public environments present various safety and security risks that must be carefully managed. One major concern is the potential for autonomous errors, where malfunctions or unpredictable behavior by robotic systems can result in accidents, equipment damage, or harm to human operators and patients. In addition to physical risks, cybersecurity threats pose a growing danger, as hackers may target robotic systems to disrupt operations or gain unauthorized access to sensitive data. Such vulnerabilities highlight the urgent need for robust safety protocols, regular system audits, and advanced cybersecurity measures to ensure the safe and secure deployment of robots across different sectors. Legal and Regulatory Barriers in robotics and AI include unclear liability, data privacy concerns, ethical AI governance, and cross-border regulations. Challenges (Fig. 11.18) arise in defining responsibility for AI decisions, enforcing fair use, and preventing misuse. Establishing global AI standards, ethical frameworks, and transparent policies is essential for responsible AI deployment. The absence of standardized laws and regulations governing robotics poses serious concerns regarding accountability and legal compliance, as highlighted by [9]. One of the primary issues is determining liability for decisions made autonomously by AI-driven robots particularly in situations where errors or accidents occur, raising questions about whether responsibility lies with the manufacturer, programmer, or operator. Additionally, the ethical use of robotics in areas such as warfare and surveillance remain a critical concern, as these technologies must be carefully regulated to ensure they do not infringe on human rights or international law. Establishing clear legal frameworks and ethical guidelines is essential to guide the responsible development and deployment of robotic systems.

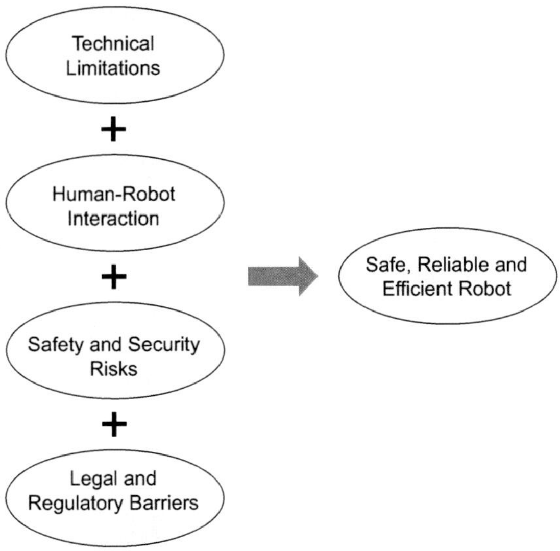

Fig. 11.18 Challenges and considerations.

11.6.2 Ethical Considerations in Robotics

Robotics and AI raise concerns around bias, job loss, privacy, accountability, and autonomous decisions. Ensuring fairness, transparency, and ethical design is vital to mitigate risks like surveillance and protect human rights fostering responsible and beneficial innovation. Job Displacement and Economic Impact arise as AI and robotics automate tasks, reducing demand for human labor in industries like manufacturing, retail, and transportation. While automation boosts productivity and creates new AI-driven jobs, it also risks wage polarization and economic inequality, requiring reskilling programs and policy reforms for workforce adaptation. Automation is rapidly transforming industries by increasing efficiency and productivity, but it also raises significant concerns related to employment and workforce dynamics. One major issue is the potential for workforce reductions, as AI-powered robots increasingly take over roles in manufacturing, logistics, and service sectors a trend noted by [19]. This shift not only threatens job security for many workers but also contributes to a widening skill gap, as the demand grows for advanced technical skills that many non-specialized workers may not possess. Addressing these challenges will require proactive strategies, including reskilling programs and educational reforms, to ensure a more inclusive and adaptive labor market. Human Privacy and Data Security in AI and robotics involve risks like data breaches, unauthorized surveillance, and misuse of personal information. AI systems collect vast user data, raising concerns about consent, encryption, and cybersecurity. Ensuring strict regulations, ethical AI design, and robust security measures is crucial for protecting user privacy.

11.6.3 Future Roadmap for Robotics and AI

The future of Robotics and AI focuses on enhanced autonomy, ethical AI, and human-centric innovations. Advancements in machine learning, edge computing, and quantum AI will improve real-time decision-making and adaptability [14, 32]. Ethical AI frameworks, transparency, and bias mitigation will ensure responsible AI deployment. Regulations will evolve to address data security, liability, and AI ethics. Robotics will integrate human-AI collaboration, enhancing industries like healthcare, manufacturing, and smart cities. Sustainability will be a key focus, promoting energy-efficient AI. Interdisciplinary research will drive AI's next evolution, ensuring safer, more efficient, and globally beneficial robotic systems. AI and robotics are evolving with autonomous systems, deep learning, and real-time decision-making. Edge AI, quantum computing, and neuromorphic chips enhance processing power, while human-robot collaboration improves safety and efficiency. Innovations in computer vision, NLP, and swarm robotics enable smarter automation. Future trends focus on ethical AI, sustainability, and adaptive intelligence, driving breakthroughs in healthcare, smart cities, and industrial automation. Future advancements in robotics will increasingly focus on enhancing cognitive abilities, improving energy efficiency, and fostering deeper human-robot collaboration. AI-driven robots are expected to possess advanced learning and adaptive capabilities, enabling them to operate effectively in dynamic and unpredictable environments. Alongside these developments, significant efforts will be directed toward creating energy-efficient systems through the use of advanced batteries and innovative energy-harvesting technologies, as highlighted by [28]. Additionally, the evolution of human-robot symbiosis will be a key area of focus, with the development of more intuitive and responsive interfaces that facilitate seamless interaction and cooperation between humans and robots in various professional and personal settings.

Conclusion

Robotics and AI are rapidly transforming industries driving innovation in healthcare, manufacturing, smart cities, and mobility. Yet this progress brings ethical, security, and workforce challenges. Ensuring fairness, transparency, and strong regulations is key to responsible deployment. Protecting data, preventing bias, and reskilling workers will foster trust and equity. Collaborative robots can balance automation with job preservation, while energy-efficient designs and green AI aid sustainability. Generative AI paired with reinforcement learning and explainable AI will shape adaptive, ethical systems that align with human values. With global cooperation, robotics can evolve safely and sustainably for societal benefit.

Declarations

- The authors received no specific funding for this study.
- The authors declare that they have no conflicts of interest regarding the present study.
- No Human subject or animals are involved in the research.
- All authors have mutually consented to participate.
- All the authors have given consent to publish this work.
- The authors declare that all data sources used have been mentioned.

References

[1] Afzal, N., Rehman, M. ur, Seneviratne, L., C Hussain, I. (2025). The Convergence of AI and animal-inspired robots for ecological conservation. *Ecological Informatics*, 85, 102950. https://doi.org/10.1016/j.ecoinf.2024.102950.

[2] Ayyildiz, E. and C. Erdogan M. (2024). Addressing the challenges of using autonomous robots for last-mile delivery. *Computers & Industrial Engineering*, 1S0, 110096. https://doi.org/10.1016/j.cie.2024.110096.

[3] Callari, T.C., Vecellio Segate, R., Hubbard, E.-M., Daly, A., C Lohse, N. et al. (2024). An ethical framework for human-robot collaboration for the future people-centric manufacturing: A collaborative endeavour with European subject-matter experts in ethics. *Technology in Society*, 78, 102680.https://doi.org/10.1016/j.techsoc.2024.102680.

[4] Chandra, V., Dutta, S. and C. Albanese, C.T. (2006a). Surgical robotics and image guided therapy in pediatric surgery: Emerging and converging minimal access technologies. *Seminars in Pediatric Surgery*, 15(4), 267–275. https://doi.org/10.1053/j.sempedsurg.2006.07.006.

[5] Chandra, V., Dutta, S. and C. Albanese C.T. (2006b). Surgical robotics and image guided therapy in pediatric surgery: Emerging and converging minimal access technologies. *Seminars in Pediatric Surgery*, 15(4), 267–275. https://doi.org/10.1053/j.sempedsurg.2006.07.006.

[6] Deng, H., Xu, J., Nie, J., Wang, H., Sun, Y. et al. (2024). Application of task-autonomous dental robot for lateral window preparation in the maxillary sinus. *Journal of Cranio-Maxillofacial Surgery*. https://doi.org/10.1016/j.jcms.2024.11.005.

[7] Dhanda, M., Rogers, B.A., Hall, S., Dekoninck, E., C Dhokia, V. et al. (2025a). Reviewing human-robot collaboration in manufacturing: Opportunities and challenges in the context of industry 5.0. *Robotics and Computer-Integrated Manufacturing*, *S3*, 102937. https://doi.org/10.1016/j.rcim.2024.102937.

[8] Dhanda, M., Rogers, B.A., Hall, S., Dekoninck, E., C Dhokia, V. et al. (2025b). Reviewing human-robot collaboration in manufacturing: Opportunities and challenges in the context of industry 5.0. *Robotics and Computer-Integrated Manufacturing*, S3, 102937. https://doi.org/10.1016/j.rcim.2024.102937.

[9] Dhanda, M., Rogers, B.A., Hall, S., Dekoninck, E., and C. Dhokia V. (2025c). Reviewing human-robot collaboration in manufacturing: Opportunities and challenges in the context of industry 5.0. *Robotics and Computer-Integrated Manufacturing*, S3, 102937. https://doi.org/10.1016/j.rcim.2024.102937.

[10] Emaminejad, N. and C. Akhavian R. (2022). Trustworthy AI and robotics: Implications for the AECindustry. *Automation in Construction*, 13S, 104298.https://doi.org/10.1016/j.autcon.2022.104298.

[11] Farkh, R., Marouani, H., Al Jaloud, K., Alhuwaimel, S., Tabrez Quasim, M. et al. (2021). Intelligent Autonomous-Robot Control for Medical Applications. *Computers, Materials & Continua*, c8(2), 2189–2203. https://doi.org/10.32604/cmc.2021.015906.

[12] Fazilat, M., Zioui, N., C St-Arnaud, J. (2022). A novel quantum model of forward kinematics based on quaternion/Pauli gate equivalence: Application to a six- jointed industrial robotic arm. *Results in Engineering*, 14, 100402. https://doi.org/10.1016/j.rineng.2022.100402.

[13] Hu, L., Wei, C. and C. Yin L. (2025). Fuzzy A* quantum multi-stage Q-learning artificial potential field for path planning of mobile robots. *Engineering Applications of Artificial Intelligence*, 141, 109866.https://doi.org/10.1016/j.engappai.2024.109866.

[14] Inamdar, R., Sundarr, S.K., Khandelwal, D., Sahu, V.D., C. Katal, N. et al. (2024). A comprehensive review on safe reinforcement learning for autonomous vehicle control in dynamic environments. *E-Prime -Advances in Electrical Engineering, Electronics and Energy*, 10, 100810. https://doi.org/10.1016/j.prime.2024.100810.

[15] Jahanshahi, H. and C. Zhu Z.H. (2025). A comprehensive review of tactile sensing technologies in space robotics. *Chinese Journal of Aeronautics*, 103423. https://doi.org/10.1016/j.cja.2025.103423.

[16] Javaid, M., Haleem, A., Singh, R.P., Rab, S. and C. Suman R. (2022). Significant applications of Cobots in the field of manufacturing. *Cognitive Robotics*, 2, 222–233. https://doi.org/10.1016/j.cogr.2022.10.001.

[17] Khan, A., Meyers, J.E., Yavorek, S., O'Connor, T.E., Siasios, I. et al. (2019). Comparing Next-Generation Robotic Technology with 3-Dimensional Computed Tomography Navigation Technology for the Insertion of Posterior Pedicle Screws. *World Neurosurgery*, 123, e474–e481. https://doi.org/10.1016/j.wneu.2018.11.190.

[18] Konstantinou, C., Antonarakos, D., Angelakis, P., Gkournelos, C., Michalos, G. et al. (2024). Leveraging Generative AI Prompt Programming for Human-Robot Collaborative Assembly. *Procedia CIRP*, 128, 621–626. https://doi.org/10.1016/j.procir.2024.03.040.

[19] Liang, C.-J., Le, T.-H., Ham, Y., Mantha, B.R.K., Cheng, M.H. et al. (2024). Ethics of artificial intelligence and robotics in the architecture, engineering, and construction industry. *Automation in Construction*, 1c2, 105369. https://doi.org/10.1016/j.autcon.2024.105369.

[20] Liang, W., Ning, Z., Xie, S., Hu, Y., Lu, S. et al. (2021). Secure fusion approach for the Internet of Things in smart autonomous multi-robot systems. *Information Sciences*, 57S, 468–482. https://doi.org/10.1016/j.ins.2021.08.035.

[21] Lin, C.S., Kuo, Y.-F. and C. Wang T.-Y. (2025). Trust and acceptance of AI caregiving robots: The role of ethics and self-efficacy. *Computers in Human Behavior: ArtificialHumans*, 3, 100115. https://doi.org/10.1016/j.chbah.2024.100115.

[22] Lin, S.-L. and C. Lin, B.-C. (2024). Enhancing Safety in Autonomous Vehicle Navigation: An Optimized Path Planning Approach Leveraging Model Predictive Control. *Computers, Materials & Continua*, *80*(3), 3555–3572. https://doi.org/10.32604/cmc.2024.055456.

[23] Mannone, M., Seidita, V., C Chella, A. (2023). Modeling and designing a robotic swarm: A quantum computing approach. *Swarm and Evolutionary Computation*, 7S, 101297. https://doi.org/10.1016/j.swevo.2023.101297.

[24] Pakkala, D., Känsäkoski, N., Heikkilä, T., Backman, J. and C. Pääkkönen, P. (2025). On design of cognitive situation-adaptive autonomous mobile robotic applications. *Computers in Industry*, 1c7, 104263. https://doi.org/10.1016/j.compind.2025.104263.

[25] Pan, M., Yang, Y., Qin, X., Li, G., Xi, N., Long, M., Jiang, L., Zhao, T. and C. Liu, L. (2024). Applying the intrinsic principle of cell collectives to program robot swarms. *Cell Reports Physical Science*, *5*(8), 102122. https://doi.org/10.1016/j.xcrp.2024.102122.

[26] Sharma, S., Dubey, R., C Chaudhury, S. (2024). A bibliometric survey on impact of Blockchain in Robotics: Trends and Applications. *Computers and Electrical Engineering*, *120*, 109744. https://doi.org/10.1016/j.compeleceng.2024.109744.

[27] Srinivas Aditya, U.S.P., Singh, R., Singh, P.K., C Kalla, A. (2021). A Survey on Blockchain in Robotics: Issues, Opportunities, Challenges and Future Directions. *Journal of Network and Computer Applications*, 1Sc, 103245.https://doi.org/10.1016/j.jnca.2021.103245.

[28] Tanimu, J.A. and C. Abada, W. (2025). Addressing cybersecurity challenges in robotics: A comprehensive overview. *Cyber Security and Applications*, 3, 100074. https://doi.org/10.1016/j.csa.2024.100074.

[29] Wang, J., Shi, E., Hu, H., Ma, C., Liu, Y., Wang, X., Yao, Y., Liu, X., Ge, B. and C. Zhang, S. (2024). Large language models for robotics: Opportunities, challenges, and perspectives. *Journal of Automation and Intelligence*. https://doi.org/10.1016/j.jai.2024.12.003.

[30] Wang, S., Lim, W.M., Cheah, J.-H. and C. Lim, X.-J. (2025). Working with robots: Trends and future directions. *Technological Forecasting and Social Change*, 212, 123648. https://doi.org/10.1016/j.techfore.2024.123648.

[31] Wang, Y., Ai, Q., Zhao, W., Gao, Y., Liu, Q., Shi, T., Du, S., Wang, B., Fu, W., Yuan, Q., Jiang, B., Ma, X., Li, H. and C. Zhang, X. (2024). Safety and Reliability of a Robot-assisted Laparoscopic Telesurgery System: Expanding Indications in Urological Surgery. *European Urology*, 85(5), 506–507. https://doi.org/10.1016/j.eururo.2023.11.002

[32] Wu, J., Huang, C., Huang, H., Lv, C., Wang, Y. and C. Wang, F.-Y. (2024). Recent advances in reinforcement learning-based autonomous driving behavior planning: A survey. *Transportation Research Part C: Emerging Technologies*, 1c4, 104654. https://doi.org/10.1016/j.trc.2024.104654.

[33] You, K., Zhou, C., Ding, L. and C. Wang, Y. (2025). Construction Robotics in Extrem Environments: From Earth to Space. Engineering. https://doi.org/10.1016/j.eng.2024.11.037.

[34] Zafar, M. H., Langås, E.F. and C. Sanfilippo, F. (2024). Exploring the synergies between collaborative robotics, digital twins, augmentation, and industry 5.0 for smart manufacturing: A state-of-the-art review. *Robotics and Computer-Integrated Manufacturing*, 8S, 102769. https://doi.org/10.1016/j.rcim.2024.102769.

[35] Zhang, Z., Li, M., Wei, R., Liao, W., Wang, F. and C. Xu, G. (2024). Research on shared control of robots based on hybrid brain-computer interface. *Journal of Neuroscience Methods*, *412*, 110280. https://doi.org/10.1016/j. jneumeth.2024.11028.

12 Generative Artificial Intelligence Development, Models, Healthcare Applications, and Future Directions: A Review

Prateek Mishra[1*], Vijay Bharti[2] and Sagar Panchal[3]

Generative Artificial Intelligence (GAI) has been gaining momentum in recent years and is becoming revolutionary in many ways. This study examines the development of GAI, examining its fundamental structures, approaches, and significant advances. We examine specific applications of GAI in healthcare, emphasizing its role in areas such as drug discovery, personalized medicine, diagnostic tools, and patient care. This article also addresses the obstacles and opportunities to join together to form a single organization GAI into healthcare, such as ethical issues, data privacy, and process control. Finally, we provide a detailed overview of future models and potential developments in GAI, focusing on upcoming new models, their potential for broader use, and their implications for the healthcare sector and society at large. The evolution of generative artificial intelligence, the models that underpin it and its revolutionary uses in healthcare are all examined in this review. In this quickly changing sector, it also shows new trends and future directions.

12.1 Introduction

Artificial intelligence (AI) drives industrial advancement by enabling integration of technologies such as GPUs, IoT, cloud computing, big data, and blockchain [1]. The rise of Generative AI (GenAI) marks a significant leap, with models capable of producing novel data—text, images, and other media—based on learned patterns from training datasets [2]. This review compiles and analyzes key findings on GenAI's applications, architectures, and performance. Though rooted in myths, AI formally emerged in 1956 during the Dartmouth Conference, led by McCarthy, Rochester, Minsky, and Shannon [3]. GenAI is now revolutionizing sectors like healthcare through innovations, challenges, and future prospects explored herein.

[1-3] CSE, Asia Pacific Institute of Information Technology, Panipat, India.
E-mail: bhartivijay2@gmail.com[2]; sp5555566@gmail.com[3]
* Corresponding author: director@apiit.edu.in

DOI: 10.1201/9781003670582-12

12.1.1 Overview of Generative AI

AI is transforming healthcare by enhancing diagnostics, treatment development, and patient care. Generative AI contributes significantly to mental health, personalized medicine, drug discovery, and surgery—but also raises concerns around bias, privacy, and ethical decision-making [4]. Advances in neural networks have enabled high-quality content generation, with methods like GANs and evolutionary techniques powering automated multimedia synthesis. This chapter highlights research from the special issue *"Generative Fashions in Artificial Intelligence and Their Applications"* [7], emphasizing how Generative AI (GAI) is reshaping industries and daily life. These systems generate text, images, and other media by learning from training data. Though still evolving, they've attracted widespread interest from academia, media, policymakers, and society. This study reviews GAI research over the past decade using bibliometrics, text mining, and social network analysis to map key developments and trends [5].

12.1.2 Importance and effect of Generative AI in many industries

Generative AI is increasingly defined by its ability to autonomously create realistic digital content—including images, audio, video, and 3D models—entirely from scratch, not just modified replicas. Open-source tools like DALL-E 2 and Stable Diffusion have amplified public interest by enabling text-to-image generation and advanced editing capabilities [6]. Ongoing research continues to expand generative models' creative potential and control mechanisms. The complexity of visual traits and advanced counterfeiting techniques makes replica detection difficult [11]. Large pre-trained models like GPT-3 and DALL-E highlight the broad capabilities of generative models across diverse applications [18]. Generative AI is accelerating the shift toward Industry 5.0 by fusing advanced technologies with human-centric design. From VAEs to powerful GANs, its development is revolutionizing sectors like manufacturing, supply chains, retail, and medicine—highlighting sustainable and ethical innovation through use cases such as Tesla's AI and Autodesk's Generative Design [57]. In healthcare, GenAI enhances diagnostics, personalized treatment, and mental health support, though concerns around bias, ethics, and oversight remain [4]. Its integration into metaverse healthcare enables medical data generation, predictive simulations, and immersive patient interactions—but also raises key privacy and fairness challenges [58].

12.2 Literature Survey

AI has rapidly progressed from foundational algorithms to real-world applications and industry-wide adoption—spanning healthcare, manufacturing, and beyond. Despite ongoing challenges, it stands as a transformative technology driving innovation across diverse domains [1]. Generative AI has rapidly evolved, with foundational model shifts from 2012–2018 laying the groundwork for key advancements between 2018–2023. This historical context highlights GenAI's

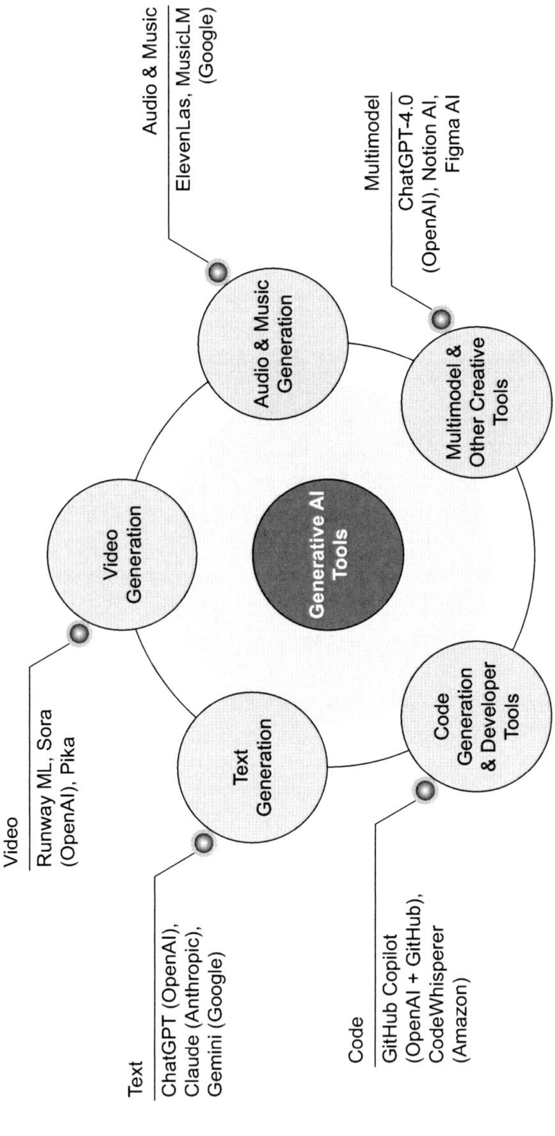

Fig. 12.1 Generative AI Tools.

accelerating progress and its expanding range of applications across sectors [2]. Generative AI is reshaping domains like computer vision, NLP, art, and healthcare—especially in data enhancement, creation, and medical image analysis [3]. It also raises ethical concerns, including deepfakes, prompting the need for detection systems and responsible AI guidelines. This paper outlines the current GenAI landscape and offers a roadmap for future research and ethical development. Proper regulation is essential to harness Generative AI's benefits and reduce risks in neuro-interventional surgery. AI already improves care, cuts costs, and saves lives. Machine learning will further advance precision medicine—offering accurate diagnoses and tailored treatments [4].

Emerging research explores how generative AI and ML can enhance patient experience, hospital operations, education, and cost efficiency. Applications also span Earth sciences, remote sensing, IoT, and cybersecurity. Large language models like ChatGPT show promise in image processing, pattern recognition, and computer vision [5]. This survey outlines key challenges in generative AI, including fake media detection, data bias, and weak alignment in evaluation, model control, and ethical design. It reviews major algorithms, notable models, and multimedia generation techniques, providing a broad overview of current limitations and future opportunities [6]. Researchers developed a model using multiple imputation ensembles (MIE) and GANs to generate synthetic fermentation data for Shindari, a traditional Jeju Beverage. This approach leverages incomplete datasets to predict microbial behavior and improve spoilage control, enhancing production processes in biotechnology [7]. Modern computer science helps historians connect disparate records and correct distortions in ancient history, but it also introduces risks like algorithmic bias and data inaccuracies [8]. A chronological survey of chatbots presents a detailed view of the technological and historical progress shaping conversational AI. It synthesizes key milestones and offers insights into chatbot evolution and cross-industry potential—providing valuable takeaways for researchers and stakeholders [9]. AI implementations inspired by neuroscience and cognition are shaping human-centered designs, promoting symbiotic interactions between users and systems. This study proposes future research directions and raises open questions for the broader community on ethical and collaborative AI development [10]. Generative AI models outperform traditional VAEs by converging faster in handwritten image modeling, with efficiency measured using inception scores and benchmarks against GAN, VAE, and VAE/GAN [13]. Broader research compares GenAI with conventional AI—examining architectures, applications, risks, and future trends—positioning it as a foundational resource for continued exploration [14]. This study explores core aspects of LMMs—architecture, training, fine-tuning, and prompt engineering—while offering a taxonomy of recent vision-language models. It also presents a unified overview of LLMs and LMMs, examines global trends in large-scale model development, and outlines future research directions [15].

12.3 Evolution and Development of Generative AI

Conversational AI has progressed from early statistical models and classic chatbots like ELIZA and ALICE to advanced agents like ChatGPT and Google Bard. Key milestones include the Turing Test, the CALO project, and transformer-based breakthroughs—driven by academic and industrial innovation [9]. Meanwhile, AI's role in healthcare has grown remarkably due to rapid advances in machine learning and computing power [8]. Conversational AI has evolved from early rule-based systems like ELIZA to advanced LLMs capable of complex medical dialogue. Key milestones include recurrent neural networks (1990s), attention mechanisms (2014), and multimodal foundation models. These advances enable real-time symptom analysis, personalized education, and clinical decision support. Current research focuses on medical LLMs using retrieval-augmented generation and systems integrating text with, medical imaging [8].

12.3.1 The evolution of AI up to the year 2025

Table 12.1 The evolution of AI up to the year 2025.

Year	*Development*	*Description*
1980	Expert Systems	AI garnered renewed interest with the development of expert systems like MYCIN, which utilized rule-based logic to assist in diagnosing diseases, especially in healthcare.
1997	Deep Blue Defeats Chess Champion	AI demonstrated its growing potential by defeating the world chess champion Garry Kasparov, highlighting its problem-solving and analytical capabilities.
2002	AI in Consumer Products	AI made its way into consumer products like robotic vacuum, marking its early presence in everyday technology.
2011	IBM Watson Triumphs in Jeopardy	IBM's Watson showcased its AI power by defeating human champions on "Jeopardy!", displaying remarkable data processing abilities that would later be applied in healthcare data analytics.
2012	DL Breakthrough	The success of DL models, particularly in image recognition, marked a pivotal moment for AI in fields like medical imaging, improving diagnostic capabilities.
2020	AI in Healthcare (COVID-19)	During the COVID-19 pandemic, AI played a crucial role in drug discovery, virus spread prediction, and vaccine development, showcasing its potential to address global healthcare challenges.
2021	Open AI's GPT-3 Released	The release of GPT-3, a language model have the potential of generating human-like text, set the stage for AI applications in healthcare such as patient interaction, clinical documentation, and telemedicine.

Contd...

Table 12.1 *Contd...*

Year	*Development*	*Description*
2022	DALL•E 2 by OpenAI	DALL•E 2, an AI model that give rise to high-quality images from text descriptions, could be applied in medical imaging and visualization for healthcare professionals.
2023	GPT-4 Released	GPT-4's release further improved AI's capabilities in processing and understanding complex medical language, offering advancements in clinical decision support systems.
2024	AI Regulations and Ethical AI	As AI continues to evolve in healthcare, governments and organizations focus on implementing regulations and developing ethical AI frameworks to ensure transparency and reduce bias in healthcare applications.

Human intelligence has evolved over millennia to the point where it now drives the creation and development of artificial intelligence. As versatile AI models emerge, the synergy between human and machine intelligence is accelerating—shaping profound outcomes. This discussion emphasizes the human role in guiding ethical, responsible, and effective AI systems [10]. AI-driven technologies are transforming healthcare by enhancing accuracy, productivity, and clinical decision-making. Digital aides track patient status, robotics improve surgical precision, and machine learning supports image analysis and treatment prediction. Tools like NLP, speech recognition, and predictive modeling enable personalized care across medical systems [23]. Generative AI is reshaping healthcare by advancing drug discovery, diagnostics, mental health care, and personalized medicine. Despite its benefits, issues like data bias, ethics, and the need for human oversight remain critical. With proper regulation, AI can deliver improved patient outcomes, cost-efficiency, and drive precision medicine forward [4].

12.3.2 Machine Learning and Neural Networks: A New Era for Healthcare

Generative AI has progressed from theoretical foundations to advanced architectures like GANs and VAEs, driving mainstream adoption across industries [12]. The report also draws parallels between human maturation and AI learning—highlighting how connectionist networks model complex skills such as language and interaction, mirroring cognitive development during childhood [32].

Neural networks adeptly process complex language features such as relative clauses, verb structures, and number agreement [33]. Advances in machine learning and deep learning are propelling AI-driven improvements in medical diagnosis and treatment [45]. In radiology, these innovations enhance lesion detection, thoracic and cardiovascular imaging, and cardiac function analysis [46].

Generative AI has rapidly advanced from early probabilistic models to sophisticated architectures like VAEs, GANs, and transformer-based diffusion systems—redefining content creation and cognitive modeling [1]. Notably, parallels with human learning, especially during childhood's plasticity-rich phase, reveal how hierarchical AI designs mirror natural skill acquisition. Connectionist networks replicate these developmental pathways, offering valuable insights into both AI evolution and cognitive science.

12.4 Core Models of Generative AI

GANs have advanced generative modeling, though their training remains computationally intensive and time-consuming [19]. Current GenAI research explores key methods—including GANs, Autoencoders, Transformers, and Diffusion models—across applications like image synthesis, NLP, and video creation, while addressing technical challenges and ethical concerns [2]. Generative AI has advanced through diverse architectures—each with strengths and trade-offs. While GANs revolutionized image generation, their training challenges have sparked interest in more efficient alternatives [19]. Transformer and diffusion models offer greater scalability and stability, enabling coherent multimodal content creation across text, image, and audio. Current research explores quantization, sparse attention, and hybrid designs that merge neural networks with symbolic reasoning to enhance efficiency and controllability [19].

Table 12.2 Models of Generative AI in Healthcare.

Model Type	*Key Features*	*Healthcare Applications*	*Citation*
GANs (Generative Adversarial Networks)	Two networks (Generator and Discriminator) trained in opposition	Medical image generation, data augmentation, disease diagnosis	[13]
VAEs (Variational Autoencoders)	Probabilistic approach, latent variable models	Image denoising, drug discovery, disease prediction	[12]
Transformer-based Models	Self-attention layers, large scale models, parallelized training	Text-based medical records analysis, drug design	[15]
cGANs (Conditional GANs)	Uses conditional information for generation	Medical image translation (e.g., MRI to CT), style transfer in medical images	[16]
WGANs (Wasserstein GANs)	Uses Wasserstein distance for training stability	High-resolution medical image generation, text-to-image synthesis	[16]
DeepFake GAN	Realistic face swap technology, video synthesis	Virtual health consultations, surgical simulation videos	[17]
BigGAN	Large scale models, high fidelity image generation	Synthetic healthcare data generation, personalized treatment plans	[18]

12.5 Healthcare Applications of Generative AI

AI is rapidly reshaping healthcare by boosting clinical care, research, and efficiency—powered by big data and advanced machine learning algorithms [24].

Generative AI is helping unlock the potential of vast healthcare datasets by detecting patterns, forecasting risks, and enabling proactive care strategies [54]. Recent advances allow it to enhance datasets, synthesize medical images, and accelerate drug discovery—using models like s GANs, VAEs, Flow-Based Models, and Probabilistic Graphical Models [55]. Despite growing adoption, challenges around reliability, safety, and acceptance persist due to GenAI's divergence from traditional medical technologies. This study reviews cutting-edge healthcare applications and outlines key considerations for effective implementation [23]. GenAI is increasingly supporting healthcare communication, training, and education, with growing potential to enhance diagnosis, treatment, and outcomes—pending validation in clinical settings [56]. Meanwhile, metaverse technologies are reshaping care through virtual therapy, telemedicine, and remote monitoring—improving accessibility, engagement, and cost-effective training [58].

12.5.1 Deep Learning in Medical Image Analysis

Deep learning (DL) methods—leveraging advanced neural networks—enable fast, accurate analysis of medical scans like X-rays, CT, and MRIs, helping detect abnormalities and support diagnosis [26]. Despite their potential, challenges remain around accessing diverse, high-quality datasets. [26]

Deep learning, particularly CNNs, has revolutionized medical imaging—automating detection, segmentation, and classification of abnormalities like tumors in MRI and CT scans. It enables precise treatment planning and reduces harm to healthy tissue [29, 30]. Despite challenges with data quality, transparency, and ethics, advances in federated learning and explainable AI offer solutions. These biologically inspired architectures excel at extracting complex patterns, making them pivotal for early disease detection and monitoring [25, 34]. In brain MRI analysis, data augmentation techniques like rotation, scaling, flipping, translation, and elastic deformation are used to synthetically expand datasets—enhancing model performance and variability.

12.5.2 Drug Discovery and Personalized Medicine

The Human Genome Project (HGP) and biomarker advances are reshaping drug discovery by revealing genetic disease mechanisms, enabling personalized treatment, and enhancing efficacy [28]. High-throughput sequencing streamlines drug target identification and clarifies interactions. Theranostics blends diagnostics with therapy for optimized care, while biomarkers aid detection and therapeutic evaluation. Insights into genetic diversity inform global health strategies, and CRISPR-Cas9—fueled by HGP—continues to drive biotech innovation. Future research should emphasize biomarker integration, ethical frameworks, and

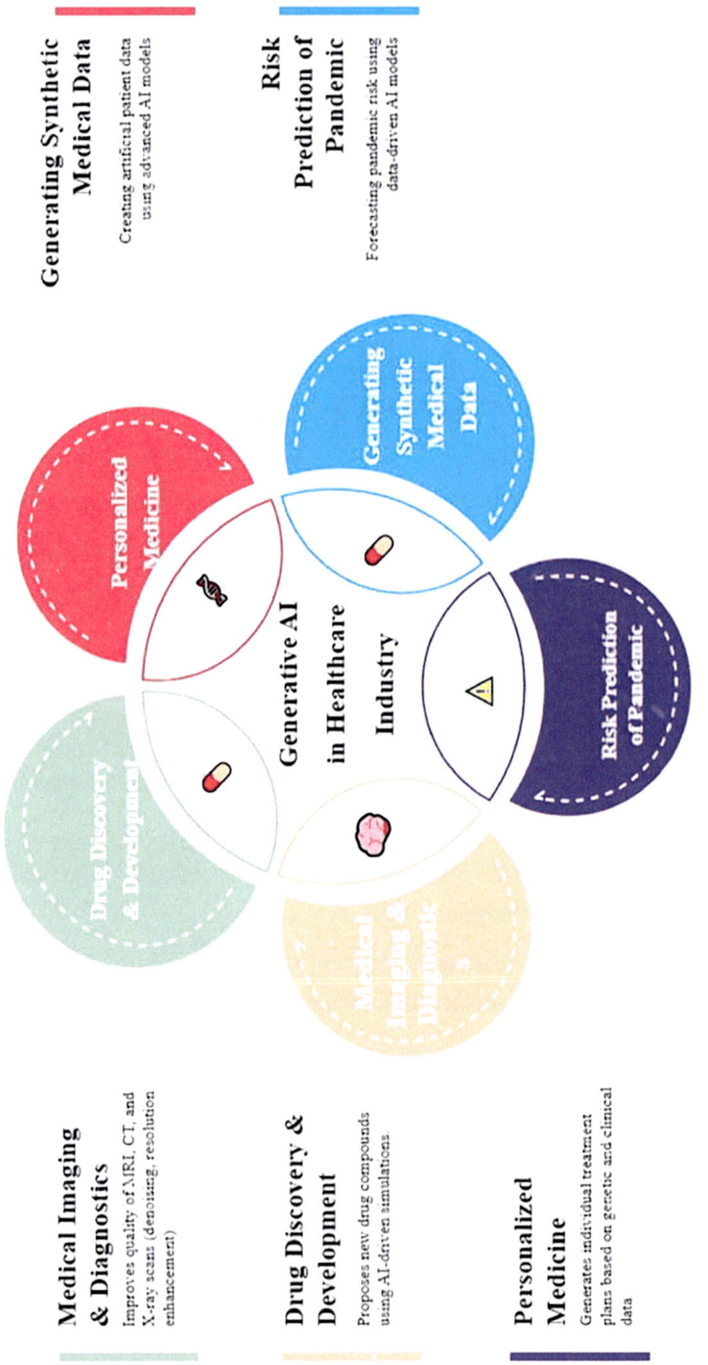

Fig. 12.2 Applications of Generative AI in the Healthcare Industry.

diversity-informed approaches. AI's ability to analyze diverse patient data—genetic, medical, and lifestyle—is key to advancing personalized medicine. It helps optimize drug design and delivery for maximum efficacy and minimal side effects. Future research should focus on enhancing algorithms to better integrate and interpret complex patient profiles for precise, tailored treatments [27].

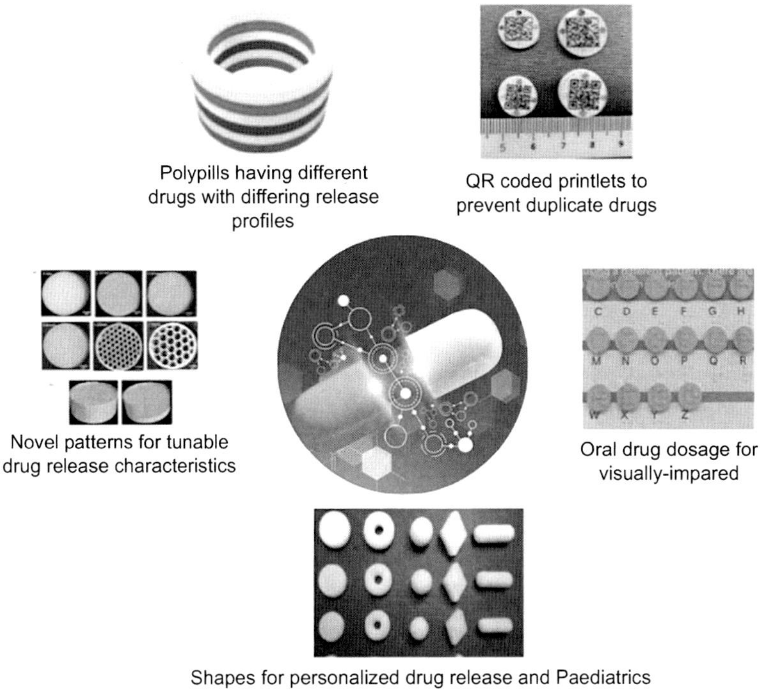

Fig. 12.3 Customizable Polypills for Personalized Drug Release.

12.5.2.1 Key Aspects of Personalized Medicine in Drug Discovery

Genomic technologies like high-throughput screening and gene expression analysis accelerate drug discovery by assessing toxicity and efficacy [47]. Pharmacogenomics refines treatments by predicting drug response based on genetic variations [48], while personalized therapy shifts focus from symptoms to genotypes [49]. Genomics also aids precise drug target identification [50], and AI boosts development by predicting efficacy and safety—enhancing personalized medicine [51].

Generative AI—especially GANs—is increasingly vital to modern pharmaceutical research, enabling synthetic data generation and the design of novel compounds with targeted properties [57].

12.5.3 Medical imaging and diagnostic tools

Medical imaging remains central to healthcare—supporting diagnosis and monitoring through techniques like X-ray, CT, MRI, PET, SPECT, and ultrasound, each with distinct advantages and risks [59]. Advances such as PET/CT and magnetic particle imaging continue to improve accuracy and safety. Ensuring optimal patient care requires thoughtful use of modalities, considering radiation exposure and diagnostic value.

Medical imaging plays a vital role in non-invasive diagnostics, using modalities like X-ray, CT, MRI, PET, SPECT, and ultrasound—each balancing resolution, cost, accessibility, and safety [59]. Emerging techniques like optical imaging, AI-enhanced analysis, and hybrid systems (PET/CT, PET/MRI) enhance diagnostic accuracy. Selecting the optimal modality requires consideration of radiation exposure, comfort, and clinical value.

12.6 Challenges in Generative AI

Generative AI faces multifaceted challenges, each matched by actionable solutions. High computational costs can be reduced via optimized architectures, cloud resources, and distributed training [20]. Data quality issues call for balanced collection, diversity, and fairness checks [21]. Overfitting and GAN mode collapse are mitigated using regularization, improved loss functions, and stable architectures like Wasserstein GANs [19, 17]. Interpretability improves with explainable AI systems [14], while secure methods and encryption address privacy risks [22]. Ethical concerns require robust guidelines, detection mechanisms, and regulatory oversight [23]. AI can significantly improve healthcare outcomes through data-driven precision medicine—provided it's properly regulated [4]. Generative AI leverages vast medical datasets for drug discovery, imaging, and predictive modeling using methods like GANs, VAEs, and Flow-Based Models. Despite its promise, concerns remain around legal implications, ethics, and the reliability of AI-generated data in clinical decision-making [4].

12.7 Future Directions and Opportunities

Generative AI integration into autonomous systems like drones, self-driving vehicles, and robotic swarms enhances adaptability and security—but requires addressing key challenges such as scalability, responsiveness, and adversarial resilience [35]. Efficient model deployment on edge devices demands lightweight architectures. Ensuring transparency and explainability is vital for trust in autonomous decision-making. Privacy-preserving methods, including federated learning, support secure data collaboration. Ethical frameworks and regulatory standards remain crucial for responsible use in high-impact domains [35].

GenAI -powered self-healing autonomous systems can perform real-time fault detection, diagnosis, and recovery—boosting resilience in critical applications [36].

Using models like GANs and VAEs, these systems adapt to failures autonomously. Future research should refine these mechanisms to reduce human intervention and improve robustness [36].

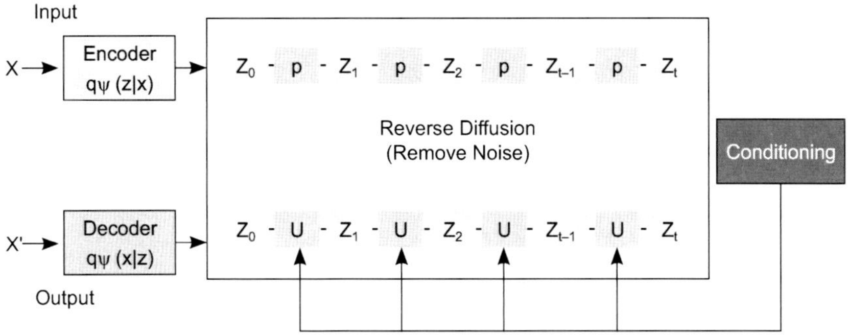

Fig. 12.4 Adversarial Generative Models.

By allowing GenAI is revolutionizing autonomous systems—such as drones, robotic collectives, and self-driving vehicles—by enabling advanced flexibility, environmental awareness, and real-time decision-making in areas like emergency response and logistics. To ensure safe and reliable deployment, research must address key challenges in scalability, resilience, and operational integrity.

Developing lightweight GenAI systems for real-time performance on resource-limited edge devices is a key priority [35]. Enhancing defense against adversarial threats demands innovative anomaly detection and robust training. Integrating explainable AI ensures transparency in autonomous decisions, while secure multi-party computation and federated learning uphold data privacy [35].

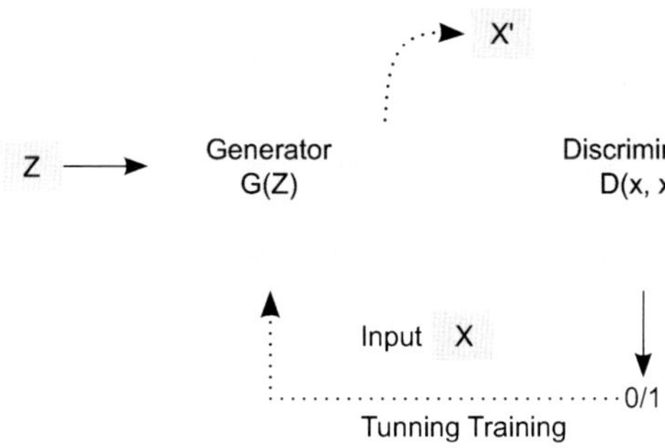

Fig. 12.5 Creative Diffusion Framework.

GenAI integration marks a paradigm shift in self-healing autonomous systems—enhancing resilience through proactive fault detection, diagnosis, and recovery using advanced architectures like Transformers, PINNs, and Neuro-Symbolic AI [36]. These innovations are particularly transformative in high-risk domains such as deep-sea exploration, nuclear facilities, and autonomous transport, where reliability is critical.

12.7.1 Real-time content generation and interactive storytelling

Generative AI enables dynamic, real-time content creation and adaptive storytelling—delivering personalized, immersive experiences that respond to user input [38]. Future research should enhance responsiveness and creative agility while maintaining narrative coherence. Ethical concerns around data privacy, consent, and governance must also be addressed to ensure responsible deployment [38].

Generative AI is reshaping interactive storytelling by enabling adaptive, user-responsive narratives through transformer models and reinforcement learning [38]. Key challenges include developing metrics for evaluating narrative quality and curbing harmful content. Future research should explore multimodal systems that integrate text, audio, and visuals, while addressing ethical concerns like bias and IP rights. Instructional storytelling stands out for its potential to deliver personalized, emotionally engaging learning experiences [38]. The integration of real-time Real-time generative AI is reshaping healthcare and storytelling through dynamic, context-aware narratives powered by diffusion transformers and multi-agent LLMs [60]. These models support therapeutic interventions, personalized diagnostics, and immersive training. Key challenges include mitigating misinformation and balancing latency with responsiveness. Future research should focus on explainability protocols for medical outputs and federated learning for privacy-preserving deployment [60].

12.7.2 AI-driven real-world applications

AI integration in healthcare —via machine learning, NLP, and image recognition—is revolutionizing diagnostics, treatment, and patient care [39]. Future efforts must prioritize ethical AI systems, safeguard data privacy, and strengthen real-time decision-making. Cross-disciplinary collaboration is essential for scalable, globally impactful solutions [39].

Advanced robotics, such as the da Vinci Surgical System, have revolutionized minimally invasive surgery by enhancing precision, dexterity, and control [40]. Their flexible maneuverability and high-definition 3D visualization support accurate anatomical identification and decision-making—especially in delicate procedures—ultimately enhancing surgical outcomes [40].

AI empowers autonomous vehicles to process real-time sensor, camera, and radar data—enabling obstacle detection, pedestrian prediction, and adaptive navigation in complex environments [41]. Advancing these systems requires improved algorithms to boost safety, efficiency, and learning across varied driving scenarios [41]. AI, big data, and analytics are revolutionizing healthcare, banking, agriculture, and urban planning by enabling early detection, personalized services,

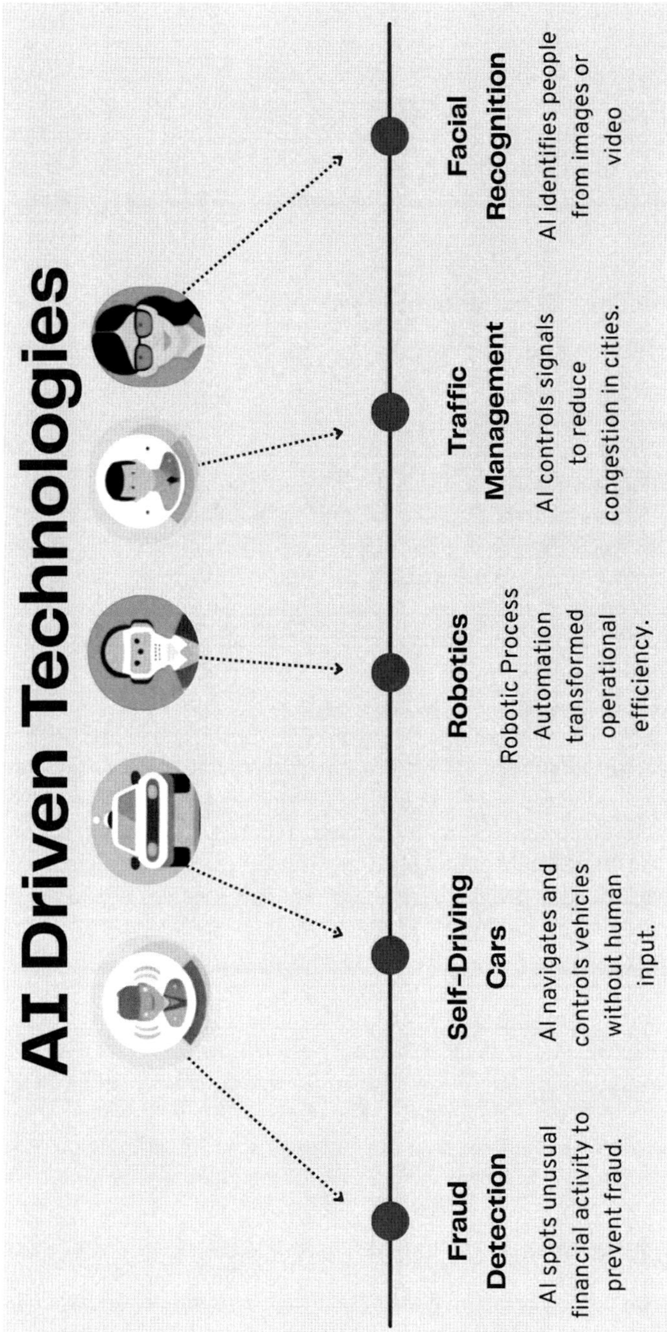

Fig. 12.6 AI Driven Different Technologies.

and efficient resource use—driving industry-wide decision-making and cost reduction [51]. In healthcare, mHealth facilitates remote access through mobile platforms, while WBANs face safety challenges from electromagnetic exposure [52]. AR/VR support enhanced diagnostics and surgery via real-time visualization. Lifetime machine learning boosts battery management by adapting to new data for reliable, real-time health monitoring [53]. Metaverse technologies offer immersive telemedicine, training, and patient engagement [58]. AI also anchors Industry 4.0 by integrating IoT, GPUs, cloud, and blockchain, advancing applications across decades [1].

12.7.3 Multimodal generative AI models

Multimodal learning models combine diverse data types for prediction, facing challenges in learning shared representations and enabling cross-modal generation. Deep generative models—especially variational autoencoders—effectively handle heterogeneous inputs and extract meaningful features. Recent studies showcase their potential in overcoming these complexities [42]. Human-AI Collaboration (HAIC) is increasingly vital for enhancing efficiency and innovation across sectors like healthcare, finance, and education [43]. This study presents a framework for evaluating HAIC systems using a decision tree to select metrics based on collaboration modes—AI-Centric, Human-Centric, or Symbiotic. By integrating qualitative and quantitative indicators, it captures the dynamic nature of HAIC and lays groundwork for more targeted future research on its practical impact [43]. As AI becomes increasingly integrated into everyday life, concerns around misuse—such as discrimination, privacy breaches, and security threats—are rising, especially in sensitive areas like recruitment, where bias risks persist [44]. To address these challenges, the paper emphasizes the need for comprehensive ethical regulations. It reviews current policy efforts, including NSF initiatives supporting AI research institutes and relevant executive directives, offering recommendations to guide federal agencies toward responsible AI governance [44].

Conclusion

Generative AI is reshaping industries, with healthcare witnessing profound impact through breakthroughs in medical data generation, drug discovery, and diagnostic imaging. Models like GANs, VAEs, and transformers drive tailored, high-precision applications. As hybrid systems mature, they promise major advances in personalized care and diagnostics. Realizing GenAI's full potential hinges on ethical governance, regulation, and continuous innovation.

Declarations

- Originality: No other journal or conference is currently considering this work for publication, and it is an original piece of research that has never been published before.

- Authorship: The study has benefited greatly from the conceptualization, methodology, analysis, writing, and revisions of all listed authors.
- Ethical Compliance: This study complies with ethical standards and does not use human or animal participants, or where appropriate, appropriate institutional review board (IRB) permissions were acquired.
- Data Availability: All of the data used in this study were either acquired with the required authorizations or are publicly available. The sources of the data are properly cited.
- Conflicts of Interest: The authors disclose that none of their personal or financial interests could have an impact on the research presented in this paper.
- Funds: The Acknowledgments section includes a list of all funds received for this study.
- AI-Assistance: The paper makes clear the role of generative AI tools when they were utilized (for example, for ideation or language improvement).

References

[1] Lu, Y. (2019). Artificial intelligence: a survey on evolution, models, applications and future trends. *Journal of Management Analytics*, 6(1), pp.1–29.

[2] Sengar, S.S., Hasan, A.B., Kumar, S. and Carroll, F. (2024). Generative artificial intelligence: a systematic review and applications. *Multimedia Tools and Applications*, pp.1–40.

[3] Balasubramaniam, S., Chirchi, V., Kadry, S., Agoramoorthy, M., Gururama, S.P. et al. (2024). The Road Ahead: Emerging Trends, Unresolved Issues, and Concluding Remarks in Generative AI—A Comprehensive Review. *International Journal of Intelligent Systems*, 2024.

[4] Thakur, N. (2024). Evolution of Generative AI in Healthcare. *In Revolutionizing the Healthcare Sector with AI* (pp. 26–53). IGI Global.

[5] Dwivedi, R. and Elluri, L. (2024). Exploring Generative Artificial Intelligence Research: A Bibliometric Analysis Approach. *IEEE Access*.

[6] Castelli, M. and Manzoni, L. (2022). Generative models in artificial intelligence and their applications. *Applied Sciences*, 12(9), p.4127.

[7] Alalaq, A.S. (2024). The History of the Artificial Intelligence Revolution and the Nature of Generative AI Work.

[8] Al-Amin, M., Ali, M.S., Salam, A., Khan, A., Ali, A. et al. (2024). History of generative Artificial Intelligence (AI) chatbots: past, present, and future development. *arXiv preprint arXiv:*2402.05122.

[9] Arslan, S.S., 2024. Artificial human intelligence: The role of humans in the development of next generation AI. *arXiv preprint arXiv:*2409.16001.

[10] Bharti, V. and Goel, R. (2024). Comparative Analysis of Deep Learning Approaches for Detecting Copy-Move Forgery. *In 2024 International Conference on Computational Intelligence and Computing Applications (ICCICA)* (Vol. 1, pp. 286-291). IEEE.

[11] Asimiyu, Z. (2024) Exploring the Evolution and Fundamentals of Generative AI: Key Advancements and Implications.

[12] Turhan, C.G. and Bilge, H.S. (2018). Variational autoencoded compositional pattern generative adversarial network for handwritten super resolution image generation. *In 2018 3rd International conference on Computer Science and Engineering (UBMK)* (pp. 564–568). IEEE.

[13] KILINÇ, H.K. and KEÇECİOĞLU, Ö.F. (2024). Generative Artificial Intelligence: A Historical and Future Perspective. *Journal of Engineering & Smart Systems*, 12(2).

[14] Huang, D., Yan, C., Li, Q. and Peng, X. (2024). From Large Language Models to Large Multimodal Models: A Literature Review. *Applied Sciences*, 14(12), p.5068.

[15] Huang, W., Bai, M., Han, A., Suzuki, T., Zhao, Q et al. Deep Generative Model in Machine Learning: Theory, Principle and Efficacy. In ICLR 2025 Workshop Proposals.

[16] Wang, Y., Pang, M., Chen, S. and Rao, H. (2024). Consistency-gan: Training gans with consistency model. *In Proceedings of the AAAI Conference on Artificial Intelligence* (Vol. 38, No. 14, pp. 15743–15751).

[17] Gatla, R.K., Gatla, A., Sridhar, P., Kumar, D.G. and Rao, D.N.M. et al (2024). Advancements in Generative AI: Exploring Fundamentals and Evolution. *In 2024 International Conference on Electronics, Computing, Communication and Control Technology (ICECCC)* (pp. 1-5). IEEE.

[18] Modrekiladze, B. (2024). Dual Space Training for GANs: A Pathway to Efficient and Creative Generative Models. arXiv preprint arXiv:2410.19009.

[19] Mohammed, A.S. and Patil, S. (2022). Investigating the Optimal Cloud Computing Infrastructure for Training Large-Scale Generative Models. *International Journal for Multidisciplinary Research (IJFMR)*, 4(6).

[20] Bond-Taylor, S., Leach, A., Long, Y. and Willcocks, C.G. (2021). Deep generative modelling: A comparative review of vaes, gans, normalizing flows, energy-based and autoregressive models. *IEEE transactions on pattern analysis and machine intelligence*, 44(11), 7327–7347.

[21] Esan, D.O., Owolawi, P.A. and Tu, C. (2023). Generative Adversarial Networks: Applications, Challenges, and Open Issues.

[22] Morales-Juarez, E. and Fuentes-Pineda, G. (2024). Efficient generative adversarial networks using linear additive-attention Transformers. arXiv preprint arXiv:2401.09596.

[23] Park, C.W., Seo, S.W., Kang, N., Ko, B., Choi, B.W. et al. (2020). Artificial intelligence in health care: current applications and issues. *Journal of Korean Medical Science*, 35(42).

[24] Garcea F., Serra A., Lamberti F. and Morra, L. Data augmentation for medical imaging: A systematic literature review. *Computers in Biology and Medicine*. 2023 Jan 1;152:106391.

[25] Chlap, Phillip, "A review of medical image data augmentation techniques for deep learning applications." *Journal of Medical Imaging and Radiation Oncology* 65.5 (2021).

[26] Goceri, E. (2023). Medical image data augmentation: techniques, comparisons and interpretations. *Artificial Intelligence Review*, 56(11), pp.12561–12605.

[27] Amir-Aslani, A. and Mangematin, V. (2010). The future of drug discovery and development: shifting emphasis towards personalized medicine. *Technological Forecasting and Social Change*, 77(2), pp. 203–217.

[28] Khan, A.R., Khan, S., Harouni, M., Abbasi, R., Iqbal, S. et al. (2021). Brain tumor segmentation using K-means clustering and deep learning with synthetic data augmentation for classification. *Microscopy Research and Technique*, 84(7), pp. 1389–1399.

[29] Dufumier, B., Gori, P., Battaglia, I., Victor, J., Grigis, A. et al. (2021). Benchmarking CNN on 3d anatomical brain MRI: architectures, data augmentation and deep ensemble learning. arXiv preprint arXiv:2106.01132.

[30] Isensee, F., Jäger, P.F., Full, P.M., Vollmuth, P. and Maier-Hein, K.H. et al. (2021). nnU-Net for brain tumor segmentation. In Brainlesion: Glioma, Multiple Sclerosis, Stroke and Traumatic Brain Injuries: 6th International Workshop, BrainLes 2020, Held in Conjunction with MICCAI 2020, Lima, Peru, October 4, 2020, Revised Selected Papers, Part II 6 (pp. 118–132). Springer International Publishing.

[31] Li, Q., Yu, Z., Wang, Y. and Zheng, H. (2020). TumorGAN: A multi-modal data augmentation framework for brain tumor segmentation. *Sensors*, 20(15), p.4203.

[32] Elman, J.L. (1993). Learning and development in neural networks: The importance of starting small. *Cognition*, 48(1), pp.71–99.

[33] Bharti, V. and Goel, R. (2024). Comparative Analysis of Deep Learning Approaches for Detecting Copy-Move Forgery. *In 2024 International Conference on Computational Intelligence and Computing Applications (ICCICA)* (Vol. 1, pp. 286-291). IEEE.

[34] Cao, L. "AI robots and humanoid AI: Review, perspectives and directions," 2024, arXiv:2405.15775.

[35] Tang, A., Li, K., Kwok, K.O., Cao, L., Luong S. et al. "The importance of transparency: Declaring the use of generative artificial intelligence (AI) in academic writing," *J. Nursing Scholarship*, vol. 56, no. 2, pp. 314–318, Mar. 2024.

[36] He, Y., Chai, S. and Xu, Z. "A novel approach for state estimation using generative adversarial network," in Proc. IEEE Int. Conf. Syst. Man Cybern. (SMC), Oct. 2019.

[37] Khang, A. (2023). Al and IoT-Based Technologies for Precision Medicine.

[38] Gao, J., Yang, Y., Lin, P. and Park, D.S. (2018). Computer vision in healthcare applications. *Journal of Healthcare Engineering*, 2018.

[39] Gulati, U. Ishaan and Dass R. "Intelligent car with voice assistance and obstacle detector to aid the disabled," *Procedia Comput Sci*, vol. 167, pp. 1732–1738, Jan. 2020.

[40] Suzuki M. and Matsuo Y. A survey of multimodal deep generative models. *Advanced Robotics*. 2022 Mar 19;36(5-6):261–278.

[41] Fragiadakis, G., Diou, C., Kousiouris, G. and Nikolaidou, M. (2024). Evaluating human-AI collaboration: A review and methodological framework. arXiv preprint arXiv:2407.19098.

[42] Luckett, J. Regulating generative AI: A pathway to ethical and responsible implementation. *Journal of Computing Sciences in Colleges*. 2023 Aug;39(3):47–65.

[43] Kufel, J., Bargieł-Łączek, K., Kocot, S., Koźlik, M., Bartnikowska, W. et al. (2023). What is machine learning, artificial neural networks and deep learning?—Examples of practical applications in medicine. *Diagnostics*, 13(15), p.2582.

[44] Retson, T.A., Besser, A.H., Sall, S., Golden, D. and Hsiao, A. et al. (2019). Machine learning and deep neural networks in thoracic and cardiovascular imaging. *Journal of thoracic imaging*, 34(3), pp.192–201.

[45] Wang, L. (2018). High-throughput screening technologies. *Trends in Pharmacological Sciences*.

[46] Roden, D.M. (2019). Pharmacogenomics: An introduction. *Current Opinion in Cardiology*.

[47] Collins, F.S. and Varmus, H. (2015). Precision medicine initiative. *New England Journal of Medicine*.

[48] Fukui, T., et al. (2020). Genomics in drug target discovery. Drug Discovery Today.

[49] Hughes, J.P. (2020). AI in drug development. Drug Development Research.

[50] Patel, A., Cholkar, K. and Mitra, A.K. (2014). Recent developments in drug delivery systems for personalized medicine. *Journal of Drug Delivery Science and Technology*, 24(1), 12–21.

[51] Ponnusamy, V., Vasuki, A., Clement, J.C. and Eswaran, P. (2022). AI-Driven Information and Communication Technologies, Services, and Applications for Next-Generation Healthcare System. *Smart Systems for Industrial Applications*, 1–32.

[52] Zhao, J., Qu, X., Wu, Y., Fowler, M. and Burke, A.F. et al. (2024). Artificial intelligence-driven real-world battery diagnostics. *Energy and AI*, 18, 100419.

[53] Moulaei, K., Yadegari, A., Baharestani, M., Farzanbakhsh, S., Sabet, B. et al. (2024). Generative artificial intelligence in healthcare: A scoping review on benefits, challenges and applications. *International Journal of Medical Informatics*, 105474.

[54] Helen, D. and Suresh, N.V. (2024). Generative AI in Healthcare: Opportunities, Challenges, and Future Perspectives. *Revolutionizing the Healthcare Sector with AI*, 79–90.

[55] Yim, D., Khuntia, J., Parameswaran, V. and Meyers, A. (2024). Preliminary evidence of the use of generative AI in health care clinical services: systematic narrative review. *JMIR Medical Informatics*, 12(1), e52073.

[56] Iqbal, I., Shafqat, I., Krishna, S. and Rauf, M. Role of Generative AI in Industry 5.0: A Transformative Force.

[57] Vashishth, T.K., Sharma, V., Sharma, K.K., Kumar, B., Chaudhary, S. et al. (2024). Impact of Generative AI on Metaverse-Enabled Healthcare Industries. *In Examining the Metaverse in Healthcare: Opportunities, Challenges, and Future Directions* (pp. 167–196). IGI Global.

[58] Vashishth (2024) – "Impact of Generative AI on Metaverse-Enabled Healthcare Industries", in Examining the Metaverse in Healthcare: Opportunities, Challenges, and Future Directions.

[59] Smith, J.A. and Johnson, B.C. (2023). Advances in medical imaging modalities. *Journal of Medical Imaging.*

[60] Chaddad et al. (2022): "Explainable, Domain-Adaptive, and Federated Artificial Intelligence in Medicine",

13 Leveraging Data Science and Generative AI to Explore Human Behaviour and Health Issue

Shailendra Singh Gaur[1], Kushagra Kalra[2] and Parinay Goel[3*]

By merging data science with behavioral psychology, this study explores how Big Five personality traits—Openness, Conscientiousness, Extraversion, Agreeableness, and Neuroticism—influence students' learning and workplace readiness. It aims to identify how specific traits impact adaptability, cooperation, and decision-making in professional settings. Survey data from students across disciplines were collected via customized Google Forms, focusing on Big Five traits and subtle academic-social behaviors. Responses were cleaned and preprocessed using Python libraries (pandas, NumPy, scikit-learn). K-Means clustering was applied to uncover natural personality groupings based on behavioral patterns.

A generative AI application was designed to deliver personalized feedback on identified personality clusters—simulating role-specific behaviors and workplace readiness. By generating adaptive, context-aware content, GenAI enables scalable visualization of performance variations across trait profiles and supports developmental insights.

These insights highlight clear links between behavior trends, learning outcomes, and workplace traits. For instance, high Conscientiousness correlates with strong organization and time management, while elevated Neuroticism suggests lower adaptability and stress resilience.

The model evaluates students' workplace readiness, offering a scalable online solution for personality and behavior assessment in academic and professional settings. Future improvements include refined clustering algorithms, granular behavioral markers, and advanced methods like PCA and deep learning to boost classification accuracy.

Generative AI's evolving capabilities will increasingly support real-time adaptive personality development and personalized professional guidance.

13.1 Introduction

Modern behavioral science has evolved into a data-driven field, deeply intertwined with advanced technologies that enable high-precision analysis at scale. This

[1-3] Information Technology, BPIT, GGSIPU, New Delhi, India.
E-mail: shailendrasinghgaur@bpitindia.com[1]; kushagrakalra530@gmail.com[2]
* Corresponding author: parinaygoel623@gmail.com

DOI: 10.1201/9781003670582-13

project explores how personality traits—based on the Big Five model (Openness, Conscientiousness, Extraversion, Agreeableness, Neuroticism)—affect students' academic behavior and workplace readiness. By applying this framework, the study aims to predict performance outcomes across professional settings, especially under high-stakes conditions.

13.1.1 The Big Five Personality Traits

- Openness to Experience: Reflects creativity and curiosity. High openness suggests adaptability and interest in novelty; low openness favors tradition and restraint. Conscientiousness: Indicates organization and reliability. High levels align with responsibility and self-discipline; lower levels suggest spontaneity but may lead to disorganization.
- Extraversion: Measures sociability and energy. Extroverts thrive in social settings; introverts prefer solitude or small groups.
- Agreeableness: Relates to empathy and cooperation. Highly agreeable individuals are helpful and understanding; low agreeableness may signal assertiveness and competitiveness.
- Neuroticism: Assesses emotional stability. High neuroticism links to sensitivity and anxiety; low levels reflect calmness and resilience.

13.1.2 Setting Up Google Forms for Data Collection

Google Forms is a reliable tool for systematically collecting personality data. It enables researchers to design tailored surveys aligned with their study goals. Key setup stages include:

Survey Design: Craft questions that accurately assess Big Five traits, using Likert scales and open-ended formats for both qualitative and quantitative insights.

1. Branching Logic: Apply conditional flows to personalize survey paths based on initial responses (e.g., deeper social questions for extroverts).

Table 13.1 Survey Data Description.

Feature	*Description*	*Type*	*Scale*
Age	Age of the respondent	Numerical	-
Gender	Gender of the respondent	Categorical	-
Location	Residential region of the respondent	Categorical	-
Openness Score	Average score for 10 openness-related questions	Numerical	1–5
Conscientiousness Score	Average score for 10 conscientiousness-related questions	Numerical	1–5
Extraversion Score	Average score for 10 extraversion-related questions	Numerical	1–5

Contd...

Table 13.1 *Contd...*

Feature	*Description*	*Type*	*Scale*
Agreeableness Score	Average score for 10 agreeableness-related questions	Numerical	1–5
Neuroticism Score	Average score for 10 neuroticism-related questions	Numerical	1–5

13.1.3 Data Management and Storage

Once responses are collected via Google Forms, efficient data management is essential for analysis. Google Sheets automatically stores submissions in real time, allowing researchers to access, organize, and prepare data for processing.

- Google Sheets Integration: Google Forms responses are instantly logged into a linked Google Sheet, enabling real-time data access and analysis for researchers.
- Data Organization: Survey responses can be sorted into separate sheets based on criteria like participant groups or survey phases. Google Sheets offers filtering, sorting, and validation tools to streamline analysis. Initial steps include data cleaning—removing duplicates, handling missing entries, and normalizing responses.

13.1.4 Data Processing and Analysis

For deeper insights, survey data from Google Sheets is exported as CSV files and imported into statistical tools or Python environments like Google Colab or Jupyter Notebooks. This enables advanced analysis using libraries such as pandas and scikit-learn.

- Basic Analysis in Google Sheets: Google Sheets supports descriptive statistics (mean, median, mode, standard deviation) and pivot tables for summarizing large datasets by traits or responses—offering quick behavioral insights.
- Advanced Analysis Tools: For deeper insights, Google Sheets data is exported to CSV and processed in Python using Google Colab. Libraries like scikit-learn and pandas enable machine learning tasks such as pattern recognition, classification, and predictive modeling—key for analyzing personality traits from survey responses.

13.1.5 Visualization and Reporting

Data visualization plays a fundamental role in interpreting findings and presenting them clearly to users.

- Summary View on Google Forms–Ready-to-use built-in features in Google Forms easily produce bar charts and pie charts that summarize survey results. These visual summaries are handy for getting quick insights and can be shared as an immediate overview of major findings with stakeholders.

- Custom Visualizations–Google Sheets is another source of various charting options, such as the most common ones including line graphs, histograms, and scatter plots through which the distribution of personality traits is shown among the respondents. Those users who want even more sophisticated visualizations could export their data from Google Sheets and put them into Tableau or Power BI offering more advanced interactive data presentations .

13.1.6 Collaboration and Project Management

Collaboration tools play an important role in organizing a team with multiple contributors on a project and tracking progress in a truly efficient way.

- Version Control (GitHub): GitHub enables collaborative development by tracking code changes and managing multiple project versions. It streamlines teamwork, allowing contributors to update analysis scripts without separate environments—ensuring seamless integration and transparency.
- Communication (Microsoft Teams): Microsoft Teams facilitates real-time communication, file sharing, and coordination among researchers. It supports efficient data interpretation, updates, and collaborative decision-making throughout the project.

13.1.7 Predictive Analytics and Personality Classification

The project applied K-Means clustering to group individuals based on personality traits, using the elbow method to determine the optimal number of clusters.

- Personality Prediction Models: The project aims to classify individuals as introverts, extroverts, or ambiverts based on survey responses. K-Means clustering was chosen for its ability to group individuals by behavioral patterns without requiring pre-labeled data, making it ideal for unsupervised personality profiling.
- The model identifies personality clusters purely from survey responses, without relying on predefined classifications.. This approach captures unique behavioral patterns and allows natural grouping based on individual traits.
- The Elbow Method for Finding the Optimal Number of Clusters (k): The elbow method identifies the ideal number of clusters (k) by plotting the within-cluster sum of squares (WCSS) against various k values. The "elbow" point—where further increases in k yield minimal WCSS reduction—marks the optimal cluster count, balancing model accuracy and complexity while avoiding overfitting.

13.1.7.1 Prediction Process

- Data Preprocessing: Survey responses are first cleaned and normalized to ensure consistency. This processed data is then input into the K-Means algorithm for clustering based on personality traits. Cluster Creation: K-Means groups individuals by behavioral traits, forming clusters that reflect distinct persona types based on survey responses—without relying on predefined labels.

- K Determination: This method calculates the ideal number of clusters for the considered space by analyzing how the WCSS varies with different k values.

13.1.7.2 Applications and Future Enhancements

- Behavioral Patterns: K-Means scoring reveals behavioral patterns, helping researchers infer whether individuals align more with introverted, extroverted, or ambiverted profiles based on their survey responses.
- Effects: These findings can be directly applied to workplaces, educational programs, and consumer behavior studies—enabling tailored interventions and strategic planning based on personality-driven patterns.
- Future Enhancements: To boost accuracy, future work may incorporate additional behavioral features and adopt more advanced clustering techniques. Enhancements like PCA, hierarchical clustering, or hybrid models can refine personality grouping and reveal deeper trait patterns.

13.2 Generative AI

Generative AI is transforming behavioral science by enabling predictive modeling and personality simulation using real-world data. Techniques like NLP, GANs, and GPT-based models uncover nuanced traits and dynamic behavior patterns. These tools generate survey-driven insights, enhancing personality prediction and real-time behavioral understanding across diverse environments.

13.2.1 Generative AI in Behavioral Science

Generative AI is integrated into data science to enhance research on human-environment interaction. Its core aim is pattern recognition for predicting behavioral responses. Example applications include agents.

13.2.2 Generate Synthetic Behavioral Data

Generative AI can enrich survey datasets by generating synthetic profiles with diverse personality traits, helping balance class distributions. This enhances model accuracy and supports better generalization in predictive behavioral analysis.

13.2.3 Predicting Personality Changes Due to Different Social Conditions

Generative AI models simulate how individual personalities evolve under varying psychological and social conditions. These simulations support targeted interventions in mental health, career counseling, and training programs tailored to socio-cultural contexts.

13.2.4 Enhanced Clustering and Personality Classifying

Traditional clustering often overlooks hidden personality patterns. Generative AI models multi-dimensional behavioral data to uncover latent traits, improving classification accuracy and reducing bias from predefined categories.

13.2.5 AI-Enabled Behavioral Recommendation Engines

AI engines analyze individual behavior patterns to suggest career paths, learning strategies, and personal development plans. Organizations can use these insights to optimize employee satisfaction, team dynamics, and leadership training.

13.2.6 Real-Time Modeling of Behavior Evolution

Generative AI enables the creation of adaptive models that track personality changes over time. These models support longitudinal studies by revealing how traits evolve through life events, education, and professional experiences.

13.2.7 Sentiment Analysis and Emotional Intelligence Testing

NLP models analyze text and speech to detect emotional states, enhancing psychological research and real-time sentiment tracking. Broader applications include consumer behavior, political psychology, and mental health assessment.

13.2.8 Personalized Mental Health Applications

Generative AI chatbots and virtual assistants offer personalized therapy recommendations by recognizing unique communication patterns and stress indicators. These tools support CBT, workplace mental wellness, and student counseling programs.

Integration with Data Science Methods: Generative AI enhances traditional data science by:

- Generating synthetic features for predictive models
- Reducing dimensionality to identify key traits
- Detecting behavioral anomalies linked to mental health

Integrating generative AI into behavioral science enhances personalized predictions and enables real-time analysis for career growth, education, and mental health support. This empowers data-driven decision-making for researchers and organizations to better understand and guide human behavior.

13.3 Literature Review

Personality classification has garnered wide interest across psychology, behavioral science, and machine learning. This chapter synthesizes past research and methods, emphasizing data-driven clustering techniques for personality assessment and prediction.

13.3.1 Personality Models in Behavioral Science

The Five Factor Model—Openness, Conscientiousness, Extraversion, Agreeableness, and Neuroticism—is a widely accepted framework for analyzing behavior and decision-making. Goldberg (1993) popularized the OCEAN acronym, now a cornerstone in personality research across academic, mental health, and workplace settings and further refined this model through NEO-PI-R, a comprehensive inventory that links personality traits to outcomes like job performance and life satisfaction.

13.3.2 Clustering Techniques for Unsupervised Personality Classification

K-Means clustering is a rising trend in personality classification, effectively grouping individuals by traits without prior labeling—making it ideal for discovering natural patterns in behavioral data.

1. K-Means Clustering: K-Means remains widely used for personality classification from survey and behavioral data. Researchers commonly rely on the elbow method to determine the optimal number of clusters (k), enhancing the accuracy of trait-based grouping.
2. Xu et al. (2017) used K-Means to segment personality types based on online behavioral data, demonstrating its capacity for unsupervised categorization. Tarnowski et al. (2020) applied the same technique to emotional response patterns, identifying personality typologies through clustering along affective channels.

13.4 Elbow Method in Cluster Analysis

Thorndike (1953) introduced the elbow method to determine optimal clusters in unsupervised learning. It involves plotting WCSS against cluster count, with the "elbow" point indicating the ideal balance between simplicity and accuracy.

Sugar and James (2003) reinforced the elbow method's validity by showing that adding clusters significantly reduces WCSS, supporting its use for optimal cluster selection in unsupervised learning.

13.4.1 Personality Classification in Educational and Workplace Settings

Personality-based insights support tailored training and guidance in education and workplace settings, helping students and employees achieve better outcomes through trait-informed preparation. Barrick and Mount (1991) demonstrated that personality traits are relevant in predicting the success of a job and within that the

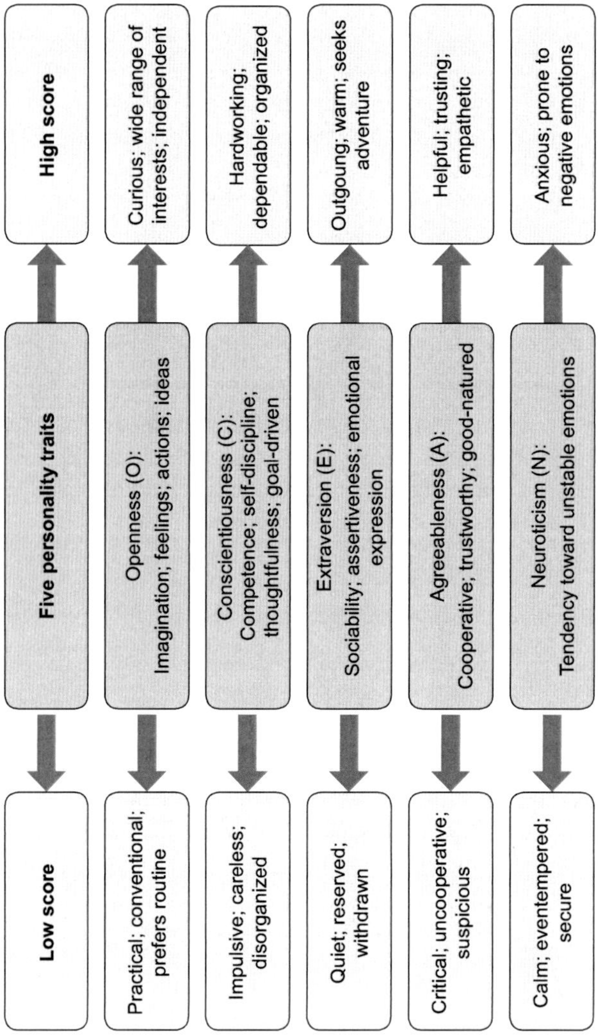

Fig. 13.1 Goldberg 5 Personality OCEAN Model.

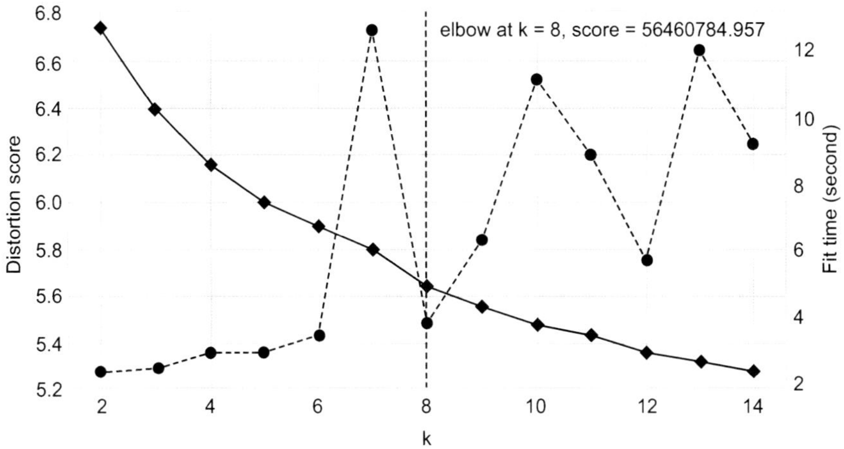

Fig. 13.2 Elbow for K-Mean Clustering.

Big Five traits significantly predict job performance. Their meta-analysis found Conscientiousness to be a consistent success indicator across diverse roles.

Chamorro-Premuzic and Furnham (2005) highlighted the role of personality traits in shaping academic and career success. They underscored the need for educational settings to use personality assessments to personalize training programs that leverage individual strengths.

13.4.2 Advantages and Limitations of K-Means and Elbow Method

Personality Traits in Education & Career Development: Research emphasized that personality traits influence academic and career success, advocating for personalized training programs in education that align with individual strengths through targeted assessments.

Limitations of K-Means and Elbow Method: K-Means assumes spherical, equally sized clusters, which may not reflect real data. The elbow method is subjective—identifying the "elbow" point can be unclear. Additionally, K-Means is sensitive to initial centroid selection, often producing varied results across runs.

13.4.3 Contributions to the Current Project

This project extends current research by applying K-Means and the elbow method for unsupervised personality clustering. Unlike label-dependent or complex models, it offers a simple yet effective framework to group survey respondents based on behavioral traits—supporting educational and workplace readiness insights without requiring prior personality definitions or advanced feature engineering.

13.5 Influence of Health Issues on Human Behavior

Table 13.2 Comparison of Clustering Techniques.

Clustering Technique	*Description*	*Advantages*	*Limitations*	*Applications in Personality Classification*
K-Means Clustering	A centroid-based algorithm that partitions data into a predefined number of clusters (k).	• Computationally efficient • Easy to implement • Works well with large datasets	• Assumes spherical clusters • Sensitive to initial centroids • Requires predefined k	Used to categorize individuals into personality types based on survey data.
Hierarchical Clustering	Builds a tree-like structure of clusters based on distance, allowing for varying numbers of clusters.	• Does not require predefined number of clusters • Provides dendrogram to visualize relationships	• Computationally expensive for large datasets • Can be sensitive to noise	Applied to identify hierarchies of personality traits and their relationships.
DBSCAN (Density-Based Spatial Clustering of Applications with Noise)	Groups points based on density, marking low-density points as outliers (noise).	• Can identify clusters of arbitrary shapes • Handles noise effectively	• Struggles with varying cluster density • Sensitive to the choice of parameters (ε, minPts)	Used to identify personality traits in large datasets, especially with noise or outliers.

Mental and physical health play a crucial role in shaping cognitive functions, decision-making, social interaction, and emotional resilience—all core to personality traits and job performance. The following factors are examined in relation to personality dimensions:

13.5.1 Mental health and personality

- **Stress and anxiety:** Elevated stress increases Neuroticism while lowering Conscientiousness and Agreeableness. Chronic stress impairs emotional regulation, decision-making, and impulse control. Depression correlates with reduced Extraversion and Openness, diminishing motivation, social engagement, and overall productivity—affecting focus and communication in academic and workplace settings.
- **Cognitive Load:** High cognitive demands disrupt decision-making and impair behavior in academic and workplace settings. Elevated mental load leads to fatigue, reduced creativity, and weakened interpersonal skills.
- **Solitude:** Extended isolation reduces Extraversion, raising social anxiety and weakening communication skills. Affected individuals often show higher Neuroticism and lower Agreeableness—traits linked to poor teamwork and reduced collaboration in shared environments.

13.5.2 Physical Health and Behavioral Patterns

- **Disruption in sleep:** Sleep loss impairs judgment, cognition, and emotional responsiveness. It's strongly linked with higher Neuroticism and reduced Agreeableness and Conscientiousness—resulting in lower productivity and weaker interpersonal dynamics.
- **Diet and Nutrition:** Poor nutrition lowers energy, focus, and overall productivity. Unhealthy eating habits often lead to mood fluctuations and cognitive inconsistencies—manifesting as irritability and reduced motivation in personality expression.
- **Chronic Illnesses:** Chronic diseases affect resilience, adaptability, and stress tolerance, often leading to increased Neuroticism and reduced Openness due to ongoing physical pain and emotional strain.
- **Exercise:** Regular physical activity boosts Conscientiousness and Extraversion, while lowering stress-linked Neuroticism. This is largely due to endorphin release, which improves mood and emotional well-being.
- Greater awareness of mental and physical health factors enriches personality classification—enhancing its predictive power for educational performance and workplace readiness.

Methodology

This study applies K-Means clustering to survey data for predicting personality types—introvert, extrovert, or ambivert—without pre-labeled inputs. Participants provided demographic details and rated themselves on Big Five traits (Openness,

Conscientiousness, Extraversion, Agreeableness, Neuroticism) using 10-item, 5-point scale questionnaires.Survey responses were cleaned, normalized via Min-Max scaling, and averaged to derive trait scores. K-Means grouped individuals based on these features, with the optimal number of clusters determined via the elbow method (WCSS analysis). Cluster validity was assessed using Silhouette Score and Davies-Bouldin Index for compactness and separation.

This explores how personality clusters align with work behavior, academic success, and soft skills. It provides insights into trait–career fit and educational readiness. The model will undergo cross-validation to prevent overfitting and ensure generalizability across diverse populations.

Table 13.3 Search Strategy Criteria.

Criteria	*Details*
Purpose	Identify survey respondents' personality traits and classify them into categories using unsupervised learning.
Inclusion Criteria	Participants aged 18–60, survey responses with complete data, willingness to participate, and consent.
Exclusion Criteria	Incomplete survey responses, participants under 18 or over 60, and individuals who withdraw consent.
Data Collection Method	Online survey distributed via email, social media, and institutional networks.
Survey Questions	Based on the Big Five (OCEAN) personality traits: Openness, Conscientiousness, Extraversion, Agreeableness, and Neuroticism.
Scale Used	Likert scale ranging from 1 (Strongly Disagree) to 5 (Strongly Agree).
Data Analysis Tool	Python libraries (e.g., pandas, NumPy, sklearn) for preprocessing and clustering using K-Means.

Math formulae

Formulae for Calinski-Harabasz Index (CHI)

Calinski-Harabasz Index $= -Tr\ (Bk)/Tr\ (Wk) \times N - k/k - 1$

Where:

Bk is the between-cluster dispersion matrix

Wk is the within-cluster dispersion matrix

k is the number of clusters

Formulae For Davies-Bouldin Index (DBI)

$\text{DBI} = (1/k) \times \Sigma\ (\max((\sigma i + \sigma j)/d(ci, cj)))$

Where:

k: The total number of clusters.

σi: The average distance of points in a cluster is from its centroid. This represents the internal dispersion of cluster i.

σj: The average distance of points in cluster j from its centroid.

$d(ci, cj)$: The distance between the centroids of cluster i and j. This represents the separation between the clusters.

$\max((\sigma i + \sigma j)/d(ci, cj))$: For each cluster i, this finds the maximum value of the ratio (within-cluster dispersion + within-cluster dispersion)/(distance between cluster centroids) over all other clusters j.

Σ: Summation over all clusters i from 1 to k.

13.6 Conclusion and Result

This study demonstrates the utility of Big Five personality traits combined with K-Means clustering and the elbow method to classify individuals based on survey responses. PCA enabled visual interpretation of distinct clusters. Evaluation metrics—Davies-Bouldin Index (6.61) and Calinski-Harabasz Index (82918.38)—confirmed meaningful grouping. The findings support personality classification as a predictive tool for understanding how introverts, extroverts, and ambiverts may perform in high-pressure professional environments. While the findings are encouraging, the study has limitations. Google Forms may introduce interpretive bias due to question perception. Additionally, K-Means assumes rigid cluster boundaries that oversimplify human personality. Future work should explore richer features, alternative clustering methods, and larger, more diverse datasets to improve classification accuracy and depth. This research lays foundation for future work on personality-based classification, offering valuable insights into academic and professional contexts. It aims to advance understanding of human behavior across modern organizational settings.

13.6.1 Clustering Overview

Survey responses were analyzed using K-Means clustering, with PCA applied for visualizing trait distributions. Eight clusters (Cluster 0–7) emerged, highlighting diverse profiles across Big Five traits.

13.6.2 Visualization of Clusters

- **PCA Visualization:**
  - Clustering is visualized in 2D space (PCA1 vs. PCA2), as shown in Figure 13.3, revealing behavioral groupings.
  - Distinct personality differences emerge across participant clusters.
- **Cluster-Specific Trait Analysis:** Agreeableness, Conscientiousness, and Openness—across clusters. Key observations include:
  - **Cluster 0:** Balanced traits with slight emphasis on Agreeableness and Openness
  - **Cluster 1:** Notably low Neuroticism; other traits moderately expressed
  - **Cluster 2:** Elevated Extraversion and Agreeableness
  - **Cluster 3:** High Conscientiousness, reflecting strong organization and diligence

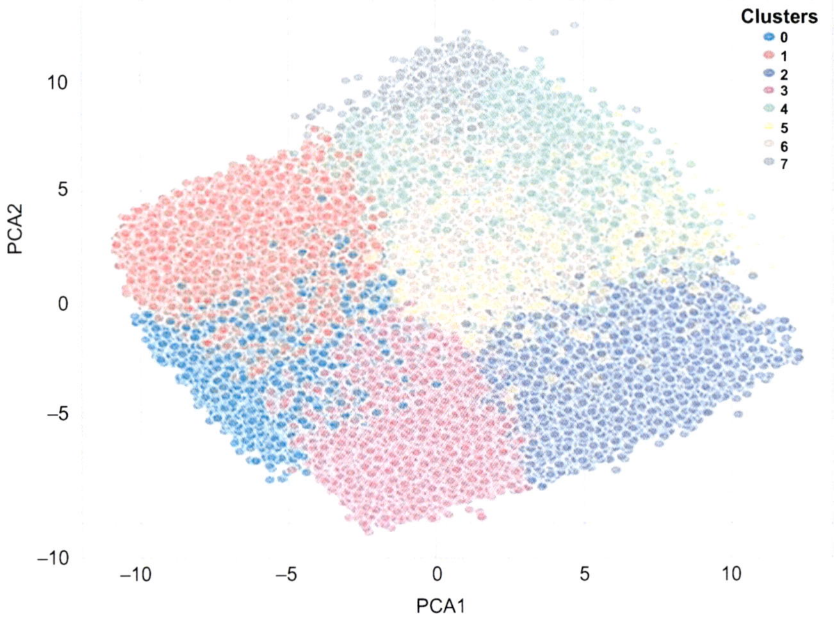

Fig. 13.3 Personality Cluster after training the Model.

- **Cluster 4:** Elevated Neuroticism and Openness, suggesting emotional sensitivity and creativity
- **Cluster 5:** Uniform trait expression with no significant variation
- **Cluster 6:** High Agreeableness and Conscientiousness, indicating empathy and reliability
- **Cluster 7:** Low scores across traits, possibly representing outliers or atypical behavior patterns

13.6.3 Cluster Evaluation Metrics

1. **Davies-Bouldin Index (DBI):**
   - Score: 6.61
   - Interpretation: The rather high DBI score indicates some amount of ambiguity of clusters where they could be said to be distinguished, but refinement may still be needed in the clustering separation.
2. **Calinski-Harabasz Index (CHI):**
   - Score: 82,918.38
   - Interpretation: A high CHI score indicates that the clusters are well-defined and compact, which further signifies that the algorithm captures patterns meaningful to the data adequately.

13.6.4 Insights from Clustering

These are the emerging patterns of behavior that are clustered:

- **Behavioral profiles:** Clusters with high Conscientiousness (e.g., Cluster 3 and Cluster 6) suggest individuals well-suited for structured, responsible tasks—indicating strong career readiness.
- Clusters with elevated Neuroticism (e.g., Cluster 4) may reflect emotional sensitivity, potentially limiting performance in high-pressure or resource-constrained environments.
- Cluster 7 warrants deeper analysis to identify traits prevalent among outliers with uniformly low scores across Big Five dimensions.

Applications: It is useful for institutions' academics and employers to mold better strategies for individualized education and training, as well as workplace accommodation.

13.6.5 Limitations

- **Cluster Separability:** While CHI clearly indicates clustering, DBI indicates that it would lead to some overlapping between the clusters. Future research could explore other clustering techniques that could increase separability or the addition of other features for purposes of separability.
- **Validation:** It shows strength in external validation because expert feedback or evaluation against strict benchmark datasets will enhance reliability of the clustering results.

13.6.6 Future Directions

- **Model Refinement:**
  - Future iterations can employ improved clustering techniques such as DBSCAN
  - Clustering along with hierarchical approaches as a hybrid show promise to give better classification accuracies.
- **Behavioral Contexts:** Incorporating academic results and job feedback strengthens links between personality types and potential outcomes—supporting growth, development, and predictive accuracy.

References

[1] Costa, P.T. and McCrae, R.R. (1992). Revised NEO Personality Inventory (NEO-PI-R) and NEO Five-Factor Inventory (NEO-FFI): Professional Manual. *Psychological Assessment Resources*.

[2] Goldberg, L.R. (1990). An alternative "description of personality": The Big-Five factor structure. *Journal of Personality and Social Psychology*, 59(6), 1216–1229.

[3] MacQueen, J. (1967). Some methods for classification and analysis of multivariate observations. *In Proceedings of the Fifth Berkeley Symposium on Mathematical Statistics and Probability*, 1(14), 281–297.

[4] Rokach, L. and Maimon, O. (2005). Clustering methods. In O. Maimon & L. Rokach (Eds.), *Data Mining and Knowledge Discovery Handbook* (pp. 321–352). Springer.

[5] Pedregosa, F., Varoquaux, G., Gramfort, A., Michel, V., Thirion, B., Grisel, O. and Duchesnay, É. (2011). Scikit-learn: Machine learning in Python. *Journal of Machine Learning Research*, 12, 2825–2830.

[6] Google. (n.d.). Google Forms Help: Create, manage, and analyze surveys. Retrieved from https://support.google.com/forms/

[7] McKinney, W. (2010). Data structures for statistical computing in Python. *In Proceedings of the 9th Python in Science Conference* (pp. 51–56).

[8] Wold, S., Esbensen, K. and Geladi, P. (1987). Principal Component Analysis. *Chemometrics and Intelligent Laboratory Systems*, 2(1-3), 37–52.

[9] Tableau. (n.d.). Interactive Data Visualization. Retrieved from https://www.tableau.com

[10] Forbes (https://www.forbes.com)

[11] Generative AI (https://generativeai.net/)

[12] WHO(https://www.who.int/)

[13] Kim, Y., Park, H., Yoo, S. and Kim, D. (2018). The OCEAN representation of the five dimensions. Figure retrieved from ResearchGate.(https://www.researchgate.net/figure/The-OCEAN-representation-of-the-five-dimensions-Source-Kim-et-al-2018_fig2_371853641)

Index

A

Algorithmic Bias 13, 102 , 105, 108, 133, 134, 140, 143, 197
Artificial Intelligence (AI) 1, 185, 186, 188, 194

B

Behavioral Analysis 217
Big-Five Personality Traits 213, 214, 225
Biomedical Engineering (BME) 15
Blockchain 159-168, 185-187, 194, 208

C

ChestX-ray14 72, 74-76, 80, 82, 84, 88

D

Data Science 134, 213, 217, 218
Data security 108, 138, 159, 160, 164, 165, 168, 171, 180, 181, 190
Deep Learning 11, 24, 27, 48, 58, 58, 62, 75, 77, 85, 96, 100, 113, 149, 150, 199
Diagnostic Accuracy 4, 59, 72, 73, 89, 92, 97, 105-107, 149, 204
Diffusion Models 8, 31, 32-34, 40, 42, 45, 49, 58, 59, 60, 62, 67, 103, 147-150
Digital Health 28, 29, 143
Drug Discovery 1, 6, 7, 8, 13, 24, 32, 74, 114, 133, 142, 143, 147, 149-151, 156, 194, 195, 198-201, 203

E

Electronic Health Records (EHRs) 22, 23, 26
Emerging technologies 15, 29, 175, 185-187
Encoder-Decoder Networks 98
Ethical AI 51, 152, 171, 173, 174, 181, 184, 185, 187-190, 199, 206
Ethical Consideration 3, 32, 67, 113, 136, 137, 153, 178, 184, 190

G

Generative Adversarial Networks (GANs) 6, 8, 31, 59, 60, 74, 81, 89, 103, 149
Generative Artificial Intelligence (GenAI) 31
GPT 6, 42, 59, 61, 96, 102, 103

H

Healthcare 1, 2, 24, 27, 72, 131, 132, 175, 179, 182, 194
Healthcare Applications 194, 200
Healthcare diagnostics 51, 75, 91, 94, 102
Healthcare Engineering 15, 16, 20, 25, 26
Healthcare systems Engineering (HSE) 18
Health Monitoring 20, 139, 208
Human Oversight 78, 105, 108, 133, 138, 184, 199
Human robot collaboration 171, 178, 180, 181, 187, 188, 190

I

Image Translation 8, 36, 58, 59, 62, 63, 67, 96, 200
Interoperability 23, 25, 79, 108, 131, 138, 153, 159-161, 164, 168

K

K-Means Clustering 213, 219, 222, 223, 225
Key Generative Models 33

L

LLM 42
Machine Learning (ML) 6, 12, 24, 33, 60, 75, 113, 115, 136, 171, 178, 185, 188, 190, 197-199, 201, 206, 208, 215, 218
Machine Learning Models 60
Masked Language modeling 33
Medical Diagnostics 26, 74, 76, 77, 81, 85, 89, 90, 91, 94, 95, 101, 102, 105
Medical Imaging 8, 19, 73, 84, 95, 150, 152, 155
MRI 2, 8, 19, 27, 59, 63, 73-75, 80, 96, 102, 116, 149-151, 200, 201, 204
Multimodal AI 76, 105

N

Natural Language Processing (NLP) 23, 33, 45, 59, 65, 147, 148

P

Personality Classification 216, 218, 219, 22, 223, 225
Personalized Medicine 6, 15, 17, 29, 53, 67, 74, 115, 151, 154, 194, 195, 199, 201, 203
Predictive Analytics 2, 18, 23, 24, 26, 29, 91, 116, 130, 131, 139, 151, 161, 164, 165, 168, 171, 216
Prompt engineering 94, 101, 102, 105, 197

R

Regulatory challenges 29
Remote Monitoring 10, 18, 21, 25, 27, 28, 140, 142, 143, 201
Retinal Diseases Images 113
Retrieval-Augmented generation 101, 102, 105, 198
Robotic Process Automation 142, 143
Robotics 1, 3, 6, 28, 131, 133, 137, 138, 142, 143, 159, 160, 163, 171, 173, 175, 176
Robotic Surgery 5, 26, 141

S

Super Resolution Generative Adversarial Networks (SRGAN) 113
Surgical Robotics 3, 4, 13, 173

T

Telemedicine 15, 19, 28, 29, 75, 78, 135, 142, 169, 182, 198, 201, 208
Transformer 6, 7, 34, 42, 43, 44, 59-61, 79, 89, 102, 147, 151, 154, 200

V

Variational Autoencoders 6, 31, 34, 59, 60-62, 64, 74, 81, 82, 89, 103, 200, 208
Variational Inference 33, 34
Virtual Health Assistant 140, 141, 155

W

Work Flow Automation 23, 94

X

X-rays 15, 26, 72-75, 80-86, 88, 89, 96, 102, 201

About the Editors

Deepika Kumar is an Associate Professor and Head of Department, Computer Science & Engineering at Bharati Vidyapeeth's College of Engineering, New Delhi. She has a PhD in Machine Learning and Bioinformatics. She has more than 16 years of teaching experience. Her research interests are Machine Learning, Artificial Intelligence and Bioinformatics. She has been granted two patents and published more than 30 research papers in various SCI, SCIE, Scopus indexed journals and conferences. She has also published a book *Dimensionality Reduction, Feature Extraction, and Manifold in Machine Learning*. She received "Best Researcher Award" for consecutively four years for her contribution in research at Bharati Vidyapeeth's College of Engineering, New Delhi.

Gargi Mishra has a Master's degree from the Indian Institute of Technology, Roorkee, and a PhD in Machine Learning from GGSIP University, New Delhi. With over 15 years of experience in teaching, technical writing, and research, she is currently an Associate Professor at Bharati Vidyapeeth's College of Engineering, New Delhi, in the Department of Computer Science and Engineering. Her research interests include artificial intelligence, machine learning, and computer vision.

Jude D Hemanth is a Full Professor in the Department of ECE at Karunya University, Coimbatore, India. He holds a B.E. in ECE, an M.E. in Communication Systems, and a Ph.D. in Computational Intelligence and Image Processing. He has authored over 280 research papers in reputed journals and conferences, with a cumulative impact factor exceeding 520, and has published 49 edited books with leading publishers. Dr. Hemanth serves as Associate Editor for several SCIE-indexed journals, including IEEE JBHI, IEEE Transactions on ITS, Soft Computing, IET Image Processing, and Heliyon. He is the editor for 2 series on *Biomedical Engineering*, and *Robotics and Healthcare*, each with major publishers, and a board member for the ASTI series. He has led and collaborated on funded research projects from the UK (GCRF), CSIR, and DST (India), and is affiliated as a Research Scientist with labs in Argentina, Brazil, Tunisia, Romania, and Spain. Dr. Hemanth has delivered 200+ keynote talks worldwide and is a certified NVIDIA Deep Learning instructor.

Made in the USA
Las Vegas, NV
15 September 2026

216a42d9-4246-417f-a9e4-e3931a217c35R01